Development Policies of Central and Eastern European States

The states from Central and Eastern Europe that joined the EU in 2004 and 2007 provide a fascinating series of case studies for scholars interested in politics, IR and development studies. The interest comes from the fact that never before had so many recipients of EU aid joined the Union and taken on the commitment to become aid donors. The journey from recipients of aid to aid donors is interesting because, not only does it tell us about development policy in CEE states, this policy area gives us an insight into governmental structures in CEE states, foreign policy priorities, public opinion, the role of NGOs/civil society and how well CEE states have taken on board the EU acquis (the EU's rule book). The book also explores whether the development cooperation programmes of the majority of CEESs reflect the so-called "transition experience" of moving from authoritarianism and socialism to democracy and modern liberalism. It also explores the extent to which these donors are aligned with the approaches of the DAC donors. Finally, by extending the scrutiny to the bottom-up development activities of non-state actors and public opinion, the book will analyse the dynamics of the solidarity of the former 'East' with the global 'South'.

This book was published as a special issue of *Perspectives on European Politics and Society*.

Ondřej Horký-Hlucháň is a Research Fellow in the Institute of International Relations, Prague.

Simon Lightfoot is Senior Lecturer in European Politics, University of Leeds.

Fewer and fewer donor country studies have been published in recent years. In particular, the aid policies of the New Member States have been in the shadows for a long time. This volume is not only timely but also plays the important role of demystifying some of the central roles which were conferred to the development assistance programmes of these emerging donors.

Prof. dr. Paul Hoebink
Director Centre for International Development Issues Nijmegen, Radboud University
Nijmegen, The Netherlands

This volume provides a clear and sophisticated analysis of actors, processes, and policies of the new (or re-emerging) donors in Central and East Europe. It draws on a number of different theoretical approaches, provides new empirical material, and challenges existing assumptions. By doing so, not only does it fill a gap in the academic literature, but is set to become an essential reading for all those who want to have a better understanding of the new global aid architecture.

Maurizio Carbone
Professor of International Development and Jean Monnet Professor of EU External
Relations Director of PhD Programme in Politics, School of Social and Political
Sciences, University of Glasgow, Scotland

Development Policies of Central and Eastern European States

From Aid Recipients to Aid Donors

Edited by
Ondřej Horký-Hlucháň and Simon Lightfoot

LONDON AND NEW YORK

First published 2013
by Routledge
2 Park Square, Milton Park, Abingdon, Oxfordshire OX14 4RN

Simultaneously published in the USA and Canada
by Routledge
711 Third Avenue, New York, NY 10017

First issued in paperback 2015

Routledge is an imprint of the Taylor & Francis Group, an informa business

© 2013 Taylor & Francis

This book is a reproduction of *Perspectives on European Politics and Society*, vol. 13, issue 1. The Publisher requests to those authors who may be citing this book to state, also, the bibliographical details of the special issue on which the book was based.

All rights reserved. No part of this book may be reprinted or reproduced or utilised in any form or by any electronic, mechanical, or other means, now known or hereafter invented, including photocopying and recording, or in any information storage or retrieval system, without permission in writing from the publishers.

Trademark notice: Product or corporate names may be trademarks or registered trademarks, and are used only for identification and explanation without intent to infringe.

British Library Cataloguing in Publication Data
A catalogue record for this book is available from the British Library

ISBN 13: 978-1-138-94510-4 (pbk)
ISBN 13: 978-0-415-63912-5 (hbk)

Typeset in Times New Roman
by Taylor & Francis Books

Publisher's Note
The publisher would like to make readers aware that the chapters in this book may be referred to as articles as they are identical to the articles published in the special issue. The publisher accepts responsibility for any inconsistencies that may have arisen in the course of preparing this volume for print.

Contents

Citation Information	vii
1. From Aid Recipients to Aid Donors? Development Policies of Central and Eastern European States *Ondřej Horký & Simon Lightfoot*	1
2. The Transfer of the Central and Eastern European 'Transition Experience' to the South: Myth or Reality? *Ondřej Horký*	17
3. Visegrad Countries' Development Aid to Africa: Beyond the Rhetoric *Dominik Kopiński*	33
4. Hungarian International Development Cooperation: Context, Stakeholders and Performance *Balázs Szent-Iványi*	50
5. Development Discourse in Romania: From Socialism to EU Membership *Mirela Oprea*	66
6. Involving Civil Society in the International Development Cooperation of 'New' EU Member States: The Case of Slovenia *Maja Bučar*	83
7. Assessing the Aid Effectiveness of the Czech Republic: Commitment to Development Index and Beyond *Petra Krylová, Miroslav Syrovátka & Zdeněk Opršal*	100
8. Development Cooperation of the Baltic States: A Comparison of the Trajectories of Three New Donor Countries *Evelin Andrespok & Andres Ilmar Kasekamp*	117
Index	131

Citation Information

The chapters in this book were originally published in *Perspectives on European Politics and Society*, volume 13, issue 1 (April 2012). When citing this material, please use the original page numbering for each article, as follows:

Chapter 1
From Aid Recipients to Aid Donors? Development Policies of Central and Eastern European States
Ondřej Horký & Simon Lightfoot
Perspectives on European Politics and Society, volume 13, issue 1 (April 2012) pp. 1-16

Chapter 2
The Transfer of the Central and Eastern European 'Transition Experience' to the South: Myth or Reality?
Ondřej Horký
Perspectives on European Politics and Society, volume 13, issue 1 (April 2012) pp. 17-32

Chapter 3
Visegrad Countries' Development Aid to Africa: Beyond the Rhetoric
Dominik Kopiński
Perspectives on European Politics and Society, volume 13, issue 1 (April 2012) pp. 33-49

Chapter 4
Hungarian International Development Cooperation: Context, Stakeholders and Performance
Balázs Szent-Iványi
Perspectives on European Politics and Society, volume 13, issue 1 (April 2012) pp. 50-65

Chapter 5
Development Discourse in Romania: From Socialism to EU Membership
Mirela Oprea
Perspectives on European Politics and Society, volume 13, issue 1 (April 2012) pp. 66-82

CITATION INFORMATION

Chapter 6
Involving Civil Society in the International Development Cooperation of 'New' EU Member States: The Case of Slovenia
Maja Bučar
Perspectives on European Politics and Society, volume 13, issue 1 (April 2012) pp. 83-99

Chapter 7
Assessing the Aid Effectiveness of the Czech Republic: Commitment to Development Index and Beyond
Petra Krylová, Miroslav Syrovátka & Zdeněk Opršal
Perspectives on European Politics and Society, volume 13, issue 1 (April 2012) pp. 100-116

Chapter 8
Development Cooperation of the Baltic States: A Comparison of the Trajectories of Three New Donor Countries
Evelin Andrespok & Andres Ilmar Kasekamp
Perspectives on European Politics and Society, volume 13, issue 1 (April 2012) pp. 117-130

From Aid Recipients to Aid Donors? Development Policies of Central and Eastern European States[1]

ONDŘEJ HORKÝ* & SIMON LIGHTFOOT**
*Institute of International Relations, Prague, Czech Republic
**School of Politics and International Studies, University of Leeds, UK

ABSTRACT   *This article provides an overview of the emergence of development aid donors in Central and Eastern Europe (CEE). It explores the definitions employed to characterize these donors before going on to examine the challenges faced in creating a development policy in the CEE states. It outlines how a soft acquis from the EU, weak governmental structures, low political will and low public understanding prevented the policy from acquiring strong roots. As a result, the economic crisis, which is used to frame the debate, has knocked all the states in the region off course. Finally, it situates the papers in this special issue in the wider context of the overview and the wider literature and summarizes the main questions raised by the special issue: development cooperation as an expression of foreign policy interests, the normative role of the other international and European actors, the advantages of the CEE development cooperation programmes, and their embodiment in a wider societal context.*

The states from Central and Eastern Europe (CEE) that joined the European Union (EU) in 2004 and 2007 provide an interesting case study for this special issue. The interest comes from the fact that never before had so many recipients of EU aid joined the EU and taken on the commitment to become aid donors. The journey from recipients of aid to aid donors is interesting not only because it tells us about development policy in the CEE states, but also because this policy area gives us an insight into governmental structures in the CEE states, foreign policy priorities, public opinion, the role of NGOs/ civil society and how well the CEE states have taken on board the EU acquis (the EU's rule book).

Even though they continue to receive larger amounts of aid from the EU and other European Economic Area (EEA) countries than in the pre-accession period, these flows are not accounted for as 'official aid' any more and, hence, the countries have rapidly fostered their identity as aid donors, in part due to the demands of EU membership. Whilst many states in the region have a history of development aid under communism, that aid was highly political. Therefore, the states under study had to build their development cooperation programmes from scratch. As a result, the model the majority of these states went for was one similar to that used by the 'old' members of the EU and the Development Assistance Committee of the Organisation for Economic Cooperation and Development (OECD DAC), in part due to the influence of the EU as the largest world donor and the OECD DAC as the principal forum of donor countries, respectively.

However, research on the international development cooperation programmes of the CEE states has focused mainly on the 'new' EU member states as a homogeneous group from a European integration perspective and it has often overlooked their national preferences and particularities (although we note that this is a tendency often found when looking at the non-DAC donor group in general, see Kim and Lightfoot 2011). This special issue presents papers that seek to enlarge the regional and theoretical scopes of the research by studying both the global context and the domestic roots of the development policies of the CEE states. This multilevel comparative perspective enables the answering of research questions left over by previous inquiries: Are the CEE states' rather pragmatic approaches to development cooperation an expression of their narrow national interests or their appurtenance to the global political community? What are the respective influences of the EU, OECD, United Nations and other international actors? Do the development cooperation programmes of the majority of the CEE states reflect the alleged specificity of their transition experience from authoritarianism and socialism to democracy and economic liberalism, or a simple alignment to the approaches of the 'Western' donors? Finally, by extending the scrutiny to the bottom-up development activities of non-state actors and public opinion, this issue studies the dynamics of the solidarity of the former 'East' with the global 'South' at the societal level.

Classifying the CEE States as Donors

How we define the states under study is crucial. Two supranational organizations play a role in the development policy of the ten CEE states: the OECD and the EU (Manning 2006, Kragelund 2008).[2] The OECD DAC operates as an important site for the construction and dissemination of transnational research and policy ideas across a wide range of contemporary issues (Mahon and McBride 2009, p. 84). In the 1960s, the DAC was created to coordinate and promote aid from the Western donor community. It also developed common rules and definitions for what constituted Official Development Assistance (ODA) and, in doing so, helped to shape the development policy in member states and beyond (Riddell 2007, p. 18). In particular, the DAC makes extensive use of an international peer review system (see Mahon and McBride 2009, p. 86). Kragelund argues that membership of the OECD affects central themes in development such as democracy and the market economy, as the OECD is not only a 'club of the rich', but also a community of shared values and interests (Kragelund 2008).

The EU takes on board the soft norms of the OECD DAC and operationalizes them via the *acquis communautaire* (Orbie and Versluys 2008). On the other hand, the influence between the EU and the OECD DAC is mutual since the EU represents the majority of the DAC members. A number of the CEE states, too, are OECD members or have plans to join. However, the fact that the 'new' EU member states are not OECD DAC members reduces their influence on shaping the DAC's norms and, consequently, the norms of the EU. In addition, in the case of the OECD, peer pressure is the principal, if not the only, way for the EU to enforce soft law[3] among its member states (Horký 2011). These are the rules and laws that govern the EU. For example, the targets agreed by the EU for ODA in the 'new' member states, 0.17 per cent of GNI by 2010 and 0.33 per cent by 2015, can be seen as a major driving factor in pushing these states to give aid, despite their initial reluctance to accept them as binding (Carbone 2007). Donors can also channel their ODA via the European Commission as multilateral aid (Kragelund 2008); however, this is more of an obligation than an opportunity for the member states since the major part of the development cooperation provided by the Commission is funded by the compulsory contribution of the states to the EU budget.

Other international organizations such as the United Nations Development Programme (UNDP) and the Canadian International Development Agency (CIDA) and individual donor countries have played an important role in building the capacities of the CEE states, but since these actors do not set norms, their influence is limited. The EU and OECD memberships are hence the crucial criteria in classifying the countries of the CEE region. The CEE countries under study here are all EU member states, but only four are currently OECD members. These form Group 1 in Kragelund's classification and comprise the Czech Republic, Hungary, Poland and Slovakia. The other category (Kragelund's Group 3) is made up of non-OECD EU members, which include the three Baltic states, Slovenia, Bulgaria and Romania. Nevertheless, OECD membership and OECD DAC membership must be duly differentiated.

The aim of this special issue is to examine the journey that the CEE states have been on since joining the EU (see Dauderstadt 2002, Krichewsky 2003, Carbone 2004 for the pre- accession period; Grimm and Harmer 2005, Kuuish 2006, Bucar *et al.* 2007, Lightfoot 2008 for immediate post-accession analysis). Some of these so called post-communist states had a long history of providing aid bilaterally or via the Council for Mutual Economic Assistance (CMEA), with not only the former Czechoslovakia and Bulgaria providing aid in significant amounts (Browne 1980, p. 227), but also Romania, whose donor experience has been disregarded in contemporary policy and research (Oprea, this issue). After the end of the Cold War, these states underwent major economic transformations, which saw their aid budgets cut dramatically (Carbone 2007, p. 47). Most of their capacities and experiences were 'lost in transition' and, despite their path dependency from the socialist period (Szent-Iványi and Tétényi 2008), their new development cooperation programmes are discursively reframed and, therefore, it is more appropriate to call these states 'new donors', rather than 're-emerging donors' (see Grimm *et al.*, 2008).

This phase of their development was met with a strong degree of optimism. For example, in 2004, the Czech Republic had an ODA flow of 0.11 per cent and could seem to be on the track to meet the 0.17 per cent target in 2010. The Polish government had a plan to join the DAC by 2010 (Manning 2006, p. 343, Horký 2010b). In 2007, Riddell identified Latvia, Lithuania, Estonia and Hungary as having become donors over the past few years (Riddell 2007, p. 52). Kragelund argued that although aid made up a very small share of the EU/OECD members' expenditure, all four announced plans to increase aid in line with their EU commitments. He also notes that they have all shown interest in adapting their own aid procedures to DAC standards, and that their official aid rhetoric resembles that of the DAC to a large extent (Kragelund 2008, p. 559). Indeed, in 2007, the Czech Republic underwent an informal mini peer review by the OECD DAC, followed recently by Poland and Slovakia. These reviews are demand driven (i.e., requested by the country) and funded by them. At the time, however, both the pragmatic motivations for undergoing such a review as well as the declaratory aspect of their commitments were underestimated.

Whilst the non-OECD group of EU states had much smaller economies, they still had ambitious targets for ODA flows. Manning (2006), then chair of the OECD DAC, argued that for both these groups, DAC 'standards' will be a key point of reference. He also argued that both groups were keenly interested in what the donor behaviour encouraged in the Paris Declaration of 2005 might mean for them and in particular for how they could maintain a degree of visibility for their growing aid efforts in a world of greater harmonization (Manning 2006, pp. 373–374). It should be noted that Estonia and Slovenia have been invited to become OECD members. However, the lost appeal of the carrot of accession in the post-2004 period (see Horký 2011) and the adverse effects of the economic recession in all the CEE states, except Poland, on their public expenditure has shown the limits to this initial optimism.

Development Policies in CEE States in the Post-Accession Period

It is becoming increasingly common in the EU-15 to question whether labels such as 'Eastern Europe' are useful when looking at the region due to the divergent nature of the countries of the region (*The Economist* 2010). Indeed, the seemingly geographically neutral label was never accepted by the Central European countries for they were being put in the same basket as their less developed ex-Soviet Eastern neighbours, and especially Russia. Labels such as 'new member states' are also criticized as being outdated now – these states are part of the EU-27 and not a separate club. Moreover, Croatia is on the verge of becoming the 28th member. The economic crisis and the concurrent public debt crisis with the crisis of the euro have also shown the diversity of patterns and sustainability of social and economic development within the EU, with several 'newcomers' outpacing some member states that acceded to the EU during the previous waves of enlargement in many aspects. Having said that, previous research (Bučar and Mrak 2007, Lightfoot 2010) argued that the situation in development policy was different and, therefore, the similarities between the states were sufficient to make such a comparison. In part, the similarity is shaped by the fact that all states, whether OECD members or not, have a different commitment to reach ODA targets as agreed by the EU in 2005, an element of a two speed Europe (Horký 2011), and their starting position was uneven even in comparison to the weak performers of the EU-15, such as Greece or Portugal.

In 2005, Grimm and Harmer argued that 'whilst budget constraints will persist and will affect ODA volumes, international obligations within the EU framework suggest that there will be a steady growth of ODA from Central Europe in coming years, albeit from a smaller economic basis than in the EU-15' (Grimm and Harmer 2005, p. 5). The growth of the ODA part on the then growing gross national income (GNI) of these states supported this optimism with many countries from the region making massive statistical strides. Much of this journey was occurring as they made the change from recipient of aid to donor of aid with their accession to the EU and the compulsory contribution to the EU budget.[4] Table 1 summarizes the evolution of aid quantity in the CEE states before their accession, before the 2008 global financial and economic downturn, and on the eve of the debt crisis in 2010.

However, after 2006, despite the real term increases in ODA, all the 'new' EU member states were struggling to achieve the ODA percentage targets; although not for the first time, we should note that this was not just confined to the newcomers from the CEE. Already by 2008, aid from many European countries was stagnant or had fallen (Addison and Mavrotas 2008, p. 8). The AidWatch summary is worth quoting at length:

> 2008 saw ten out of the twenty-seven European countries either decrease or fail to raise their aid levels in relation to GNI. Amongst the EU-15, Austria recorded the biggest decrease. However, even within other EU-15 countries progress towards achieving the 0.51% GNI was negligible for many. Greece has already thrown in the towel and lowered its target for 2010 to 0.35% GNI. If current trends continue, Greece will fail to meet even this drastically reduced commitment. Germany, France, Italy, Portugal and Belgium are other members of the club showing little hope of hitting their targets (AidWatch 2008).

> The following non-DAC OECD countries reported changes in net ODA as follows: Czech Republic (-3.5 per cent); Hungary (−42.9 per cent) after high debt relief levels in 2006 for Iraq; Poland (+5.2 per cent); Slovak Republic (+0.1 per cent) (AidWatch 2008).

> The 2009 report makes even less good reading and is again worth quoting at length: Half of the EU-12 decreased their aid levels and a further two did not register any improvements on last year's figures. Amongst the new Member States, Bulgaria and Malta are by far the worst performers, with decreases of

Table 1. Evolution in aid quantity in the CEE countries, 2001–10

ODA/GNI ratio (in %)	2001	2006	2010
Poland	0.02	0.10	0.08
Czech Republic	0.05	0.11	0.12
Slovak Republic	0.06	0.09	0.09
Hungary	0.02	0.10	0.09
Lithuania	0.02	0.06	0.10
Latvia	0.02	0.06	0.06
Estonia	0.01	0.06	0.10
Romania	N/A	N/A	0.07
Bulgaria	N/A	0.06	0.09

Source: Authors' compilation from AidWatch (2011), PASOS (2007).

27%. Hot on their heels were Estonia, which dropped by 19%, Poland by 10%, Hungary 9%, and the Czech Republic by 1%. Looking at the individual commitments, the picture is even darker. Only two CEE states, Slovenia and Lithuania, are on track to meet their targets (AidWatch 2010).

However, informal feedback for Slovenia suggests that 'the budgets for the next two years don't look very promising' (Interview with author, Brussels 2010). An update in 2010 was even more gloomy, despite some small increases in ODA in Slovakia and no official change in Estonia and Slovenia. Among the other CEE states, the Czech Republic saw an overall 5 per cent cut in government budget, Hungarian ODA continued the downward trend it started in 2007 and cuts were announced in the ODA budget in Latvia. In Lithuania, Poland and Romania, non-governmental organizations (NGOs) identified cuts being made in the Ministry of Foreign Affairs (MFA).

Clearly, statistics must be treated with some caution. One ironic factor of the recession was that for some states, the share of development aid as a percentage of the budget increased due to the decline in GNI. Therefore, it is worth looking at total aid flows as well. For example, all activities reported as Romanian ODA in 2008 amounted to €100 million, although the target for 2010 was more than €200 million. In 2010, the Romanian MFA announced a doubling of bilateral ODA from €2 million to €3.8 million. However, of this amount, the Head of Division for ODA said that €2 million would be used for implementing projects in the Republic of Moldova. This pledge for Moldova came after the Romanian government cut the ODA budget by more than 60 per cent and halved its staff in 2009. There are, therefore, serious questions about the geographical focus and impact on poverty of Romanian aid. It should also be underlined that the quantity of aid is not necessarily linked to its quality and, therefore, its overall effectiveness in any of the CEE countries.

Whatever the composed effects of the debt crisis and post-accession 'aid fatigue', only the Czech Republic, Estonia and Lithuania have seen a slight increase in their ODA/GNI ratio over the 2006–10 period. However, it is also important to examine their performance in the EU-27 perspective. As AidWatch put it:

> Figures show that three countries alone are responsible for more than three quarters of the €15 billion aid gap in 2010: Italy (responsible for 43.8% of the gap), Germany (26.4%) and Spain (6.4%). As for the EU12, no single country (except for Cyprus) has managed to reach its interim target of 0.17% of GNI. The worst performers in 2010 include Latvia (fulfilling only 35% of its 2010 obligations), Romania (41%), Poland (49%), Slovak Republic (50%) and finally Bulgaria and Hungary (both fulfilling merely 53% of their 2010 obligations). (AidWatch 2011, p. 5)

In spite of their low performance, the 'new' member states accounted for only 5.6 per cent of the gap, that is, less than Greece alone (AidWatch 2011, p. 11). In a two-speed Europe framework, the role of the newcomers in the EU development cooperation architecture remains and will remain marginal in terms of aid volume, but their shortcomings ask for a deeper analysis at the level of the individual member states since none of them is on track to meet the 2015 commitments to reach a 0.33 per cent ODA/GNI ratio.

Analysis of Domestic and International Factors on Targets of Aid Quantity and Quality

The literature identifies a number of factors that are said to lock in levels of aid and these range from domestic political contexts to institutional factors. Before we go on to explore these factors, it is worth first putting the drop in ODA outlined above into the context of the economy in 2009–10. Whilst the drastic cuts in Latvian ODA make sense in the light of an 18 per cent fall in GDP between 2009 and 2010, they make less sense in Slovenia, a state richer than Portugal. Latvia's economy is now reliant on an International Monetary Fund (IMF) loan and development organizations in the country face a bleak future following the government's announcement that development aid will be reduced to zero in the coming year. The situation in the countries of the Visegrad Group (V4) is interesting. Hungary was hit hard by the financial crisis, yet the Czech Republic and Slovakia weathered the storm relatively well. In Poland, GDP actually grew in 2009 and 2010. On the other hand, as of the end of 2011, these countries seem to be worse hit by the effects of the euro crisis than those at the core of the eurozone. The major factor that plays a role here is fiscal deficits, with Carbone confirming that historically, aid flows fall fastest in countries with large fiscal deficits (Carbone 2007, p. 64). This has been a particular problem for Hungary and Latvia during the global recession. This may also help explain why states with large fiscal deficits, such as Greece, Portugal and Italy, have also seen reductions in their ODA budgets. If the economic downturn shows a 'W' curve, instead of a single 'V' one, the forecast for the CEE countries is even gloomier (see Dale 2011 for a political specific, but interesting, overview of the economic situation in the region).

It is clear that in a recession, states will have other priorities, many of which will have a much higher salience than development issues. Therefore, the key to maintaining levels of ODA is political will and an active development constituency, that is, the network of actors active in shaping and/or implementing development cooperation programmes. In general, in all countries, lack of political will is recognized by non-governmental development organizations (NGDOs) as the main problem in dealing with ODA issues. Political parties have been identified as influencing the levels of aid (Therien and Noel 2000, Tingley 2010). Meislová (2010), in a study of the 2010 election in the Czech Republic, found that development issues played a marginal role in the election manifestos of the main parties. This lack of political will is linked to limited public awareness and limited involvement of NGOs and civil society at large. Low public awareness has a negative effect on support for development cooperation. This conclusion was borne out in a special Eurobarometer report on EU development aid. It found a noticeable disparity between the views of the EU-15 and EU-12 groups. It found that in Estonia, Hungary, the Czech Republic, Latvia and Slovakia, respondents were more reluctant to take a strong stance on the question whether it was important to help people in poor countries, although the overall proportion believing that this was important remains very high (Eurobarometer 2007, p. 26). The Eurobarometer concluded that there appears to be a lack of knowledge in many 'new' member states concerning development issues, a point that is discussed throughout this special issue.

This lack of knowledge is exacerbated by the weakness of the development constituency in these states. The quantity of aid is directly related to the ability of the domestic development community to mobilize resources. Therefore, civil society has a critical role to play in development policy (see Lister and Carbone 2006). NGOs in the CEE states are seen to be generally less well developed than those in the majority of the EU member states (see Palubinskas 2003, Börzel 2010). NGDOs have additional problems, such as an insecure funding base, weak national organizations and competition with global NGDOs. Funding problems in particular have been a major concern in recent years due to government cutbacks, with all NGDO platforms reporting cuts in their budgets. While the civil society organizations have been paid enough attention, the role of the parliaments and ministries other than the MFAs, which are generally responsible for development cooperation in the CEE countries, has been less studied. The understanding of development aid by the other members of the cabinet may be diametrically different from that of the MFA officials, not speaking of the NGDOs, among which the understanding of aid as charity is still widespread, which makes the discussion of policy coherence for development in the CEE countries almost irrelevant (Horký 2010a).

Another problem is the weakness of the development cooperation departments within the state structures, resulting in their poor political power to influence changes. Hallet argues that the political weight of the foreign affairs or development minister in a government and the general public support for development aid are important factors in maintaining support for ODA targets within governments (Hallet 2009). The degree of institutional incapacity varies across the region, but can be found to some degree in all the states. Unlike the EU-15, where development cooperation is managed by well-established bureaucracies, it is handled in a generally ad hoc manner by the fledgling proto-structures in most of the CEE countries. Because there are few lasting governmental instruments, their development assistance has been very shock-prone and sporadic. The recent downturn of 2008–09 demonstrates this fragility; while 13 of the EU-15 member states were able to raise ODA from 2007–08, only four of the EU-12 states raised their levels. It could be argued that the structural solidarity of the institutions in the older member states has permitted them to pursue ODA funding at this time, while the 'undernourished' new member states' institutions have not had the strength to guide ODA through the crisis' obstacles (AidWatch 2009). For example, Poland has had an act to create a legal framework for development assistance in preparation since 2004, but the act has not yet been implemented.

The lack of formal structure can make things easier to change. Hallet argues that as budget planning processes might be sluggish in their response to economic cycles, the adjustment of aid budgets can be expected to have some time lag. Therefore, he concludes that a swift reaction of aid budgets to the ups and downs of economic activity is unlikely (Hallet 2009). However, development aid budgets are political decisions and thus, ultimately, depend on political factors. The crucial ones in the case of the CEE countries are the location of the budget and whether the budget is decided annually. In the Czech Republic, the ODA budget is implemented by the Czech Development Agency with some marginal remnants left to the line ministries under the policy coordination of the MFA and with the application of multi-year, yet non-binding, financing frameworks for development activities. In Poland, the line ministries still have their own ODA activities and report to the MFA ex-post. The main players are the Ministry of Finance and the Ministry of Education. The ODA unit at the MFA has been strengthened and manages its own portfolio of ODA projects. Poland plans to establish a Polish Bureau for Development Cooperation and a special bank account, Development Cooperation of Poland, as well as the multi-annual programming and funding framework and the management guidelines for the implementation of Polish ODA. In the Slovak Republic, the MFA acts as a coordinator of the ODA provided by the Slovak Republic via a Coordination Committee for Development Assistance (see Vittek and Lightfoot 2009). This committee was established in order to ensure the active participation of the line ministries in the Slovak ODA. The MFA has the strategic decision making role in both ODA Funds through the majority in their Steering Committees (SCs) – all ODA disbursements have to be approved by the SCs (Hanspach 2004). Recently, the foundation of SlovakAid has led to a similar system as in the Czech Republic. In Romania and Bulgaria, there is almost total lack of institutional support and capacity. In Bulgaria, for example, there is no legal framework for ODA activities, which is one of the reasons we have omitted Bulgaria from this special issue. In sum, this produces a situation, where, in the Slovak parliamentary discussion following the first reading of the Development Act, the former Minister of Foreign Affairs, Eduard Kukan, could state: 'Nobody will get mad if we will not fulfil the targets and we have to defend it internationally that we cannot be compared with Scandinavian and other countries active in this area for years and that we can reach required percentages gradually' (Drażkiewicz 2008). This point is crucial and relates to both the domestic points outlined above plus the relative weakness of the acquis in the field. The concern for many NGOs in all the CEE states is that not only do nearly all the CEE states appear not likely to meet their ODA targets, but there is little enthusiasm for a road map to get the states to their targets.

An Overview of the Special Issue

Having provided an overview, this section outlines the rest of the special issue. As announced, each paper tackles at least one of the following issues: the articulation between the global and domestic context, including the multitude of participating actors; the possible application of the transition experience in development cooperation programmes as compared to the approaches of the DAC donors; and, finally, the consequences for the relations between the 'East' and the global 'South'. The papers, therefore, provide the first systematic analysis of the development policies of the CEE states since enlargement. They build on the key literature that was published in the first few years after accession by offering thematic as well as country studies.

Ondřej Horký from the Institute of International Relations in Prague has recently scrutinized the Europeanization of the Czech development cooperation, that is, the top-down implementation of the EU's rules in the Czech bilateral development cooperation programme (see Horký 2011 for an overview, Horký 2010c for further details). In this issue, he complements his focus on the Czech case, and also the

EU-12 states in general, with the scrutiny of the bottom-up upload of the 'value add' of their 'transition experience' to the EU level. Indeed, according to the representatives of the post-communist states, their transition experience would be applicable also in the South, and more specifically in the countries touched by the so-called Arab Spring of 2011. In his article, The Transfer of the Central and Eastern European 'Transition Experience' to the South: Myth or Reality?, Horký builds on the conceptual distinction between the political and technical levels of development cooperation and argues that the alleged transfer of the 'transition experience' is a marginal phenomenon of the 'new' member state's development policies and, hence, more of a myth than reality. He puts forward arguments as to why the transfer of the transition experience in another cultural and temporal context is extremely difficult and limited to the narrow fields of civil society and public administration. Horký concludes that the potential of the 'transition experience' to inform the development policy of the EU is hampered by the marginal influence of the EU-12 states in the EU development policy architecture and also by their national commercial and security interests, which prevent them from politicizing development cooperation at the EU level and contributing thus to its overall development effectiveness by including human rights and the promotion of democracy as an integral part of a more coherent EU's external action. The 'myth' thus serves partly as a mask for the low level of public support for the current form of development cooperation in the post-communist societies, which contrasts with the commitments of their governments that they have easily accepted as a part of their EU and OECD membership.

Dominik Kopiński from the Institute of International Studies at the University of Wrocław comes to a similar conclusion in his paper, Visegrad Countries' Development Aid to Africa: Beyond the Rhetoric. He argues that against the commitments of the V4 governments to focus their aid on the Least Developed Countries (LDCs), and in Sub-Saharan Africa particularly, the emphasis of the V4 countries on their immediate commercial and alleged security interests in their neigbourhood, that is, other CEE countries and the Balkan countries, is not only in contradiction of public opinion, which hampers the popular and long-term political support of development policies as such, but even of their long-term interests, as attested by the growing engagement of Brazil, Russia, India and China (BRIC) and other emerging powers with Africa. As the involvement of many 'new' member states in Iraq and, lately, in Afghanistan attests, the applicability of the theory of path dependency to the (re)emerging donors advanced by Balász Szent-Iványi and András Tétényi (2008) is not an absolute one and the current African policies of the Visegrád countries are rather a symptom of a 'low lack of strategic vision and *ad hoc* formulation of foreign policy'.

In the following article, Hungarian International Development Cooperation: Context, Stakeholders and Performance, Balázs Szent-Iványi of the Corvinus University in Budapest starts to explain this gap by contributing to the growing literature on Europeanization. The EU membership had 'little noticeable effect in shaping Hungary's development policy since 2004'. Instead, it serves its foreign policy and economic interests. Hungarian bilateral development aid is low in volume, donor-driven, tied, fragmented, with a low poverty focus and its impacts are unevaluated, all of which run contrary to the principles of the EU development policy and in line with the aforementioned research on the Czech Republic. Perhaps,

DEVELOPMENT POLICIES OF CENTRAL AND EASTERN EUROPEAN STATES

the most important point of Szent-Iványi's study is the scrutiny of the socialization of the actors within the Hungarian development constituency since the coercion effect of the EU on Hungary in this particular policy field was very limited. On the base of semi-structured interviews, he tracks the socialization of the officials between Brussels and Budapest and concludes that even though the relevant officials have learnt to 'talk the talk' of the EU institutions and DAC donors, their social learning is very shallow, in part due also to the high turnover at the MFA. Szent-Iványi then confirms that Hungarian aid is influenced by broader foreign policy interests, which concurs with the low or missing Hungarian capacities to provide aid to the LDCs and Africa. Finally, he points out the frequent paradox of the shallow Europeanization of the latecomers in the EU's development policy arena: The governments defend the preference for the domestic actors with the argument of building the development constituency, which serves as an excuse for putting the poverty focus aside.

Mirela Oprea's (World Vision) insightful and theoretically informed study, Development Discourse in Romania: From Socialism to EU Membership Cooperation, contributes to the accumulation of these paradoxes among the (re)emerging donors, which have been left aside by the first wave of research, mostly carried out superficially by at least partly political actors and even scholars from the 'old' member states.[5] Oprea pays full attention to the discursive framing of the 'new' member states' development policies, a crucial step in both the predominantly normative field of contemporary development and also European studies. She argues that the externally driven Europeanization process has led to the discursive and institutional erasure of the rich and impressive record of Romanian development cooperation, whatever may have been its ideological premises. She concludes that the 'new' member states 'are not encouraged to become members of the donor community – they are encouraged to join the community of Western donors and abide to the dominant development discourse represented by OECD-DAC norms and practices embraced by and filtered through EU soft development law'. She recognizes the benefits of Europeanization, but points out that 'a possible opportunity cost for this massive import of development ideology is a tapering space for alternative development thinking'. We encourage the use of this perspective in further research since by giving space to submerged yet still present discourses, it can help to highlight non-Europeanization as a *resistance* to Europeanization, caused by the EU discursive hegemony not only in the development field, but also in other policy areas.

While more research using less orthodox methodologies such as critical discursive analysis, Foucauldian archeology or oral history is needed to go further in this direction, at the current stage of research, an analysis of civil society and its relations with the state can also help to understand the track record of the CEE countries' development policies. Maja Bučar from the University of Ljubljana offers a detailed study of the evolving and lively Slovenian NGDO constituency in her paper, Involving Civil Society in the International Development Cooperation of 'New' EU Member States: The Case of Slovenia. Using a theoretical framework that distinguishes between the different functions of development NGOs in the West, she applies it to the NGDO landscape in Slovenia and tracks the growing formalization and division of tasks between civil society as represented by Sloga, the national NGDO platform, on the one hand, and the Slovenian MFA as a policy-maker on the other hand. In the context of the Slovenian EU presidency, which has required the joint capacities of both the government and the NGOs, she points out the specificity of the emerging donors' development constituencies. Despite their frequent discomfort with government policies, the NGOs and the state are allies that help to promote the development agenda in the country with their joint forces. Following Bučar's argument, the watchdog and lobbyist functions of civil society are marginal, which, however, along with the financial dependence of the NGOs on the state, may lead to widening the gap between the NGOs and the public, and thus to the further depoliticization and unsustainability of aid giving.

A technically oriented analysis of aid in the CEE countries complements the already complex picture. Assessing the Aid Effectiveness of the Czech Republic: Commitment to Development Index and Beyond by Petra Krylová, Miroslav Syrovátka and Zdeněk Opršal from the Palacký University in Olomouc[6] applies the methodology of the Commitment to Development Index (CDI) to the Czech case. At this stage of research, it tackles only its aid component, although upcoming research will offer a more precise picture of the external relations of the CEE countries with the South and approximate their performance in the field of policy coherence for development. The paper gives a detailed quantitative analysis of Czech aid and, by adjusting its components with the CDI methodology, reveals that the quality adjusted aid provided by the Czech Republic accounts for only 0.06 per cent of GNI, instead of the unadjusted 0.12 per cent with a larger reduction in the case of multilateral cooperation, due mostly to the large quantity of aid provided to Afghanistan. For the first time, the paper also collects information on private donations, where the reduction is even larger: from US$8million to US$1million. Despite the reductionism caused by the use of qualitative methodology and the difficulties in collecting data because of non-compliance with OECD DAC statistical reporting, the Czech Republic ranks at the bottom of the DAC donors, between the United States of America and Japan, which puts Czech aid in an interesting perspective.

In the final paper of this issue, Development Cooperation of the Baltic States: Commonalities and Differences, Evelin Andrespok (University of Helsinki) and Andres Ilmar Kasekamp (University of Tartu) give a comparative account of the development cooperation programmes of Estonia, Latvia and Lithuania. Unlike the V4 countries or Romania, these countries were part of the Soviet Union and, therefore, their direct contact with the South was more limited in the past. Consequently, they initiated development cooperation only as part of the EU accession process. Nevertheless, despite the recent 20th anniversary of the dissolution of the Soviet Union, the Cold War legacy is still a key yet unspoken determinant of the foreign policies of the Baltic States, including the territorial priorities of their development policies in the ex-Soviet Union. In line with this, the Baltic States have eagerly latched onto the European Neighbourhood Policy as a vehicle for their bilateral development cooperation. But in spite of their historical commonalities, the three states in question present striking differences. While Estonia appears to have progressed furthest in fostering and Europeanizing its development cooperation, the Latvian efforts have suffered due to deep cuts in the state budget following the 2009 economic recession. The current eurocrisis indicates that the paths of the 'new' as well as the 'old' member states may diverge further and finally blur the clear categorizations established immediately after EU accession.

Conclusion

How then can we summarize the journey undertaken so far by the CEE states on the road to becoming aid donors? This special issue highlights the rather pragmatic approaches to development cooperation adopted by these states (see also Szent-Ivanyi 2011). To a large extent, development policy is an expression of their narrow national interests, although with a clear nod towards the EU and OECD DAC norms. These organizations, to use a popular political expression, have helped nudge the CEE states towards taking on board many aspects of the global development norms. It should also be noted that for their stage of maturity as donors, many do not compare badly against the more established DAC members. It is clear that few donors provide aid on a purely altruistic basis (Younas 2008) and that foreign policy concerns shape aid policy (Alesina and Dollar 2000, Woods 2005). It should be noted that unlike the post-communist states, many 'old' member states have their foreign policy interests in their former colonies, which are also the poorest regions of the world and, consequently, their development policies are more prone to legitimization by altruistic values.

As far as our second research question is concerned, we have confirmed the correlated influence of the EU and, to a lesser extent, the OECD. Besides the shallow Europeanization as a top-down process, the foreign policy concerns of the EU-10 states becoming visible at the EU level are a newer phenomenon. Orbie and Versluys (2008) show that the CEE states have two clear priorities for EU development policy. The first is the strengthening of the 'eastern dimension' of EU external relations as a part of the European Neighbourhood Policy and the second appears to be related to the objectives of development cooperation, which many of the EU-12 see as an instrument to achieve broader foreign and security policy aims, rather than to reduce poverty as an end in itself (Orbie and Versluys 2008, p. 87). We have seen the EU-12, especially those states from the CEE that have limited historical connections to developing countries in Africa and tend to direct their bilateral aid to neighbouring states within Europe, adding to the voices within the EU questioning the EU's special relations with the African, Caribbean and Pacific (ACP) states, which are perceived as a colonial legacy. At the same time, we have seen an increasing focus on the Eastern dimension. The majority of aid from the EU-12 states goes to Moldova, Ukraine and Georgia, along with the former Yugoslavia, and they wish to see a strengthening of EU action in this area. The creation of the Eastern Partnership in 2008 by Poland and Sweden was a significant development (see Copsey and Pamorska 2010) and the Eastern dimension is also a recurring priority of the CEE states' EU presidencies at the expense of Africa, Asia and Latin America. In sum, despite the limited aid volumes, it is clear that whilst the influence of international actors is visible on the CEE countries, we are starting to see the influence in the opposite direction, too.

The non-compliance with the EU soft law, both in terms of quantitative and qualitative commitments that have historically reflected the preferences of the 'old' member states in development policy, may raise some concerns about the future of the development policy of the EU as a whole, and more generally in the context of the declining influence of the EU in the world. But it also presents some opportunities. While there seems to be a very limited amount of transition experience of the CEE countries that is ready to be delivered through the current forms of technical assistance and political support of the civil society, their interrelation in the historical experience might inform a more coherent external action of the EU in the future. With the current global dynamics, the question for the CEE countries might be to not stick literally to the 'old' DAC rules, but to engage directly with the current challenges presented by the declining aid flows in relation to other financial flows as well as the competition of the ever 'newer' donors such as the big powerful states in the South or private foundations that have largely outpaced the slowly emerging CEE donors. More focus on policy coherence for global development might be a lodestar for them.

Finally, the answer to the last research question of this special issue – development cooperation as an expression of 'East'–South solidarity – is also related to the slow acceptance and implementation of international norms. The low awareness of the extreme poverty in the South and of the interrelatedness of the North, including the 'East', with the South is a challenge that prevents the CEE countries, for example, from pursuing greater coherence in their policies in areas such as trade, security or climate. This weakness does not concern only citizens, but also civil society and, more importantly, politicians. If the values of global development are not shared, or if there is insufficient information, institutions and actors to turn development awareness into action, external pressure on implementing the norms will be inefficient. Rather, it leads to their superficial acceptance and, in relation to the ongoing debt crisis, we have also seen, setbacks. It is not then surprising that the governments try to reflect their pragmatic interests in development policy and ensure their ownership of the policy against its declared goal. This need for a correspondence between values and interests is probably not only a condition for the sustainable development policies of the CEE states, but for global development policy as a whole.

Notes

[1] The papers in this special issue were presented in a two part panel discussion, The 'East' Meets the 'South': Global and Development Policies of Central and Eastern European States, at the annual convention of the Central and East European International Studies Association (CEEISA) in Istanbul in June 2010. A number of these papers were also presented at the EADI/DSA Conference in York in September 2011 under the auspices of the EADI Working Group, Development Aid of Non-DAC Donors. We would like to thank all the people who attended the panels for their constructive comments and especially our referees, who did such a thorough job on all the papers.

[2] The Mediterranean countries, Cyprus and Malta, which make up part of the EU-12, are excluded from our analysis.

[3] Part of the problem is that the acquis here is seen to be 'soft law' or political, rather than legal, commitments and political will is lacking, especially during the recession.

[4] It is worth noting that just two years before joining the EU, Poland was still receiving $1,160 million in development aid, which, as an ODA/GDP percentage, worked out to 0.6 per cent (Grimm and Harmer 2005, p. 10).

DEVELOPMENT POLICIES OF CENTRAL AND EASTERN EUROPEAN STATES

[5] We would argue that missing field research and politically driven, bluntly pro-EU wishful thinking has led to the excessive optimism on the convergence of the 'old' and 'new' member states' development policies in non-academic or semi-academic research.

[6] Palacký University has probably the only full interdisciplinary study programme in the CEE countries, from the Bachelor's to the PhD level.

References

Addison, T., and Mavrotas, G. 2008. Development finance in the global economy: The road ahead. In: Tony Addison and George Mavrotas, eds. *Development finance in the global economy: The road ahead.* Basingstoke, UK: Palgrave, 1–24.

AidWatch, 2008. *No time to waste.* Brussels, Concord.

AidWatch, 2009. *Lighten the load.* Brussels, Concord.

AidWatch, 2010. *Penalty against Poverty: More and Better EU aid can score Millennium Development Goals.* Brussels, Concord.

AidWatch, 2011. *Challenging self-interest: Getting EU aid fit for the fight against poverty.* Brussels, Concord.

Alesina, A., and Dollar, D., 2000. Who gives foreign aid to whom and why? *Journal of economic growth,* 5 (1), 33–63.

Börzel, A.T., 2010. Why you don't always get what you want: EU enlargement and civil society in Central and Eastern Europe. *Acta politica,* 2010, 45, 1–10.

Browne, S., 1980. *Foreign aid in practice.* London: Pinter.

Bucar, M., and Mrak, M., 2007. Challenges of development cooperation for EU new member states. *Paper presented at the ABCDE World Bank conference,* 17–18 May, Bled, Slovenia. Available from: http://siteresources.worldbank.org/INTABCDESLO2007/Resources/PAPERABCDEBucarMrak.pdf [Accessed 11 November 2009].

Bučar, M., *et al.,* 2007. *Towards a division of labour in European development co-operation: Case studies.* Bonn: Deutsches Institut fur Entwicklungspolitik.

Carbone, M., 2004. Development policy. In: N. Nugent, ed. *EU enlargement.* Basingstoke, UK: Palgrave, 242–252.

Carbone, M., 2007. *The European Union and international development.* London: Routledge/UACES.

Copsey, N., and Pomorska, K., 2010. Poland's power and influence in the European Union: The case of its Eastern policy. *Comparative European politics,* 8 (3), 304–326.

Dale, G., 2011. *First the transition, then the crash.* London: Pluto Press.

Dauderstadt, M., 2002. Eastern enlargement and development policy. In: M. Dauderstadt, ed. *EU Eastern enlargement and development cooperation.* Bonn: Friedrich-Ebert-Stiftung.

Drążkiewicz, E., 2008. *Official Development Assistance in Visegrad countries.* Warsaw: Polish Green Network.

The Economist, 2010. "Eastern Europe" Wrongly labelled, The Economist Jan 09.

Eurobarometer, 2007. Europeans and development aid. Eurobarometer 280. Available from: http://ec.europa.eu/public_opinion/archives/ebs/ebs_280_en.pdf [Accessed 11 November 2009].

Grimm, S., and Harmer, A., 2005. Diversity in donorship: The changing landscape of official humanitarian aid: Aid donorship in Central Europe. *HPG background paper,* September.

Grimm, S., *et al.,* 2008. European development cooperation to 2020: Challenges by new actors in international development. *Working Paper 4.* Bonn: European Association of Development Research and Training Institutes (EADI). Available from: http://www.edc2020.eu/index.php?id=69 [Accessed November 2011].

Hallet, M., 2009. Economic cycles and development aid: What is the evidence from the past? ECFIN Economic Brief 5, European Commission's Directorate-General for Economic and Financial Affairs, November.

Hanšpach, D., 2004. V4 countries and development cooperation: (Re)emerging donors in (re)united Europe and the role of UNDP. *Medzinárodne otázky* (international issues), XIII (4/2004), 23–41.

Horký, O., 2010a. Policy coherence for development of the Czech Republic: Case studies on migration and trade. In: Paul Hoebink, ed. *European development cooperation: In between the local and the global.* Amsterdam: Amsterdam University Press, 235–258.

Horký, O., 2010b. Development cooperation in the Czech foreign policy. In: Michal Kořan, ed. *Czech foreign policy: Analysis.* Prague, Institute of International Relations, 347–361.

Horký, O., 2010c. The Europeanization of development policy: Accommodation and resistance of the Czech Republic. DIE Discussion Paper, 18/2010. Available from: http://www.die-gdi.de/CMS-Homepage/openwebcms3.nsf/(ynDK_contentByKey)/ANES-8BCEK3/$FILE/DP%2018.2010.pdf [Accessed 29 November 2011].

Horký, O., 2011. The impact of the shallow Europeanisation of the 'new' member states on the EU's actorness: What coherence between foreign and development policy? In: Stefan Gänzle, Sven Grimm and Davina Makhan, eds. *EU policy for global development: Superpower in the making?* Basingstoke, UK: Palgrave Macmillan.

Kim, S., and Lightfoot, S., 2011. Does 'DAC-ability' really matter? The emergence of non-DAC donors: Introduction to policy arena. *Journal of international development*, 23 (5), 711–721.

Kragelund, P., 2008. The return of the non-DAC donors to Africa: New prospects for African development. *Development policy review*, 26 (5), 555–584.

Krichewsky, L., 2003. *Development policy in the accession countries: Report,* 2nd edn. Vienna, Trialog.

Kuuish, R., Andres Kasekamp, Piret Ehin, Kristi Raik, Riina Kuusik, Vadim Kononenko, Eero Mikenberg, Kai-Helin Kaldas, Margus Kolga, Aili Ribulis, Toomas Hendrik Ilves. 2006. Estonia's development cooperation: Power, prestige and practice of a new donor. In: *Estonian Foreign Policy Yearbook*. Tallinn, Eesti Välispoliitika Instituut, 51–67.

Lightfoot, S., 2008. Enlargement and the challenge of EU development. *Perspectives on European politics and society*, 9 (2), 128–142.

Lightfoot, S., 2010. The Europeanisation of international development policies: The case of Central and Eastern European states. *Europe-Asia studies*, 62 (2), 329–350.

Lister, M., and Carbone, M., 2006. Integrating gender and civil society into EU development policy. In: M. Lister and M. Carbone, eds. *New pathways in international development: Gender and civil society in EU policy*. Aldershot, UK: Ashgate, 1–14.

Mahon, R., and McBride, S., 2009. Standardizing and disseminating knowledge: The role of the OECD in global governance. *European political science review*, 1 (1), 83–101.

Manning, R., 2006. Will 'emerging' donors challenge the face of international co-operation? *Development policy review*, 24 (4), 371–83.

Meislová, M., 2010. Czech Republic's 2010 elections and foreign development cooperation. *Contemporary European studies*, 2, 29–41.

Orbie, J., and Versluys, H., 2008. The European Union's international development policy: Leading and benevolent? In: J. Orbie, ed. *Europe's global role*. Farnham, UK: Ashgate, 67–90.

Palubinskas, G., 2003. Democratization: The development of nongovernmental organizations (NGOs) in Central and Eastern Europe. *Public administration and management*, 8 (3), 150–163.

PASOS, 2007. The challenge of the EU development co-operation policy for new member states. Report prepared for EP Development Committee, EXPO/B/DEVE/2007/33 NOVEMBER2007 PE 385.540 EN. Available from: http://www.pasos.org/www- pasosmembers-org/publications/the-challenge-of-the-eu-development-co-operation-policy-for-new-member-states [Accessed 11 November 2011].

Riddell, R., 2007. *Does foreign aid really work?* Oxford, UK: Oxford University Press.

Szent-Ivanyi, B., and Tetenyi, A., 2008. Transition and foreign aid policies in the Visegrad countries: A path dependant approach. *Transition studies review*, 15 (3), 573–587.

Szent-Ivanyi, B., 2011. Aid allocation of the emerging Central and Eastern European donors. *Journal of international relations and development*, forthcoming.

Therien, Jean-Philippe, and Noel, Alain, 2000. *Political parties and foreign aid. American political science review*, 94 (1), 151–162.

Tingley, D., 2010. Donors and domestic politics: Political influences on foreign aid effort. *The quarterly review of economics and finance*, 50 (1), 40–49.

Vittek, M., and Lightfoot, S., 2009. The Europeanization of Slovak development cooperation? *Contemporary European studies*, 1, 21–37.

Woods, N., 2005. The shifting politics of foreign aid. *International affairs*, 81 (2): 393–409.

Younas, J., 2008. Motivation for bilateral aid allocation: Altruism or trade benefits. *European journal of political economy*, 24 (3), 661–674.

The Transfer of the Central and Eastern European 'Transition Experience' to the South: Myth or Reality?

ONDŘEJ HORKÝ

Institute of International Relations, Prague, Czech Republic

ABSTRACT *The Central and Eastern European (CEE) states claim that their post-communist transition experience is a value-add to their development cooperation programmes. They argue that the lessons learnt from their relatively successful political and economic reforms have the potential to inform policy-makers in both the post-communist East and the post-colonial South. This article closes a research gap by building on the conceptual distinction between the political and technical levels of the development process. First, it scrutinizes the inherent contradictions and limitations of the transfer of the 'transition experience' through development cooperation, and then it assesses the extent and impact of transition inspired development projects run by the CEE governments, non-governmental organizations (NGOs) and companies. It is argued that the prevalent political character of the transition and the technical nature of the current EU development policy has significantly reduced the possibility of transfer, which is seen in the limited scope and impact of projects that build on specific transition experiences. As seen from the Czech case, the contrast between strong political discourse, limited institutional settings and weak implementation practices shows that the shallow transfer of the 'transition experience' is mere rhetoric. This is shown by their use of tied technical assistance for the promotion of their political, security and commercial interests in the middle-income countries of East and South Eastern Europe.*

And I'm very much looking forward to hearing some of the observations that those who've fought long and hard for democracy may have as we face similarly transformative moments around the world.

US President Barack Obama, Warsaw, 28 May 2011

1. Introduction[1]

In May 2011, the President of the United States (US), Barack H. Obama, visited Warsaw. He not only met with 17 political leaders of the Central and Eastern

European (CEE) countries, he also held a discussion with the former leaders of the Solidarity movement and other Polish experts on democratization, human rights and development. In the context of the Arab Spring, the popular uprisings in Tunisia, Egypt, Libya and other countries of North Africa and the Middle East, Obama expressed his hope that Poland, a leader of Europe and a success story in political and economic terms, would share its experience with other world regions (The White House 2011). The 'transition experience' of the CEE states has never before been given such attention from both the media and the political world, and it was proudly reiterated by the highest Polish representatives during the President's visit.[2] Significantly, though, while discussing the event, the newspapers did not report the statements about what Poland could teach the world except for those in Obama's introductory speech (*Gazeta Wyborcza* 2011a).

The hype about the 'transition experience', which was initiated mainly by the Arab Spring events and preceded by the announcement of the Polish Ministry of Foreign Affairs that it would send Lech Wałesa, the former leader of *Solidarność,* to Tunisia as soon as in mid-April 2011 (*Gazeta Wyborcza* 2011b), has certainly highlighted the supposed know-how of Poland and other post-communist countries. If they really have the ability to help the Arab world with their recent democratic transitions, it would mean that the transition of a part of the CEE is over and that the region has definitely become a part of the West that is officially recognized by the US. Similarly, at the European level, the transition experience has been put forward by the Czech, Hungarian and Polish Presidencies in the Council of the European Union (EU). Moreover, the European Commission (2010) has materialized the 'transition experience' for the first time by publishing the *European Transition Compendium.* This 300 page 'address book' of the 'new' member states' experiences in different fields can attest to their added value, prove their maturity and, hence, secure for them a place *à part entière* in the EU development policy despite their poor performance in the field of international development (Horký 2010b). Yet, evidence of the transfer of the 'transition experience', not speaking about its feasibility, is still missing.

The academia, including the author of this article, did not fail to replicate the political discourse. At the most, researchers have criticized the low capitalization of the 'transition experience' of the post-communist states without, however, scrutinizing the very possibility of its transfer (Szent-Iványi and Tétényi 2008). This paper closes this research gap by building on the conceptual distinction between the political and technical levels of the development process. Not only does it assess the extent and impact of transition inspired development projects run by the CEE governments, non-governmental organizations (NGOs) and companies, it also scrutinizes the inherent contradictions and limitations of the transfer of the 'transition experience' through international development cooperation. If not indicated otherwise, the geographical term, 'Central and Eastern Europe', is reduced here to the 10 post-communist 'new' EU member states, excluding Cyprus and Malta. In fact, the notion of 'countries in transition' or 'transition economies' (IMF 2000) has faded out since the entry of some of them into the EU, which has resulted in the split of the former East between the global North and the global South – between aid donors and aid recipients.[3]

The article proceeds as follows. The first part reviews the references to the 'transition experience' in academic literature, policy research and political documents at the EU level. It points out the implicit contradiction between the political character of the transition and the technical character of development cooperation as a vehicle intended to spread the supposedly original experience beyond the borders of the CEE. The second part applies the conceptual framework of depoliticization to the activities carried out by the EU, the 'new' member states, their sub-regional groupings, multilateral organizations, and especially by the Czech Republic as a country case. It presents the paradoxical situation in which the institutional reform of development cooperation, conforming to Europeanization, has closed rather than enabled opportunities for transfer of the transition experience. The analysis of a project that openly strived to transfer the Czech transition experience in the social sector to Serbia illustrates the abovementioned contradictions and the inability of technical assistance to initiate lasting political changes in the partner country. The article concludes that the shallow transfer of the 'transition experience' has some limited reality to it, but it remains above all mere rhetoric or a 'myth' that is complementary to the shallow Europeanization of the development cooperation policies of the 'new' member states and to their national interest in the middle income countries of East and South Eastern Europe.[4]

2. Between the Political and the Technical: The Contradictions of the 'Transition Experience' in Development Cooperation

In spite of the growing amount of academic research on the transition and the development cooperation of the 'new' EU member states, the references to the transfer of the 'transition experience' – whose nature is analysed later in this part – have been sporadic. Even serious attempts to bring the transition and development cooperation onto the academic agenda have been unsuccessful in joining the two issues together.[5] Some identify the transfer of the 'transition experience' as the new member states' most evident comparative advantage, but they insist that the states have not yet capitalized on it (Szent-Iványi and Tétényi 2008). Others note that according to their informants, the transition experience would be too specific to EU enlargement to be applicable outside the Western Balkans (Lightfoot 2010, p. 341). The most detailed account of the subject was published in an academic journal by a development practitioner (Hanšpach 2005), but the identified sectors where the transition experience is the most relevant corresponded to the actual political priorities of the Czech Trust Fund, implemented by the United Nations Development Programme (UNDP) Regional Centre in Bratislava. More interestingly, the year before the Arab Spring, Katarzyna Żukrowska (2010) edited a book on the 'transformation' in Poland and in North Africa, which goes beyond the traditional focus on the development policies of the CEE countries.[6] However, the book, which was funded by the Polish Ministry of Foreign Affairs, does not live up to expectations and both the comparative ambition of the book and the promise of recommendations on the basis of the Polish case remained unfulfilled.

Policy-oriented research has focused mainly on the transfer of the transition experience through democratization and human rights policy and it has given the EU newcomers the label of 'democracy's new champions' (Kucharczyk and Lovitt 2008). Studies that are more related to development cooperation have usually originated at the national level. A research report commissioned by the Czech Ministry of Foreign Affairs on the Eastern policy of the EU stated unsurprisingly that the 'new' member states surely had 'specific transition know-how', but it questioned its relevance. Nowadays, the Eastern European countries would be best described as having the context of a 'specific symbiosis of capitalism and post-communism' that is different from the Central European context of the 1990s (Schneider 2009, p. 11). Another study has scrutinized the experience of the Czech Republic as an aid recipient (Mareš et al. 2006). Its recommendations highlight the role of aid as a catalyst, the importance of local ownership, the combined use of external and local knowledge, and the design of a clear exit strategy. These elements are already an integral part of the current international development discourse and commitments such as the Paris Declaration, but quite paradoxically, these recommendations are rarely respected by the Czech development cooperation programmes (Horký 2010a).[7]

Finally, the 'transition experience' in development cooperation has been a part of the official discourse of the EU since the 2004 enlargement.[8] Most importantly, Article 33 of the European Consensus on Development states that 'the EU will capitalise on new Member States' experience (such as transition management) and help strengthen the role of these countries as new donors' (European Commission 2005). From the beginning, the transition experience, referred to here using the technical phrase, 'management', has been coupled with the need to Europeanize the 'new donors'.[9] The technical character of the transfer was underlined in a follow-up of the Accra Agenda for Action (High Level Forum 2008), in which the Council welcomed the initiative of the Commission to map the transition experience in the *European Transition Compendium* and asked the Commission as well as the member states to include it in their technical assistance and to foster the partner countries' ownership of it (Council of the EU 2009b).[10] At that point, the only concern about this application was raised by civil society – that the transition experience might overshadow other contributions to the EU development policy (TIS 2009), whatever they might be. Plus, a single participant of a conference dedicated to the topic pointed out the potential difficulties in using development cooperation as a vehicle for the transition experience: the limited volume of aid compared to other financial flows and the relatively resistant mentality in the transition countries (Ministerstvo zahraničních vecí and UNDP 2009).

Despite the consensus on the relevance of the transfer of the 'transition experience', the political declarations are not without contradictions, as attested to by a discussion paper by the Czech EU Presidency, which defined the purpose of the *European Transition Compendium*. It is difficult to imagine how the *political* transition, including the change of regime from autocracy to democracy, the removal of the *nomenklatura*, the 'historical policy' and the empowerment of the society at the grass-roots level (Council of the EU 2009a), could be carried out through *technical* assistance and hence in close cooperation with the governments of the 'partner countries' in the spirit of the Paris Declaration and the Accra Agenda for Action. In a similar vein, a later non-paper by eight 'new' member states, led by the Czech Republic, about the follow-up to the publication of the *Compendium*, has defined transition cooperation as a 'specific *technical* support which uses the experience [...] from *political* and economic reforms' (Non-paper 2011, my emphasis). This contradiction should make us cautious since the history of development cooperation offers numerous examples of seemingly technical cooperation leading to disastrous consequences, including the political repression in Lesotho or even a silent support for the preconditions of a genocide (Ferguson 1997, Uvin 1998). However, in the context of the transfer of the 'transition experience', the contradiction has not been openly tackled so far and, therefore, this article proposes to distinguish between the technical and the political levels to envisage three ideal-typical channels of transferring the potential 'transition experience' (Table 1). I start by scrutinizing and defining the 'transition experience' according to these three channels before moving on to the supplementary conditions for its transfer.

Firstly, at the *technical* level and as a part of the development cooperation between central governments and local authorities, technical assistance is concerned mostly with the 'transition experience' of institutional reforms, capacity building and conformity to new European and international standards such as those in the fields of public administration in general and state accounting or environmental protection in particular. Since the transfer of knowledge requires the consent of the partner country governments, it cannot produce major institutional and political shifts in favour of democracy and human rights. This is not to say, however, that this type of administration-to-administration assistance is apolitical. Indeed, it strengthens the role of the state, which may have positive as well as negative impacts on the population: For example, it can reinforce the state's capacities to enforce limits on air polluters, but at the same time, it may help build the capacities of the state to promote pro-market measures that might lead to land grabs and that are not beneficial to the population. Nevertheless, technical assistance is understood here as apolitical in the sense that it does not necessarily change the power balances between the different political parties and movements of the recipient country.

Secondly, the *political* experience from the aiding country's transition can be fully transferred without the approval of the recipient country's central or local government by supporting the latter's civil society at the grass-roots level or the dissident and opposition movements at the top of its political hierarchy. We have seen that, perhaps, the most important feature of the CEE transitions consists of the conviction that positive social and economic changes cannot occur without building democracy and increasing popular participation in the government. Most activities in exporting this type of 'transition experience' are typically concerned with the training of independent – read anti-government – media or strengthening the capacities of legal or illegal NGOs. Often, this type of assistance can consist of giving cash to persecuted dissidents. Even though this can be reported to the Organisation

Table 1. Channels of transferring the 'transition experience' and their content

Channel	Content
Technical	Transfer of technical knowledge from one public administration to another
Political	Political support of civil society without the consent of the government
Hybrid	Challenging the incoherence of the EU external and development policies

Source: Author.

for Economic Cooperation and Development's (OECD's) Development Assistance Committee (DAC) as Official Development Assistance (ODA), its goals hardly fit the principles and objectives of development cooperation as defined by the European Consensus on Development – ownership, partnership and focus on the Millennium Development Goals (MDGs) (European Commission 2005).[11] Again, these are, of course, ideal types, and some seemingly technical public administration reforms such as the introduction of an ombudsman or a reform of the judiciary system may induce adjustments in power in favour of the citizens at the expense of the elites, but in this case, the reforms would probably be accepted by the partner countries as a part of some kind of political conditionality, as, for example, the conditionality in the framework of the European Neighbourhood Policy (ENP).

Thirdly, there are indeed *hybrid* cases where development cooperation would include political dialogue, democratization and human rights promotion (which are also principles and goals of the European Consensus on Development), but their feasibility is very limited since this would include strengthening the political conditionality of the EU development policy. Arguing with their 'transition experience', the 'new' member states are willing to strengthen political conditionality as such since they find that the European Commission and the 'old' member states are not enforcing it sufficiently because of other, often commercial interests. In the same vein, the 'new' member states have been very critical of the low conditionality of the general budget support provided by the EU. But the 'new' member states' efforts to act according to their positions are hampered not only by the EU's inability to exercise political conditionality, which is in line with the traditional institutional division between foreign and development policy, but also by their limited negotiation power within the Council (Horký 2010b) and in their bilateral policies.

In addition to the three narrow channels of transfer I have outlined here, attention must be equally paid to the very content of the 'transition experience'. Transition, as defined by the *European Transition Compendium*, is understood mostly as a shift from autocracy to democracy and from a centrally planned economy to a market-based economy.[12] However, at both the political and the economic levels, the 'new' member states' institutions were formally set up or transformed as quickly as their economies were liberalized and privatized in the 1990s. For these countries, the first decade of the 21st century was characterized by the incremental implementation of the *acquis communautaire* in their national legislations and the preparation for accession to the EU. Given that the CEE countries were not the only authoritarian countries in the 1980s and that neoliberal policies were promoted by the Bretton Woods institutions worldwide, it appears that few experiences are specific to the transition of the 'new' EU member states.

That does not mean, however, that the generic experience of countries that underwent modernization is universal in the sense that it can be translated to different cultural contexts. It was already underlined that the situation in, say, Hungary in 1991 was very different from the context of Kyrgyzstan in 2011 since many CEE countries, whatever their level of development, have privatized and liberalized their economies. The experience is thus reduced to those fields in which the public sector, rather than markets, is involved. However, probably the most valuable lesson of the CEE transitions is that economic and social development cannot happen without major bottom-up political changes in the environment of geopolitical changes caused by the end of the Cold War. Moreover, the impetus of the unrepeatable geopolitical changes was so strong that the CEE countries, despite their formally democratic regimes, suffer from weak civil societies, weak popular participation and widespread corruption. In addition, there is no societal consensus on the 'transition experience', as parts of the post-communist societies are strongly critical of the uneven economic development that has been taking place since 1990. Paradoxically, the democracy-development nexus is simultaneously contradicted by the example of China, which has separated liberal democracy from capitalism, because many countries see China as an inspiring model. And finally, but no less importantly, be it in civil society or public administration, for the transfer to be a success, the partner country must be interested in the aid donor's 'transition experience', rather than in any other type of know-how, including the know-how that is offered by a more experienced donor. In conclusion, the already narrow channels of transfer with the limited relevance of the transition experience make it hardly transferable into development cooperation outside technical assistance in public administration.

3. The Transfer of the 'Transition Experience': Some Evidence from the Czech Case

It would be quite naïve to expect this article to offer solid evidence that the 'transition experience' was effectively transferred from the CEE countries to other parts of the region and beyond its borders through development cooperation and that it initiated long-lasting changes in the target societies. Indeed, it is difficult to present evidence that *any* development intervention has produced sustainable changes anywhere in the world. Moreover, few evaluations of development cooperation have been carried out in the CEE countries, whose development aid is considered to be fragmented, donor-driven and inefficient. Therefore, this article does not focus on the whole region – although other country cases using the same methodology would be very much welcome as a follow-up of this new research agenda – but merely on the Czech Republic. As Balázs Szent-Iványi (2012) rightly points out, the Czech Republic is considered one of the most advanced donors in the region in terms of quantity, quality and institutional settings of development cooperation. Its case might be instructive since if only a small amount of evidence of effective transfer of the 'transition experience' is found in the Czech Republic, it might be foolish to expect a great amount of evidence of effective transfer among later entrants such as Bulgaria and Romania. Szent-Iványi also shows that the aid accounted for as the 'transition cooperation' of the Czech Republic did not account for more than a negligible fraction of the Czech ODA (Szent-Iványi and Tétényi 2008).

However, the case of the Czech Republic also has its pitfalls. Its government restarted the foreign development aid programme as early as in 1995 along with the OECD accession, that is earlier than the other 'new' member states to whom the EU accession carrot represented the first incentive. This means that the Czech path of dependence might be stronger and, therefore, it might limit the Czech capacity to use its 'transition experience' in the current development cooperation programmes.[13] On the other hand, 'transition experience' is not necessarily concentrated around the specific tool of transition cooperation (it is now referred to as 'transition policy') and it must be identified in other bilateral and bi-multilateral development projects as well. The Czech Republic's position in the Council of the EU and the Visegrad Group is also useful for understanding its stance by applying the distinction between the technical, political and hybrid approaches to the 'transition experience'.

Officially, the Czech Republic has a hybrid approach to development cooperation that should help it to promote its transition experience abroad. In fact, the Czech law on foreign development cooperation and humanitarian aid defines poverty reduction as the main goal of development cooperation in the wording of the European Consensus on Development (European Commission 2005), but it also adds 'democracy promotion, human rights protection and good governance in developing countries' as additional goals (Vláda České republiky 2010a). Like in other Central European countries and the Baltic States, the Czech Republic's development cooperation strategy insists that development cooperation be an integral part of the foreign policy (Vláda České republiky 2010a). This hybrid approach can be explained not only by the existence of the transition policy, which is accountable as official development assistance, but also by an ideological conviction that development cooperation should be politically conditional.[14] With no direct experience with the general budget support, the Czech Republic was the member state that was most critical of its low political conditionality at the EU level in 2010. The Czech Republic was also ahead of the other member states in promoting the *European Transition Compendium* with the idea of creating a new financial tool to support the transfer of the 'transition experience' in the EU's neighbourhood. In this regard, the involvement of Czech NGOs and companies in the EU's development policy is the pragmatic side of the coin named 'transition experience', a point on which this article dwells in the conclusion. But if the official approach of the Czech Republic can be labelled as hybrid, the volume of its development cooperation is so low and fragmented that, in reality, it does not represent any leverage in its bilateral relations with the recipient countries, and due to its low capacities, an upload of preferences to the European level is improbable (Horký 2010a).[15]

In reality, the transfer of the 'transition experience' is clearly divided between its political and technical tools even though the strategy papers for transition policy and development cooperation superficially refer one to the other (Vláda České republiky 2010b, Ministerstvo zahraničních věcí 2010). The political support of civil society is carried out by the Czech NGOs that have been awarded grants by the Department of Human Rights and Transition Policy since 2004. The department is subordinated to the Political Director of the Ministry of Foreign Affairs and understood as a political (and not developmental) instrument.[16] Indeed, the most prominent activities in this respect concern the support of the opposition movements in Belarus, Cuba and Myanmar. However, none of the projects have been evaluated so far and the resistance of these regimes to democratization casts substantial doubts on the overall strategy of focusing on the opposition. On the other hand, the Department for Development Cooperation and Humanitarian Aid reports to the same Deputy Minister of Foreign Affairs that is responsible for economic diplomacy. The volume of grants for the transition policy – €2 million – should be considered minor as compared to the figure of around €25 million for the other bilateral projects, where transition experience in its technical form may be applied as well. However, if the bi-multilateral cooperation is included, the UNDP Czech Trust, with an approximate budget of €500,000 a year, is the main tool of involving the Czech transition experience in development cooperation in the form of technical assistance.

The UNDP Regional Centre in Bratislava, which coordinates the programme, is the only identified actor that openly claims that there is actual demand for the transition experience in the post-Soviet countries and the Western Balkans (UNDP 2010).[17] A typical 'product' of the Czech UNDP Trust Fund is a study tour for officials from the former Soviet bloc and Yugoslavia to the Czech Republic, or participation of Czech experts in an event abroad. Since 2004, the four priority axes include HIV and AIDS, environmental assessment, good governance at the local level, and economic reforms at the central level. NGOs and companies exclusively from the Czech Republic implement about 20 projects a year. No evaluation of the tied technical assistance has been carried out until now. Not all projects include the transition experience as such, but the projects are mainly related to the expertise on issues that has been present in Czechoslovakia and the Czech Republic and do not pay much attention to the transition context. The activities in the field of HIV and AIDS prevention and treatment, for example, started before 1990. Other fields taken up are related to the implementation of the EU's norms, especially those related to the adoption of communitarian standards that facilitate mutual trade.

So far, the 'transition experience' projects have been identified in two special, but marginal, instruments of Czech development cooperation without sufficient evidence of their impact. However, technical assistance that uses the transition experience appears also among a small minority of ordinary multi-year and, hence, potentially more sustainable bilateral projects that were formerly coordinated by the line ministries and are nowadays implemented by the Czech Development Agency. There is only one evaluation report from 2004 on a project implemented by a Czech NGO in the field of food safety that might be labelled as 'transitional' since it sought to implement measures brought about by the EU accession in Vietnam (Ministerstvo zahraničních věcí 2004). The evaluation team discovered that most of the related activities were not carried out; the project was considered a failure and it was recommended that it should be stopped before its planned end. Another project, building a migration and asylum system in Ukraine, which could have partly learnt from the Czech experience, was judged as successful. Nevertheless, it was noted that the Ukrainian public administration was not involved enough to ensure optimal sustainability of the results.

With evaluations missing, the difficulties in meeting all the conditions to transfer the transition experience are best shown in detail on one project that attempted to use the 'transition experience' in development cooperation (Horký and Němečková 2006). The name of the project, which was implemented in Serbia from 2004 to 2006 by the major Czech NGO, People in Need, can be literally translated as Support of the Institutional Transition Process and Initiation of Changes in the Care System for the Mentally Disabled in Serbia and Montenegro. The project was funded by the Czech Ministry of Labour and Social Affairs with a budget of €500,000. Its informal goal was not to transfer positive experiences from the transition of the institutions for the intellectually disabled in the Czech Republic, but rather to encourage the Serbian stakeholders to avoid the mistakes that the Czech institutions made in the

1990s. At that time, substantial funds were poured into transforming the obsolete and dilapidated institutions in the Czech Republic into almost luxurious, yet still restricted, places when what the country should have done was to close or limit the institutions for the lightly disabled and start to empower and integrate them back into society by setting up protected homes with assistants for the handicapped. During the Czech-Serbian project, a model protected home for a dozen clients was built in Stamnica, the employees of the local institution were trained by their Czech counterparts and an information centre for the Serbian population and media was opened in the capital. However, even if the rights of the intellectually disabled are nowadays tackled by the Serbian ombudsman, the situation in the overcrowded institutions has not changed and the clients are still treated in a paternalistic way, as they are considered unable to lead a decent life and denied even basic rights to privacy (Ђорђевић 2010). The reason for this is not only the absence of funding and human resources, but also the fact that the Serbians have not yet gotten rid of the prejudices that keep them distant from their disabled children and relatives.

The analysis of the Czech project in Serbia shows that even if the transition experience that development cooperation is supposed to transfer is highly relevant and original, it is hardly sustainable without long-term capacity building and changes in cultural patterns that are almost impossible to tackle from outside the recipient society. Moreover, the project in question was implemented by an NGO without a direct partnership between the relevant ministries or institutions in the Czech Republic and Serbia, which limited the sustainability of the outcomes. A big paradox of the 'transformation' of the bilateral system for providing development aid in the Czech Republic is that the decision-making was concentrated in the Ministry of Foreign Affairs, the implementation at the Czech Development Agency, and the previously 'fragmented and inefficient' aid provided directly by the line ministries was stopped. Despite many viable arguments for the centralization of Czech development cooperation, the ministries' fears that their expertise would be lost have proved to be legitimate. In practice, only the Ministry of Finance has been left a symbolic envelope for transition inspired cooperation projects, and its counterparts are to be evaluated soon. In other words, creating a bilateral aid system similar to those existing in experienced donor countries, in line with the Europeanization and OECD-ization efforts, has partly destroyed the possibility that the transition experience concentrated in the Czech public administration would ever be used in development cooperation. Even though the Ministry of Foreign Affairs has recently initiated a good governance budget line within the Czech Development Agency, it is too early to see how this experience, missing in the agency itself, can be externally mobilized in the public administration and externally handled in relation to the South.[18]

Conclusion

A review of the evidence from the Czech Republic has shown that there are a number of projects that refer to the 'transition experience', which is divided between political support for civil societies (mostly those in the authoritarian regimes) and technical assistance focused mostly on the public administration in the neighbourhood.

However, their part in the overall bilateral development cooperation of the country is marginal and their impacts remain unclear. The case study of the Czech project for the care of the intellectually disabled in Serbia has underlined the limits in the application of a negative yet highly relevant transition experience. The small scale of the projects meets the low capacities of the recipient country's local actors and its long-lasting cultural patterns, which makes the experience undergone by the Czech Republic inapplicable to the local context. In terms of the *reality* of the transfer, the final account is weak, which raises the question as to what extent the 'transition experience' is a genuine value-add of the CEE countries.

Moreover, recent developments cast doubts on the future possibility of bringing the transition experience to light in a concentrated effort by the CEE governments, as has been optimistically anticipated since 2009 by development policy-makers and practitioners (Ministerstvo zahraničných vecí and UNDP 2009). The 2011 regional conference of the Hungarian EU Presidency project, organized by the Hungarian platform of development NGOs (HAND 2010), came to the conclusion that the 'transition experience' is mere rhetoric (Szent-Iványi 2012). As a follow-up to the call of the Visegrad Group to use the transition experience 'in a systematic and coherent manner' (Ministerstvo zahraničných vecí 2011), the sub-regional non-governmental development platforms proposed anything but the possibility of using the Visegrad Fund for joint projects (FoRS et al. 2011). The recent setting up of the Centre for Experience Transfer in Integration and Reform (CETIR) as a new structure for providing technical assistance by the Slovak Ministry of Foreign Affairs (Vláda Slovenskej republiky 2011) held out a hope that a recent call for transferring the Slovak transition experience to Egypt and Tunisia would bring about something new, but the projects do not differ from the traditional political support for civil society as spelt out in the Czech calls for Egypt, Libya and Tunisia under the label of 'transition policy' (SlovakAid 2011).

If the transfer of the 'transition experience' to the South refers to little in reality and if, at the same time, it is supposed to be *the* comparative advantage of the 'new' member states in the EU development policy, it must be a myth. And in line with Roland Barthes (1957), myths should serve some purpose. In this direction, this article advances three explanations. First, the marginal 'transition experience', divided between the narrow political and technical channels, is still put forward by the CEE governments because it hides their inability to promote the hybrid approach to development cooperation, which includes democratization and human rights and which would be translated into greater political conditionality of aid. However, their low bilateral development budgets, their weak position in the Council of the EU and the compartmentalization of the EU external policies do not allow for greater coherence between development and foreign policy. In other words, the 'new' member states alone do not have the power to export the revolutions that have brought them (often merely formal) democracy and (unequal) development during the past 20 years.

Second, the 'transition experience' is a myth that helps to foster a new identity for the 'new' member states as donors and to hide their inability and unwillingness to honour their development commitments at the EU and international levels. At the same time, they cannot refuse these commitments since they constitute a part of their identity as developed countries. It may seem scandalous that the European Council defined different official development assistance targets for the 'old' and the 'new' member states in 2005, which has created an unprecedented example of an institutionalized, 'double speed Europe'. However, the limits of the 'transition experience', which seeks its application in the less modernized countries of the CEE region, show that if a policy does not obtain sufficient grass-roots support, its top-down promotion would be unsustainable. And this problem applies ultimately to the development policies of the CEE states.

Third, the 'transition experience' is an excellent fad that masks the promotion of the narrow national or purely particular interests of the CEE states, NGOs and companies. In fact, this 'shallow Europeanisation' is a synonym for a greater promotion of the states' national interests after their EU accession (Denca 2009, Horký 2010b). The 'new' donors may be critical of the depoliticized EU-Africa policy and the commercial interests of the former colonizers, but they forget their own principles when pursuing their own interests in the Eastern dimension of the ENP. Therefore, the transition experience is a perfect tool for justifying the use of tied technical or political assistance for the promotion of political, security and commercial interests in the middle income countries of East and South Eastern Europe, which could hardly be justified by the internationally accepted political discourse on extreme poverty of the MDGs.

I have argued elsewhere that if the EU cannot close the gap between the 'old' and the 'new' member states in development policy, it can hardly aspire to narrow the gap between the North and the South (Horký 2010b). The myth of the 'transition experience' is seemingly one of inclusion since it justifies the place of the newcomers. However, it is also a discourse of exclusion because it legitimates and perpetuates their difference and keeps the substantial political questions of coherence between development and foreign policy out of the EU's political agenda. All those small technical and political projects that are supposed to carry the 'transition experience', whether they are included in the *European Transition Compendium* or not, might have an important symbolic value for the CEE governments. However, the main lesson of the transition – that political and technical changes cannot be tackled separately if they are to be sustainable – has been 'lost in transition'.

Notes

[1] An earlier version of this paper was presented at the 8th CEEISA Convention in Istanbul, 15–17 June 2011, and at the 13th EADI/DSA General Conference in York, 19–22 September 2011. I am thankful to the participants as well as to Simon Lightfoot, Tomáš Profant and an anonymous referee for their suggestions and comments. This research makes up a part of the project, European Integration and the Interests of the Czech Republic, funded by the Czech Ministry of Youth, Education and Sports. The similarity between the title of this paper and the title, *Myth or Reality: The Eastern European Transition Experience* (the title of a column by Peter Kolossa [2010]) is accidental. However, Kolossa's short article, discovered at a later stage of this research, echoes well the rare concerns about the reality of the 'transition experience', as its presumed reality is usually unquestioned in other media (see, for e.g., Chimbelu 2010).

[2] However, the Czech President, Václav Klaus, immediately challenged President Obama's optimism about the transferability of the 1989 democratic experience to North Africa and the Middle East (České noviny 2011).

[3] See Lord (1999) for the problem of defining Central and Eastern Europe.

DEVELOPMENT POLICIES OF CENTRAL AND EASTERN EUROPEAN STATES

[4] The term, 'myth', is understood here in its frequent meaning of 'an unfounded, false notion'. Nevertheless, the myth leads to political consequences and, in this sense, it may be considered as a tool of ideology, according to Roland Barthes (1957), but without adhering completely to the structuralist concept of a sign.

[5] An entire EADI Summer School, co-organized by the author, was held in 2005 in Prague under the title, Experiences of the Central and Eastern European Transition Period: Challenges for Development Cooperation.

[6] The book introduces a useful distinction between transition (replacing one system with another) and transformation (change within one system) (Żukrowska 2010, p. 11). However, in many CEE languages, the corresponding expression for both of these meanings finds its root in the verb, 'transform'.

[7] The European Commission omitted the management of external aid from the questionnaire for the *European Transition Compendium* (European Commission 2010, p. 293), even though it was identified as its very first asset by the EU-12 policy-makers (Maxwell and Gavas 2011).

[8] The Czech Republic stated in its foreign policy strategy that the country 'will offer its integration and transition experience' to South Eastern Europe as soon as in 2003 (Vláda České republiky 2003, p. 12). In an input in the 2010 strategy paper on foreign development cooperation, the NGO platform, FoRS, reiterated that the transition experience was a comparative advantage of the Czech Republic (FoRS et al. 2011).

[9] See Mirela Oprea (2012) for a deconstruction of the term, 'new donors'.

[10] The compendium was reportedly undertaken on the personal initiative of a high representative in the Directorate General of Development from a 'new' member state. Nevertheless, without further details, the European Parliament has recommended using the transition experience gained in the fields of good governance and democracy as well as through the Technical Assistance Exchange Office (TAIEX) and twinning programmes – that is, rather pre-accession than development cooperation tools (European Parliament 2008).

[11] The definition of ODA by the Statistical Reporting Directives of the OECD DAC is too large and contains government expenses that do not necessarily concern development, such as the costs of hosting refugees in donor countries. This definition of ODA even gives the donor countries a large amount of liberty when it comes to reporting the costs. Therefore, the permissiveness of the OECD DAC when it accepts the donor's willingness to boost its ODA with the so-called inflated aid in order to keep its commitments cannot be taken as a normative criterion.

[12] The rhetoric of the *Compendium* is quite significant when it comes to the EU-centred framing of the 'transition'. Since the EU accession is seen as the 'final step in a process of transition' (European Commission 2010, p. 3) and the transition of Greece, Spain and Portugal, all of which had a market regime without being democratic, is placed between quotation marks on the grounds that it is only a partial transition (European Commission 2010, p. 7), the integration in the common European market is ultimately presented as the final and unquestioned universal goal that denies the ideological diversity in the CEE countries during the transition.

[13] See the review of recent developments in Slovakia further in the article.

[14] This conviction is shared by some other member states as well. The conditionality expressed in the Copenhagen criteria and imposed by the EU on the newcomers would prove its reliability elsewhere, but the absence of the accession carrot makes the whole argument unconvincing outside the context of enlargement. See also Horký (2010b).

[15] At the same time, the understanding of human rights is narrow and corresponds to the first generation of human rights as promoted during the communist regime by the Czech dissidents, who influenced Czech foreign policy.

[16] It is not surprising that the Department has commented on the proposal of the *Compendium* by stressing the insufficiently covered role of civil society.

[17] Hungary, Slovakia and Romania have founded similar trust funds, but they use them more for their own capacity building.

[18] Some Czech transition experiences in political terms and in the environment sector were codified in books (UNDP 2004, People in Need 2006) and these were supposed to be transferred in transition and development cooperation projects in various authoritarian countries and Vietnam, respectively, but a detailed analysis of these projects remains the objective of further research. At the same time, these examples

DEVELOPMENT POLICIES OF CENTRAL AND EASTERN EUROPEAN STATES

practically exhaust the transition experience in the development projects of the Czech NGOs as provided by the Czech NGO platform to the consultant that compiled the *European Transition Compendium*.

References

Barthes, R., 1957. *Mythologies*. Paris, France: Seuil.

České noviny, 2011. *Klaus: Obama chtěl střední Evropě říct, že na ni USA nezapomněly*. 28 May, Available from: http://www.ceskenoviny.cz/svet/zpravy/klaus-obama-chtel-stredni-evrope-rict-ze-na-ni-usa-neza-pomnely/643659

Chimbelu, Ch., 2010. Newer EU members add value to Europe's development policy. *Deutsche Welle*, 27 March. Available from: http://www.dw- world.de/dw/article/0,,5389002,00.html

Council of the EU, 2009a. *Discussion on the European Transition Compendium*. 22 April.

Council of the EU, 2009b. *Council conclusions on an operational framework on aid effectiveness*. 18 November. Available from: http://register.consilium.europa.eu/pdf/en/09/st15/st15912.en09.pdf

Denca, S. S., 2009. The Europeanization of foreign policy: Empirical findings from Hungary, Romania and Slovakia. *Journal of contemporary European research*, 5 (3), 389–404.

European Commission, 2005. European Union Development Policy. The European Consensus. Communication (COM (2005) 311 final), 13 July 2005. Available from: http://eur-lex.europa.eu/LexUriServ/LexUriServ.do?uri=COM:2005:0311:FIN:EN:PDF

European Commission, 2010. *European Transition Compendium*. Available from: http://ec.europa.eu/development/icenter/repository/european_transition_compendium_report_20101125.pdf

European Parliament, 2008. The challenge of EU Development Cooperation Policy for the new member states. Resolution (2007/2140(INI)), 13 March 2008. Available from: http://www.europarl.europa.eu/sides/getDoc.do?pubRef=-//EP//NONSGML+REPORT+A6-2008-0036+0+DOC+PDF+V0//EN

Ferguson, J., 1997. *The anti-politics machine: Development, depoliticization, and bureaucratic power in Lesotho*. Minneapolis, MN: University of Minnesota Press.

FoRS (Czech Forum on Development Cooperation) et al., 2011. Development cooperation of the Visegrad Group in the context of the European Union, Briefing Paper, May. Available from: http://www.fors.cz/assets/files/Dokumenty/FoRS_brief_v4_final.pdf.

Gazeta Wyborcza, 2011a. *Obama: Działania polskich opozycjonistów zainspirowały świat*. 28 May. Available from: http://wyborcza.pl/1,91446,9683454,Obama_dzialania_polskich_opozycjonistow_zainspi rowaly.html

Gazeta Wyborcza, 2011b. *Okrągły Stół na eksport do Maghrebu. Wałesa do Afryki*. 14 April. Available from: http://wyborcza.pl/1,75477,9431528,Okragly_Stol_na_eksport_do_MaghrebuWalesa_do_Afryki_.html

HAND, 2010. *New voices in development effectiveness: The Presidency project of the Hungarian Association of NGOs in development and humanitarian aid*. Available from: http://www.eucivil2011.hu/downloads/HAND_Presidency_program_intro_final.pdf

Hanšpach, D., 2005. V4 countries and development cooperation: (Re)emerging donors in (re)united Europe and the role of UNDP. *International issues and Slovak foreign policy affairs*, 14 (1), 29–41.

High Level Forum, 2008. *Accra Agenda for Action*. Available from: http://siteresources.worldbank.org/ACCRAEXT/Resources/4700790-1217425866038/AAA-4-SEPTEMBER-FINAL-16h00.pdf

Ђорђевић, Катарина, 2010. У психијатријским болницима превише пацијената, а мало особља. *Крстарица Вести*. 2 June. Available from: http://vesti.krstarica.com/?rubrika=drustvo&naslov=U+psihijatrijskim+bolnicima+previse+pacijenata%2C+a+malo+osoblja&lang=2&dan=3&mesec=6&godina=2010&sifra=b45d6ed524842ded2aca3a9a8f5b8e4c

Horký, O., 2010a. Development cooperation in the Czech foreign policy. In: Michal Kořan, ed. *Czech foreign policy: Analysis*. Prague: Institute of International Relations, 347–361.

Horký, O., 2010b. The Europeanization of development policy: Accommodation and resistance of the Czech Republic. DIE Discussion Paper, 18/2010. Available from: http://www.die-gdi.de/CMS-Home page/openwebcms3.nsf/(ynDK_contentByKey)/ANES-8BCEK3/$FILE/DP%2018.2010.pdf

Horký, O., and Němečková, T., 2006. SERBEZ – projekt transformace ústavů sociální péče v Srbsku. In: Němcová I., ed. *Případové studie pro mezinárodní ekonomické vztahy*. Praha: Vysoká Škola Ekonomická.

IMF, 2000. Transition economies: An IMF perspective on progress and prospects. *IMF issues brief* (8). Available from: http://www.imf.org/external/np/exr/ib/2000/110300.htm

DEVELOPMENT POLICIES OF CENTRAL AND EASTERN EUROPEAN STATES

Kolossa, P., 2010. *Myth or reality: The Eastern European transition experience.* Available from: http://www.freedomhouse.eu/index.php?option=com_idoblog&task=viewpost&id=295&Itemid=139

Kucharczyk, J., and Lovitt, J., eds., 2008. *Democracy's new champions. European democracy assistance after EU enlargement.* Prague: PASOS. Available from: http://www.pasos.org/content/download/58320/214140/file/Visegrad_democracy_pasos2008.pdf

Lightfoot, S., 2010. The Europeanisation of international development policies: The case of Central and Eastern European States. *Europe-Asia studies*, 62(2). 329–350.

Lord, Ch., ed., 1999. *Central Europe – core or periphery?* Copenhagen: Copenhagen Business School Press.

Mareš, P., Kreuzigerová, P., and Marian, J., 2006. *Zahraniční pomoc v Česku a Československu po listopadu, 1989.* Research report MZV – RM01/08/05.

Maxwell, S., and Gavas, M., 2011. An EU-12 perspective on European development cooperation. *European Development Cooperation Support Programme*, 2 February.Available from: http://international-development.eu/2011/02/02/informal-retreat-for-eu-12/

Ministerstvo zahraničních věcí, 2004. *Evaluace projektu Harmonizace požadavků pro certifikaci zdravotní nezávadnosti a kvality potravin ve Vietnamu včetně podpory ekologického zemědělství.*

Ministerstvo zahraničních věcí, 2010. *Koncepce transformační politiky*, 15 July. Available from: http://www.mzv.cz/jnp/cz/zahranicni_vztahy/lidska_prava/koncepce_transformacni_spoluprace.html

Ministerstvo zahraničných vecí, 2011. *Komuniké.* Available from: http://www.slovakaid.sk/wp-content/uploads/2011/04/komunike-BA-V4-01042011.pdf

Ministerstvo zahraničných vecí and UNDP, 2009. *Sharing transition experience among the EU member states, the Balkan countries, and the Commonwealth of Independent States.* Report, 25–26 June. Available from: http://europeandcis.undp.org/uploads/public1/files/Conference%20summary%20report%20-%20final-17-07-2009-1.doc

Ministerstvo zahraničních věcí and UNDP, 2011. *Zpráva z evaluace projektů zahraniční rozvojové spolupráce České republiky s Mongolskem*, 15 November. Available from: http://www.mzv.cz/public/6a/da/aa/573100_475313 1MNG_eval_report_final.pdf

Non-paper, 2011. *Harnessing the transition experience in EU's external relations: From policy to implementation*, 16 February.

Oprea, Mirela (2012). Development Discourse in Romania: from Socialism to EU Membership. Perspectives on European Politics and Society. pp.1–17, iFirst, Abingdon: Routledge.

People in Need, 2006. *Transformation – the Czech experience.* Prague: People in Need. Available from: http://www.clovekvtisni.cz/download/pdf/69.pdf

Schneider, J., 2009. *Podíl nových členských zemí na formování a uskutečňování východní politiky EU.* Research report MZV - RM 01/01/07. Available from: http://www.mzv.cz/public/ed/51/d4/472476_357498_ENP_zkracena_studie_RM01012007. pdf

SlovakAid, 2011. *Výzva na predkladanie žiadostí o dotácie na projekty oficiálnej rozvojovej pomoci SAMRS/2011/A.* 19 May. Available from: http://www.slovakaid.sk/?p=6690

Szent-Iványi, Balázs, and Tétényi, A., 2008. Transition and foreign aid policies in the Visegrád countries. A path dependent approach. *Transition studies review*, 15 (3), 573–587.

The White House, 2011. *Remarks by President Obama and President Komorowski in discussion on democracy in Warsaw, Poland.* 28 May.Available from: http://m.whitehouse.gov/the-press-office/2011/05/28/remarks-president-obama-and- president-komorowski-discussion-democracy-wa

TIS, 2009. European Transition Compendium. *Trialog Information Service*, 3 July. Available from: http://trialog-information-service.blogspot.com/2009/07/european-transition-compendium.html

UNDP, 2004. *Environmental hot spots remediation - the Czech experience.* Bratislava: UNDP Regional Bureau for Europe and the CIS. Available from: http://europeandcis.undp.org/environment/iep/show/67D7631F-F203-1EE9- BDC975C04709C847

UNDP, 2010. *Zpráva o využití dobrovolného příspěvku České republiky do Rozvojového programu OSN (UNDP) v období od 11/2009 do 10/2010.*

Uvin, P., 1998. *Aiding violence: The development enterprise in Rwanda.* West Hartford, CT: Kumarian Press.

Vláda České Republiky, 2003. *Koncepce zahraniční politiky České republiky na léta 2003–2006*, 3 March 2003.

Vláda České Republiky, 2010a. *Zákon č. 151/2010 Sb., o zahraniční rozvojové spolupráci a humanitární pomoci poskytované do zahraničí a o změně souvisejících zákonů.* Zákon č. 151/2010 Sb., 21 April.

Vláda České Republiky, 2010b. *Usnesení vlády České republiky ze dne č. 366 ke Koncepci zahraniční rozvojové spolupráce České republiky na období 2010-2017*, 24 May. Available from: http://www.mzv.cz/public/c9/7a/f/536971_428745_Koncepce_ZRS.doc

Vláda Slovenskej Republiky, 2011. *Národný program oficiálnej rozvojovej pomoci SR na rok 2011*, 26 January. Available from: http://www.slovakaid.sk/wp-content/uploads/2011/02/NP-ODA-2011.pdf.

Żukrowska, K., ed., 2010. *Transformation in Poland and in the Southern Mediterranean: Sharing experiences*. Warsaw: Poltext.

Visegrad Countries' Development Aid to Africa: Beyond the Rhetoric

DOMINIK KOPIŃSKI

Institute of International Relations, University of Wroclaw, Poland

ABSTRACT *The Visegrad Countries (the Czech Republic, Hungary, Poland and Slovakia, also called the V4) have formally agreed to gradually shift the focus of their development policy and aid allocation to Sub- Saharan Africa (SSA). Yet, contrary to their official rhetoric, African countries continue to find low priority in aid policies. Development cooperation policy in the V4 is largely focused on the close neighbourhood and current political and business stakes triumph over the 'needs and merits' logic of aid allocation. The V4 policy also runs counter to the various international obligations for which the countries have signed up. Officially, a number of African states are classified as priority countries, but in practice, they serve merely as fig leaves masking a true disinterest. This article demonstrates that in most cases, the official message coming from the governments significantly diverges from reality. It also shows that many arguments traditionally used to explain the marginal position of SSA do not hold any longer and the current stance towards African countries is more the result of a lack of strategic vision and ad hoc formulation of foreign policy.*

Introduction

For many years, Sub-Saharan Africa (SSA) was a natural habitat of aid donors belonging to the Organisation for Economic Cooperation and Development (OECD). Yet, this full-scale domination of the Western world is slowly coming to an end with the advent of the so-called South-South cooperation (Kragelund 2010, Tarrósy 2011). Emerging 'heavyweights' such as China (Lancaster 2007, Brautigam 2008, Lum et al. 2009, Chin and Frolic 2007, Davis 2008) and India (Naidu 2008, Chanana 2009) are making remarkable inroads into Africa,[1] with generous aid programmes, loans, debt relief and diplomacy paved with political symbolism. The new entrants are not just a simple addition to the current aid architecture, they offer a brand new philosophy of development assistance, which clearly runs counter to past aid giving patterns (Manning 2006). The old school conditionality, coupled with structural adjustment programmes, which gave development aid in the 1980s and 1990s a bad name and provoked waves of criticism among the African countries, have traded places with a non-interference strategy. Political conditions such as weeding out corruption, promoting human rights and improving governance and accountability are virtually non-existent in South-South development cooperation. As Woods rightly commented, 'Small wonder that the emerging donors are being welcomed with open arms' (Woods 2008, p. 1220). The 'just doing business' approach is the new buzzword these days, which is understandably causing bitter reactions in the West (Naim 2007).

Although the Asian powers have captured most of the media and academia attention, many other new emerging and re-emerging donors have increasingly shifted their focus towards SSA. This includes some of the Arab countries (Villanger 2007, Neumayer 2003, World Bank 2010), Russia,[2] a growing number of recipients-turned-donors such as Brazil (*The Economist* 2010, Cabral and Weinstock 2010) and other, less obvious new kids on the block in the foreign aid industry, such as Venezuela (Márquez 2005, Morsbach 2006, Corrales 2009). The international aid architecture has, therefore, changed significantly in the past years. This power shift has translated into real numbers. According to the OECD, development assistance from providers other than its Development Assistance Committee (DAC) donors amounted to between US$12 billion and US$14 billion in 2008, which, assuming that all of these flows were consistent with the definition of official development assistance (ODA), would represent 9–10 per cent of global ODA (Smith et al. 2010).

Also, for years, financing development in Africa has been an integral part of aid policies in the new member states of the European Union (EU). In terms of volume, the so-called Visegrad countries (V4) – the Czech Republic, Hungary, Poland and Slovakia – deserve particular attention. Their relative importance in the region has already rendered them an appealing case for academics (Horký 2006, Lightfoot 2010, Szent-Iványi and Tétényi 2008, Vittek and Lightfoot 2010). Although, as studies show, the group is quite diversified, particularly in progress with building organizational setups and legal frameworks,[3] all four countries share a number of similarities, which validates a universal approach to investigating their aid allocation and policies. All four have full membership in the OECD, which imposes certain obligations on their part with regard to formulation and delivery of development assistance. By accessing to the EU, the V4 have assumed additional responsibilities, in particular committing themselves to increasing the EU's ODA and adhering to the rules and recommendations adopted by the community.

Historically, this is not a new venture into Africa. The V4 has a long record of development cooperation, and also in the region. During the communist era, the Warsaw Pact countries supported a number of peers – either clear-cut communist countries or those on the road to socialism. This was done in the name of solidarity and to spread the communist ideology. As a matter of fact, if one uses the OECD quantitative benchmarks, the assistance was more than symbolic (Manning 2006). In many cases, it complied with the 0.7 per cent of Gross Domestic Product (GDP) target adopted by the United Nations, which, in all ODA history, has been met by only a handful of Western donors. The donorship era was interrupted abruptly when communism began to fall apart. From that point onward, pursuing ideological goals no longer made much sense. After a period of a relatively swift democratic transition, facilitated by massive external assistance from the West and followed by accession to the club of the world's richest countries, the OECD, the V4 officially joined the ranks of the donors. The transition from recipient to donor was officially over, even though, in reality, it had just begun.

It should be noted that the V4's (re)engagement with Africa took place under circumstances fundamentally different from those that informed other non-DAC, non-OECD countries such as China or Brazil. The latter began its recent venture into Africa mainly as a result of 'pull' factors, for strategic reasons such as access to raw materials and new market opportunities. Poland and the Czech Republic have never regarded Africa as a potential strategic trade or investment partner, nor have they seen any rationale for nurturing economic cooperation with any of the African states. Immersed in resolving internal problems inherited from a continuously haunting communist past and preoccupied (often bordering on obsessed) with the idea of European integration, they lost the global perspective and the conviction that moving towards Africa politically or commercially could present any viable benefits. If anything, Africa was seen more as a remnant burden from the Cold War than a land of opportunities.

Nowadays, the four countries, still relatively new, yet, as the years go by, increasingly more experienced donors, are under growing pressure to rejuvenate their development cooperation with Africa. Importantly, most of the pressure comes from the EU, a result of past commitments to increase both aid in relation to GDP and what constitutes the central focus of this article – development funding earmarked specifically for Africa. In addition, documents such as the Joint EU-Africa Strategy and the European Consensus on Development leave no doubt that from the perspective of the EU, development cooperation with Africa is to be elevated. The other source of pressure, the importance of which will most likely intensify in the coming years as global education efforts start bearing fruit, is public opinion. The public expects the V4 governments to use their tax money increasingly to assist the least developed countries (LDCs) with the most desperate needs, instead of pursuing foreign policy related goals. In many opinion polls, Africa stands out as the most needy and, thus, the most legitimate destination of aid monies (IPA 2005, quoted in Vittek and Lightfoot 2010, p. 30). According to the most recent survey conducted in Poland, 52 per cent of the Polish public is of the opinion that Africa should be prioritized in the geographical distribution of development assistance (Polacy o pomocy rozwojowej 2010).

This paper is structured as follows. The first section offers some findings on the rhetoric employed by the V4 with regard to SSA and the Millennium Development Goals (MDGs). In the second section, the rhetoric is juxtaposed against the reality, or the actual development assistance channelled to the region. Further, the paper addresses the question of why the reality cannot be easily matched with the rhetoric. The last section presents the conclusion.

1. Africa in V4 Aid Policies: Rhetoric

There is an omnipresent narrative in the V4 that assisting the LDCs in improving the livelihood of their people is what development assistance should be about ultimately. The humanitarian and moral obligation undertone is applied almost universally. This is particularly true of Africa, which is legitimately regarded as the region with the most acute development needs in the world. This official discourse is mirrored in the opinion polls, which unequivocally point towards Africa as the most preferred destination of the V4 citizens' tax monies. Annual reports, booklets, virtually all materials produced by the governments and circulated in public, take the common stance that development assistance, as the name implies, is about promoting development, and this should implicitly take place primarily in the poorest corners of the world. Furthermore, the MDGs clearly stand out as an overarching objective of the aid effort and a navigation tool for donors' practices. This position is often validated by politicians who attempt to ensure the public and external actors that Africa has a special place in their 'hearts and minds'.

Clearly, the rhetoric exhibits notable variations, with some countries demonstrating more commitment to addressing the ills of the developing world 'on paper' (Poland) and others being more restrained in the language employed in documents and on official websites (Czech Republic, Hungary and Slovakia). For example, the Czech Republic makes it sufficiently clear that it is committed to supporting the LDCs. The official Czech communication on development cooperation says: 'The strategic goal of Czech development policy is to eliminate poverty and support safety and prosperity via efficient partnerships enabling impoverished and less developed countries to achieve their goals. The starting point consists of the Millennium Development Goals (MDGs)' (*Czech Development Cooperation Booklet* 2009). The document goes on to say: 'The wide range of development activities the Czech Republic focused on in 2009 was intended to contribute to the achievement of the Millennium Development Goals.' The website of the Czech Development Agency employs rhetoric that suggests a clear focus on the LDCs: 'The Czech Republic sees a moral obligation in contributing to the coordinated international activities aimed at reducing poverty in less developed and less wealthy parts of the world.' In a similar tone, the MDGs are presented as a central focus of Czech development cooperation: 'We fully support the Millennium Development Goals defined in the Millennium Declaration of 2000 and reaffirmed at the UN World Summit in September 2005 where the international community again expressed its determination to eradicate extreme poverty, its causes and consequences.' Nonetheless, it is fair to say that in the case of the Czech Republic, the narrative is more moderate in that it is difficult to find extreme positions and excessive official statements that would diverge from reality to the extent of absurdity. Quite paradoxically, more easily traceable radical statements come from the aid opponents, among which, probably, the most outspoken is the Czech President, Vaclav Klaus, who has expressed his critical stance towards development aid on many occasions (Klaus 2010).

Slovakia, which is relatively more vocal, yet also quite moderate, not only demonstrates its strong 'verbal' commitment to working towards the MDGs, but actually provides 'evidence' that its development assistance has contributed to the MDGs (Slovak Aid 2010). Some assertions in the report are bold, but hard to verify. It is, for example, argued that 22 per cent of Slovak ODA has contributed to MDG 1 (eradicating extreme poverty and hunger) and these include 'projects focused particularly on poor countries in sub-Saharan Africa and Asia' (Slovak Aid 2010). As will be shown in the next section, it is extremely difficult to align these assertions with the crude data on aid allocation, let alone the real effects of such aid.

In Hungary, there has been a noticeable impetus to revitalize relations with Africa in development cooperation. 'We intend to pay greater attention to Africa,'

Hungarian Foreign Minister Kinga Göncz announced to African ambassadors during the Africa Day organized in 2007 in Budapest (Afrol News 2007). In the same vein, Ferenc Gemesi, the then Deputy State Secretary in the Ministry of Foreign Affairs (MFA), argued, 'It is high time that we redefined our goals and interests concerning the African continent and created a new framework for our intentions' and 'within our foreign relation aspirations we must define Africa's position in a rational and future-oriented manner'. He also asserted, 'Hungary's Africa policy has to pay special attention to the bilateral development of relations with those African partner countries that have special relevance and importance to us. We aspire to maintain our present relations and those that we have been building through the past decades' (Gömbös 2007, p. 16). The above quotes, derived from a publication named *The Future of Development Policies and Changing Priorities: Africa*, may suggest that Africa is indeed of growing importance in Hungarian political circles. In another report on the MDGs (MFA,Hungary 2004), the Hungarian government tried to provide concrete evidence that it took the MDGs seriously. There is, however, a striking contrast between the number of projects being presented as Hungarian inputs to the realization of the MDGs and the actual aid allocation. Most of the projects are either being implemented in relatively prosperous countries located in the 'wider neighborhood', where the problems enshrined in the MDG Declaration are less acute, if marginal (MDG 3 and 'women entrepreneurs in Serbia and Montenegro'), or simply outsourced to Hungarian non-governmental organizations (NGOs) (see, for example, MDG 2 and MDG 5). A good example of the yawning gap between rhetoric and reality can be found in MDG 7, where the report states: ' [. . .] the spread of HIV/AIDS is one of the greatest threats to development, especially in poor countries. 40 million people are HIV infected, 26 million in Africa alone.' Quite surprisingly, as an example of Hungary addressing the HIV issue, the Hungarian Heart Foundation project is shown, under which a pulmonary screening centre has been set up in the Voivodina region in Serbia and Montenegro.

Probably, the greatest amount of rhetoric suggesting a close alignment of aid policy with international norms and rules is employed by Poland. One of the booklets issued by the Polish MFA clearly recognizes the extraordinary financial needs of Africa. It says, 'Africa remains the continent requiring by far the biggest support of the developed countries' (MSZ 2008). In the same vein, the 2009 Annual Report notes, for example, that out of the 1.02 billion undernourished people in the world, close to a quarter live in Africa (MSZ 2010a, p. 10). The report appears to convey the message that Africa does occupy a specific place in Polish aid distribution. The cover photo presents the African community of Tafi-Todzi in Ghana, which has benefited from Polish aid. Furthermore, the very first picture in the report (p. 8) shows the participants of the project, Education and Development through Art, carried out by the Polish embassy in Addis Ababa (MSZ 2010a, p. 8). At the same time, it is interesting to note the report's attempts to shift responsibility for supporting Africa onto the EU (to which Poland pays the obligatory fees), projects undertaken by NGOs (which are largely financed by the MFA) and the Polish diplomatic outposts (which work in cooperation with local partners). In the same vein, Minister Radek Sikorski explains that as 'the global financial crisis does not facilitate our country and other members of the EU to meet the declared level of financing [. . .] it is worth to realize, however, the sheer number of collective undertakings in which Poland participates as a result of its affiliation to the EU, UN and its specialized agencies, to OECD' (MSZ 2010a, p. 5). Striking a somewhat contradictory note, the report recalls that during the meeting of the Council of the EU, General Affairs and External Relations, in Brussels on 23 and 24 May 2005, it had been agreed that the EU would increase its financial assistance for SSA and provide collectively at least 50 per cent of the agreed increase of ODA resources to the African continent (MSZ 2008). On top of that, the Joint EU-Africa Strategy adopted in December 2005 envisions strengthening collaboration with Africa in 12 thematic areas. Even the way 'the other regions' supported by Poland are listed in the report may actually suggest that the rank of the African region is elevated as compared to the rest ('West Balkans, Africa, Middle East, Asia, Latin America') (MSZ 2010a, p. 37).

2. Africa in V4 Aid Policies: Reality

The goal of this paper is to show the divergence between the rhetoric employed by the V4 governments and the reality of development aid to Africa. In other words, it aims to investigate whether the countries in question do put their money where their mouths are and, more importantly, where their obligations lie. Whereas the African countries stand out as natural aid recipients if the MDGs and other international commitments assumed by the V4 are taken seriously, the evidence points to the contrary. These findings should be naturally put in the broader perspective of the V4 failing to meet other commitments in the development cooperation area, be they volume of aid or the different aspects of its quality.

Among the Czech priority countries, which, according to the MFA, are 'representing the highest partner country category', there is only one African state, Ethiopia. Officially, the country was selected on the basis of the following arguments: 'an opportunity to build on a relatively rich tradition of mutual relations and the ongoing activities of certain Czech entities'; 'great potential for Czech nongovernmental organizations and businesses'; and 'interesting prospects for cooperation with the EU and the possibility of complementarity between humanitarian aid and development cooperation' (Czech MFA 2010). It is true that the Czech Republic and Ethiopia enjoy good political relations, which renders the choice fairly understandable; nevertheless, an alternative version has it that Ethiopia would not have made it to the list had it not been for pressure from Czech NGOs.[4] The new strategy stipulated that 'the priority countries included those states which, to the greatest extent, met conditions for providing and monitoring assistance level of need, assistance absorption capacity and the quality of development cooperation relations with the Czech Republic'. Interestingly, these criteria are met by countries such as Afghanistan (where Czech expertise and effective aid delivery are clearly limited), yet former priority countries such as Angola[5] and Zambia are effectively downgraded ('the cooperation with existing priority countries will continue, but with an altered scope and focus to the prior programming period'). Indifference towards Africa is confirmed by the overall geographical distribution. In 2009, Africa received only $9.6 million under bilateral programmes, which amounts to 9.9 per cent of the total bilateral ODA ratio (*Czech Development Cooperation Booklet* 2009, p. 21). No single African country was among the top ten recipients of Czech aid in 2009, whereas earlier, Angola had made it to the list twice – ninth place in 2007 and tenth place in 2008). The consistent low priority of African partners may contrast with the assertions of the Czech Minister for Foreign Affairs, Karel Schwarzenberg, who, in May 2007, during a meeting with African ambassadors in Prague, announced that while in 2006, the value of the bilateral assistance projects in SSA was modest and stood at only about $3 million, 'this was only the beginning'. From 2007 onwards, he promised, new bilateral projects and more funds would be allocated to Africa (Afrol News 2007). Czech NGOs also recognize the problem of under-financing of the African region and the MDGs in general and call on the government to increase the volume of aid channelled to the African countries (FoRS 2010). Nevertheless, despite significant room for improvement, in quantitative terms, the Czech Republic is the most committed to Africa among the V4, with 14 per cent of its bilateral ODA given to SSA during 2005–09 (FoRS 2010). In general, it is in accordance with the Czech foreign policy towards the region, and the Czech Republic, at least in relation to its post-communist peers, remains quite conscious of its obligations, despite the lukewarm attitude so characteristic of Central Europe. It was a Czech President who first paid an official visit to South Africa after the fall of apartheid. It was also a Czech delegation that boycotted the Lisbon Summit in 2007 hand in hand with the British in a protest against the presence of Robert Mugabe (Horký 2010, p. 290).

Slovakia has probably the least impressive record of aid to Africa among the V4 countries in terms of sheer volume. Nevertheless, some qualitative changes shed more positive light. Slovakia's first development project in Kenya was carried out only in 2003. Due to a lack of institutional capacity, the project portfolio was built up in cooperation with the Trust Fund of the United Nations Development Programme (UNDP), which implemented a series of projects, mainly in Kenya, Mozambique and Sudan. Currently, African countries feature in both the so-called 'programme' and 'project' country categories for Slovakia. Kenya falls in the former category, whereas Sudan and Ethiopia are among the 16 project countries (Slovak Aid 2009). This makes Kenya one of the three priority programme countries in the period, 2009–13, for which the country strategy paper is to be produced (Vittek and Lightfoot 2010). This is, to the author's knowledge, a solitary example to date of an African country that actually got to have its own strategy document in V4 development cooperation. Slovak Aid argues that the general low demand for projects in Africa can be at least partly explained by the security concerns of grant applicants and geographical 'distance'. This was the reason for the relatively low interest in countries such as Ethiopia and Sudan in the 2009 call for proposals. In 2010, €3.5 million has been allocated for development projects. Out of that amount, €1.13 million was secured for projects in Kenya, which should be regarded as a noteworthy policy change as this is exactly double the amount Kenya was given in 2009 (€0.56 million). The change was accompanied by the trimming down of assistance to Serbia, which has long been criticized by Slovak NGOs as reflecting purely political considerations. Among the African aid recipients, only Sudan could also expect to receive support (€0.32 million). These are clearly small amounts, but are nonetheless notable when compared to the previous record. The choice of Kenya is not without its controversies (Vittek and Lightfoot 2010). First of all, Kenya remains one of the most prosperous economies in SSA. Second, the country is already the aid darling of Western official donors and NGOs.

The deciding of priority countries in Hungary is as obscure as in the other V4 countries. To cite Kiss (2007), 'Small volume of bilateral aid is spent on too many countries, the selection of partner/target countries is fairly ad hoc, in addition, almost half of the bilateral aid is spent in Europe; neither any African nor any of the least developed countries has priority for receiving more Hungarian aid.' As noted by Paragi (2010), 'Early documentation prepared by the MFA refers to "strict and consistent" selection criteria but none of these have been listed explicitly and publicly.' The explanation of the Hungarian MFA fails to shed more light on the selection procedure. The MFA asserts: '[T]he selection of these countries will ensure coherence between our political, security and economic objectives, on the one hand, and the practice of development cooperation, on the other. The programs are intended to contribute to the sustainable social and economic development of the partner countries and to the reinforcement of bilateral relations equally' (Paragi 2010, p. 202). More recent efforts to provide a rationale for country selection are definitely better worded, but still lack clear-cut criteria. Paragi (2010, p. 202) says, 'The selection of the partner countries is the result of a multi-round coordination among the various ministries which took into consideration (i) Hungary's international environment, its interest system and its political, economic, trade and security capacities, (ii) the development and poverty level of the recipient countries and (iii) the history of the relationship between Hungary and the potential partner countries.' Under both sets of criteria, the only African country that has been given 'priority' status is Ethiopia.[6] It is perhaps also instructive to note that Paragi herself barely mentions Africa in her paper on Hungarian Development Cooperation, which may suggest that she either finds it irrelevant to the debate or that there is no government activity to comment on – both explanations proving that the role of Africa in Hungarian aid policy is negligible.

In Poland, the amount of financing available for Africa is drastically low, especially considering the country's relative strength in the region and its political aspirations. In 2011, the funds under the MFA's administration amounted to 109 million Polish Złoty (PLN), which roughly equals €27 million. Out of this amount, Africa was expected to receive 4.2 million PLN (including 1 million PLN for the Small Grants Program). This is close to the assistance available to Moldova (4 million PLN), a small European country with a population of 3.5 million. Angola has been the only priority country for Poland since Tanzania was taken off the list as a result of the embassy in Dar es Salam being shut down in 2008. Low priority for Africa in development cooperation translates into the modest number of projects carried out in the region by Polish NGOs. According to the annual report of 2009, Polish NGOs have undertaken 23 development projects in Africa. In addition, three projects were implemented by higher education and research institutions; 19 projects were carried out by Polish diplomatic missions (13 by the Polish embassy in Pretoria) (MSZ 2010a, p. 107–109). In 2009, the Ministry of Finance also disbursed a credit tranche for Angola worth 21 million PLN.

One of the leading Polish NGOs, Instytut Globalnej Odpowiedzialności (IGO), maintains that Africa's marginal position in development aid programmes is very disturbing and requires urgent action. It warned that in 2011, NGOs in Poland would receive nearly 50 per cent less money for Africa as compared to the previous year. This clearly goes against the government's promises. Whereas in 2009, NGOs could count on 3.5 million PLN to be spent on projects in Africa, in 2010, the Ministry donated only close to 2 million PLN. To the NGO community's even greater disappointment, the drop corresponds with the overall increase in the money available for other geographical areas. The aid committed to Africa amounts to only 9 per cent of the MFA's aid project budget. For instance, in 2011, Angola was to receive only one-fifth of the previous year's allocation (IGO 2011).

Matching Rhetoric with Reality?

It has been demonstrated that whereas on a rhetorical level, the V4 countries are committed to the MDGs and reducing poverty, at the same time, clearly looking at the development needs of the African countries, reality is a very different story. Africa still remains peripheral in the aid policies of all the countries in question and there are no vital signs that this will change any time soon. The divergence is to a large extent a result of the international obligations that the V4 governments have assumed and, now, under rising pressure as fully-fledged donors, are held accountable for by the international community. This section will attempt to provide some thoughts on this conundrum.

To begin with, to be sure, the outcome is partly the result of more or less explicit foreign policy goals, which, in the V4, do not necessarily coincide geographically with what the EU has in mind when it speaks of the development cooperation of tomorrow. A lion's share of the aid from the region is deployed to neighbouring countries or countries that are deemed politically relevant (such as Afghanistan). Having said that, for example, a prominent feature of the Hungarian ODA is strong region-centrism and the majority of its aid is channelled to the neighbouring countries, with particular emphasis on the Balkan States. In Slovakia, similarly, a large chunk of the aid goes to Serbia (which enjoys close political and economic ties with the Slovak Republic) and Montenegro. This pattern is observable in the Czech Republic and Poland, whose priority partners feature Belarus, the Ukraine and Georgia. Foreign policy priorities in the V4 include, inter alia, securing regional stability, promoting economic cooperation and reinforcing the donor's visibility abroad. This continues to be defended on the grounds of the comparative advantage and wealth of expertise in transition, democracy and EU accession. Therefore, it is fair to say that the patchy development cooperation with SSA is to a large extent a result of the foreign policy goals adopted by the V4. It seems that as long as aid remains largely an extension of foreign policy, Africa will remain out of the equation, unless the foreign policy formulation changes radically and turns more to opportunities that can be seized.

Asked about the lack of real commitment towards the MDGs and Africa, most V4 country officials claim they do support the region, but not necessarily directly, that is, via bilateral channels. It is true that due to the obligatory fees paid to the EU, these countries do contribute financially to the EU's external assistance programmes (contributions to other multilateral institutions remain miniscule in most cases, as, for example, 4 per cent in Poland). These sums should not be ignored as they are substantial in relation to the bilateral programmes, amounting in most countries to more than 50 per cent of the reported ODA. The argument is, however, shaky since the most external assistance to SSA is financed via the European Development Fund

(EDF), which is separate from the EU budget (although administered by the Commission) (see e.g. European Commission, 2011). The V4 countries have not made any payments to the EDF in the past and it is only from the 10th EDF that they have begun participating in the implementation. For example, Poland's first contribution of €39.39 million to the EDF took place only in 2011. It is also instructive to show that the relative share of aid channelled to Africa in the EU spending on external assistance has decreased drastically since the 1980s, despite a general increase in EU external assistance. This is to some extent a result of the expansion of aid programmes in Central and Eastern Europe prior to their accession and, more recently, in the Mediterranean region (Grimm 2004, p. 4). Even if the financial contribution to the EU's external aid is viewed as an excuse for a poor record in bilateral aid, it should be noted that the V4 countries are known for their virtual lack of coordination and coherent policy towards multilaterals. For example, in the OECD peer review report, Poland admits that it 'recognizes its lack of an overarching policy or strategy guiding its partnership with multilateral institutions and would like to address this' (OECD 2010, p. 19). Consequently, if a country is short of political leverage concerning its multilateral component, it is quite difficult to accept the reasoning that it actually supports Africa via multilateral channels.

There is a host of explanations to why Africa has remained marginal in the development cooperation policies of the V4. One of the most widely held assumptions among academics is that development assistance in the V4 is the result of path dependence. In principle, according to the definition proposed by Szent-Iványi and Tétényi, this means that 'even though politicians might aim to create policies and institutions based on different foreign models, they will never be able to escape the effects of the past, as these highly influence attitudes, thinking and even decision making' (Szent-Iványi and Tétényi 2008, p. 575). It suggests, inter alia, that the territorial allocation of development assistance and, thus, the choice of priority countries are a result of the communist legacy and cannot be altered easily, at least in the short term. A good example in Polish aid is Angola, which has been reportedly chosen as a priority country on the basis of historical links and active diplomatic representation in Luanda. This is one of many examples of how geographical focus traces the V4's communist past.

Although this narrative appears to have become popular thinking in this part of the world, the hypothesis is not bulletproof. It is correct to argue that many developing countries receiving ODA nowadays belonged, at one time or the other, to the Soviet camp (Szent-Iványi and Tétényi 2008, p.580). Nevertheless, we argue that the path dependence theory is of limited use in explaining more recent aid patterns in the V4, despite continuing to be a quite convenient way of rationalizing why the transition from recipient to donor is filled with inertia. The evidence comes, for example, from Afghanistan, a country, which, in some V4 countries (Poland in particular), acquired priority country status virtually overnight and now features as a top aid recipient. This case clearly shows that development cooperation in the V4 has potential for radical change and breaking away from the historical pattern, which is obviously not as difficult as suggested elsewhere. In the same vein, lack of interest in tightening development cooperation with African countries can only partially be explained by the communist legacy. We argue that it is rather the lack of strategic vision in foreign policy and the ad hoc style of formulation of such policy that help to explain why, when South-South cooperation is so rife today, the V4 are giving up on Africa (closing diplomatic outposts in Africa is very symbolic here).

In a similar spirit, it is argued that apart from the foreign policy goals that help to navigate most bilateral programmes in the V4, there are also cultural and linguistic affinities that may influence a large chunk of aid flows. This is partly confirmed by Vittek and Lightfoot (2010) in relation to the role of the Russian language in Slovak territorial aid allocation. This argument is definitely in line with the path dependence theory and may show an overall inertia in aid policy over the past years, but its explanatory power is coming to an end today. In the contemporary world, English is slowly becoming the lingua franca, particularly among the younger generation of aid officials and practitioners, as well as NGOs, therefore, whereas it was understandable in the take-off phase in the 1990s, today, this argument is surely outdated, particularly when employed to justify a lack of impetus to tighten development cooperation with those African countries where English is spoken. The cultural gap, compounded by a lack of mutual history, indeed poses certain difficulties and may explain a part of the hesitance towards initiating or expanding development partnerships. But again, given the impetus towards helping 'exotic' countries such as Afghanistan, this makes the perceived cultural barrier an easy target for critics. Moreover, in Poland specifically, but also in the other V4 countries, the African Studies community revolves largely around cultural-linguistic and anthropological studies. These academics would be more than happy, if approached, to help mitigate and bridge the cultural distance that keeps the two regions apart.

According to another widely held premise, financial and organizational commitment to promote development in Africa is restricted by the lack of colonial and other historical ties (Szent-Iványi and Tétényi 2008, p. 578). This also seems superficially appealing, but again, not entirely convincing. The realm of development assistance has changed drastically in the past years and whereas, previously, aid allocation was largely informed by former historical links, today, given the new breed of donors, these arguments do not always hold. Countries such as China, India and Brazil equally lack colonial ties with Africa. To be sure, Sino-African cooperation began in the 1950s, but firstly, it was on a relatively moderate scale and actually dormant for many years, and secondly, it was informed mostly by ideology (see Kopinski et al. 2011). So, lack of colonial ties does not present any particular impediment in extending aid towards the region. Interestingly enough, the new donor countries' core principle is that it is precisely this lack of colonial record which makes their development cooperation exceptional and better suited to local realities. It is not distorted by decades of ruthless colonial exploitation, followed by neo-colonial policies exercised during the course of the Cold War. Likewise, some of the traditional donors, such as Norway or Sweden, equally lack colonial ties or shared historical experience with Africa, but this does not prevent them from being among the most active and efficient financiers of development. We argue, therefore, that the lack of colonial legacy may be used as a decoy in the V4 countries and is rather a sign of their helplessness and should be viewed again as a lack of strategic vision in foreign policy, rather than a real obstacle. As many other examples demonstrate, no mutual history can paradoxically be an asset in building credible development cooperation programmes. New entrants without heavy historical burdens are often welcomed with open arms on African soil.[7]

DEVELOPMENT POLICIES OF CENTRAL AND EASTERN EUROPEAN STATES

It is understandable that the V4 are unable to fully emulate China or other donors operating outside of the traditional aid system and the OECD radar. As both EU and OECD members and, in some cases, as 'soon-to-be' DAC members, the V4 countries are significantly constrained by a myriad DAC recommendations and rules, particularly on the untying of financial aid and investment related technical cooperation to developing countries, as well as statistical procedures, the standard definition of development assistance, transparency and good practice. This clearly narrows the scope of manoeuvrability with regard to the modalities used to disburse development assistance. Donors who do not align themselves with the rules of the game take advantage of the 'lawless' environment in which they operate by, for instance, using freely tied aid, concessional loans linked to foreign direct investments, et cetera, which is particularly visible in the case of Chinese foreign aid. To balance that slightly, it can be argued that, despite being signatories to the Paris Declaration, it is difficult to point to any particular measures taken by the V4 to move closer to achieving the goals laid down in the document. On the contrary, many modalities that are continuously in use in development cooperation in the V4, such as tied aid or export credits on non-concessional terms, continue to play an important role without any real prospects of being phased out completely any time soon.

Another common argument touches upon the patchy net of diplomatic outposts that the V4 possess in Africa. Embassies and consulates and their personnel do play a strategic role in development cooperation across the world. It is infinitely more difficult to coordinate and implement aid, particularly project aid, from overseas without officials and trusted people on the ground. The problem was recently further compounded by decisions to shut down embassies in what is already a small number of African states. Poland, for example, continues to have ten embassies in Africa (five in SSA). These include Algeria, Angola, Egypt, Ethiopia, Kenya, Morocco, Nigeria, South Africa, Tunisia and Libya (which was abandoned recently by the Polish staff due to security concerns). In 2008, Polish Minister Radek Sikorski decided to close the diplomatic outposts in Tunisia (Dar es Salaam), Senegal (Dakar), Zimbabwe (Harare) and the Democratic Republic of Congo (Kinshasa), unofficially in the name of trimming down costs, officially because the cooperation with those countries was termed non-satisfactory (Współpraca gospodarcza Polski z Afryka 2011). The latter move has been explained also as a part of a strategy to set up a new model of diplomatic outposts reduced to regional hubs. Nevertheless, given the swiftness of the operation and the astonishment of many experts, it is difficult to believe that this was indeed a part of a well-prepared plan.[8] The other V4 countries have also decided to shut down many diplomatic missions on the African continent (see e.g. Richter 2010). This state of affairs offers development cooperation less opportunities to move the European and African countries closer to each other, especially since even the existing outposts are usually very understaffed, lacking experts and administrative personnel. Therefore, the argument goes, expanding aid to Africa is impossible for merely practical reasons, chief among them an insufficient capacity of diplomatic infrastructure abroad. Of course, diplomatic outposts and their functioning in the developing world is a more general problem and Africa should be singled out with caution.

The last argument advanced in the paper is about the so-called 'comparative advantage' (Bucar and Mrak 2007). All the V4 countries claim almost unanimously that their territorial distribution of aid monies has a logical rationale, which is associated with the comparative advantage the countries allegedly hold in democratic and economic transition, but also in convergence with the norms and rules of the EU – the lessons they learned during the course of their accession. The above assertion is also shared by other donors (OECD 2010). This helps explain the proximity bias in aid allocation and the largely unambiguous focus in aid delivery on neighbouring countries in Eastern and Southern Europe. It is, however, questionable what this asset really means beyond the rhetoric (Mürle 2007, p. 14–15), how it can actually be applied and what benefits it can potentially yield to aid recipients (see Horky). Furthermore, as some NGOs who advocate for more aid to Africa argue (Horky, forthcomming), the V4's experience with transition from communism to liberal democracy and from central planning to free market might also be of use to many African countries that are still struggling with various structural issues, such as tax reform and privatization.

Conclusion

This paper sought to investigate the aid allocations of the V4 countries to African countries using as a point of departure various international commitments that impose on the governments in question an obligation to increasingly shift attention and thus aid delivery to SSA, which clearly stands out in the world as a region with the most desperate development needs. The most specific of these obligations is the pledge to increase financial assistance to SSA and provide collectively at least 50 per cent of the agreed increase of ODA resources to the region. Having investigated the narrative present in most of the countries, we find a yawning gap between the rhetoric and reality. All governments (though to a different degree and with a different intensity) seem to agree that Africa is the least developing, and hence the most needy, region in the world and that the MDGs (which lack progress predominantly in Africa) are their priority. Not incidentally, this is the official line of the EU, which uses every opportunity to highlight among its members the importance of intensifying development cooperation with SSA. The message surely trickles down to the new member states, but stops short of being rightly tackled.

The evidence tells a very different story. In reality, African countries remain marginal in aid distribution and, although some find a way into the priority aid recipient categories, they serve mostly as fig leaves masking a true disinterest, not only in the region's fate, but in actual opportunities that might be exploited in SSA. This also contrasts with public opinion in the V4, which rather unanimously agrees that SSA should be given priority in aid allocations. This means that the governments not only do not put their money where their mouths are and where their obligations lie, but also fail to listen to their own citizens. With most public issues pertaining to spending taxpayers' money, this kind of divergence would be confronted at least in public discourse. However, since, in the V4 countries, development cooperation remains both an exclusive and obscure topic, restricted to officials, experts and NGOs, the situation does not lead to any foreseeable resolution. Interestingly, there is sometimes a gap between public relations-type documents, such as annual reports and bulletins, and official documents, such as strategies, which are much more sober and toned down. In some cases (as, for example, Poland), the gap extends to an absurd degree.

Certainly, the lack of progress towards the implementation of international commitments with regard to SSA and the MDGs should be viewed in a broader context. As many authors before have observed, development cooperation in the V4 continues to be an area where convergence with EU norms and rules is very sluggish. After more than a decade's experience, quality and institution wise, aid policies in the region are still nascent or in the take-off stage. Therefore, neglect of Africa may be a part of a more general, systemic weakness, rather than a problem in its own right. It should also be stressed that the record of many of the old members of the EU, both big and influential, such as Italy, and small and less relevant, such as Greece and Portugal, with regard to development cooperation with SSA, is less than impressive. This makes the V4, not lone wolves, but part of the pack.

This paper also sought to address some of the most common arguments used to defend or explain the current state of affairs. The argument that the V4 support African countries indirectly, through multilateral aid, appears shaky due to a lack of real influence on and disinterest for how the money is actually spent. Furthermore, as the paper shows, contribution to the EC budget does not equal the transfer of resources to Africa. It is also true that the path dependence theory or lack of a mutual history can be instructive in explaining aid allocation patterns, especially in the past. Certainly, foreign policy goals with their proximity bias and security concerns also play their part. We argue that more currently, this is a result of a lack of strategic vision and ad hoc formulation of foreign policy. Expanding bilateral programmes to countries such as Afghanistan proves that geographical distribution of aid can be subject to change in the V4 and is not eternally bound by path dependency. Likewise, the new entrants to the aid industry, such as Brazil, China and India, demonstrate that the foreign policy lens through which the V4 look at Africa is perhaps obsolete.

Notes

A version of this article originally appeared in the Polish Centre for African Studies (PCSA) Working Paper Series (7/2011). The PCSA is the first independent, non-governmental organization in Poland devoted to the study of contemporary Africa.

[1] If not specified otherwise, Africa is synonymous with Sub-Saharan Africa.

[2] During its G8 presidency in 2006, Russia held a special meeting with donors in Moscow, which clearly showed the 'back in the game' attitude of the Russian government.

[3] Whereas Slovakia and the Czech Republic have successfully launched aid agencies and adopted specific law underpinning aid delivery, Poland is still struggling to put in place a proper legislation. As noted by Lightfoot and Vittek (2010), in relation to Slovak officials, this may produce a different pattern of satisfaction and thus determination for political change in government circles.

[4] Written communication with Ondrej Horky, Institute of International Relations, Prague.

[5] Apparently, cooperation between the Czech Republic and Angola was troubled inter alia over visa issues for Czech aid personnel. Available from: http://www.un.org/esa/agenda21/natlinfo/countr/czech/africa.pdf [Accessed 3 May 2011].

[6] In 2005, the Hungarian government decided to forgive Ethiopia's $7.4 million debt (90 per cent of its existing debt) under an agreement signed in Addis Ababa on 28 June. The remaining obligation was to be spent on poverty reduction programmes.

[7] See the Slovak official quoted in Vittek and Lightfoot (2010).

[8] One of the advantages Poland enjoys over the other V4 countries and other Western donors with regard to Africa is the multiple presence of missionaries, mostly Catholic, who are relatively active in aid delivery and could serve as local anchors for further engagement with the region. In 2007, there were 919

DEVELOPMENT POLICIES OF CENTRAL AND EASTERN EUROPEAN STATES

Polish missionaries in Africa. Being aware of this advantage, the Polish government is seeking to increase the involvement of Polish missionaries in development aid.

References

Afrol News, 2007. Eastern Europe starts repaying Africa. Available from: http://www.afrol.com/features/25604 [Accessed 16 April 2011].

Brautigam, D., 2008. China's African aid: Transatlantic challenges, a report to the German Marshall Fund of the United States. April. Washington DC: The German Marshall Fund of the United States.

Bucar, Maja, and Mrak, Mojmir. 2007. Challenges for development cooperation for EU new member states. Paper presented at the *ABCDE World Bank conference*, April 2007 Bled, Slovenia. Available from: http://siteresources.worldbank.org/INTABCDESLO2007/Resources/PAPERABCDEBucarMrak.pdf [Accessed 22 October 2011].

Cabral, L., and Weinstock, J., 2010. Brazil: An emerging aid player. ODI briefing paper.

Chanana, D., 2009. India as an emerging donor. *Economic and political weekly*, XLIV (12), 11–14.

Chin, G.T., and Frolic, B.M., 2007. *Emerging donors in international development assistance: The China case.* York: York Centre for Asian Research.

Corrales, J., 2009. Using social power to balance soft power: Venezuela's foreign policy. *The Washington quarterly*, 32 (4), 97–114.

Czech Development Cooperation Booklet, 2009. Available from: http://www.mzv.cz/jnp/en/foreign_relations/development_cooperation_and_humanitarian/general_information/czech_development_cooperation_2009.html [Accessed 2 July 2011], p. 21.

Czech MFA, 2010. The development cooperation strategy of the Czech Republic, 2010–17. Available from: http://www.mzv.cz/public/d9/f6/92/545820_444905_Development_Cooperation_Strategy_2010_2017 final.doc [Accessed 1 May 2011].

Klaus, Vaclav, 2010. The aid is not a solution for Africa, 4 December 2010. Available from: http://euportal.parlamentnilisty.cz/PrintArticle/6884-czech-president-klaus-the-aid-is-not-a-solution-for-africa.aspx [Accessed 3 May 2011].

Davis, M., 2008. *How China delivers development assistance to Africa.* Stellenbosch, South Africa: Centre for Chinese Studies.

European Commission, 2010a. EU development policy in support of inclusive growth and sustainable development. Increasing the impact of EU development policy. Brussels, 10.11.2010COM(2010) 629 final.

European Commission, 2010b. Annual report 2010: On the European Union's development and external assistance policies and their implementation in 2009. Brussels, EuropeAid Co-operation Office.

European Commission, 2011. Annual report on the European Union's development and external assistance policies and their implementation in 2010. Brussels.

FoRS, 2010. Jak Česká republika snižuje globální chudobu. Prague. Available from: http://fors.ikan.cz/assets/files/Dokumenty/aidwatch_2010.pdf [Accessed 30 April 2011].

Gömbös, E., ed., 2007. *The future of development policies and changing priorities: Africa.* "The Future of Development Policies and Changing Priorities: Africa", conference organized by the United Nations Association of Hungary and the HUN-IDA Non-profit Co., October 28, 2005. United Nations Association of Hungary, HUNIDA. Available from: http://en.hunida.hu/left_menu/downloads/the_future_of_development_policies_and_changing_priorities_africa [Accessed 11 May 2011], p. 16.

Grimm, S., 2004. Aid disbursement and effectiveness. ODI briefing paper on European development cooperation for 2010. London: Overseas Development Institute.

Grupa Zagranica, 2007. Polska pomoc rozwojowa. Niezależne badanie przeprowadzone przez organizacje pozarzadowe. Warsaw.

Horký, O., 2006. Development policy in new EU member states. Re-emerging donors on the way from compulsory altruism to global responsibility, reflecting on a wider Europe and beyond: Norms, rights and interests. *4th convention of the Central and East European International Studies Association (CEEISA)*, University of Tartu, Estonia.

Horký, O., 2010. Sub-Saharan Africa in the Czech foreign policy. *In*: Michal Kořan, ed. *Czech foreign policy in 2007–09: Analysis.* Prague: Institute of International Relations, 347–361.

IGO, 2011. Polski rzad zlekcewaz_ył pomoc dla Afryki, Instytut Globalnej Odpowiedzialnos' ci. Available from: http://igo.org.pl/aktualnosci/polityka-rozwojowa/103-polski-rzd-zlekceway-pomoc-dla-afryki [Accessed 14 April 2011].

DEVELOPMENT POLICIES OF CENTRAL AND EASTERN EUROPEAN STATES

IPA, 2005. Slovenská verejnosť a rozvojová pomoc: Výsledky výskumu verejnej mienky, Máj 2005 (Slovak public and development aid: The results of specialised poll, May 2005). 500: Institute for Public Affairs.

Kragelund, P., 2010. The potential role of non-traditional donors' aid in Africa. *ICTSD series on trade-supported strategies for sustainable development*, Geneva: International Centre for Trade and Sustainable Development (ICTSD), Issue Paper No. 11.

Kriss, J., 2007. Hungarian international development policy in figures, executive summary. Available from: http://www.trialog.or.at/images/doku/aidwatch_hand_engl_summary.pdf [Accessed 15 May 2011].

Lancaster, C., 2007. *The Chinese aid system*. Washington, DC: Center for Global Development.

Lightfoot, S., 2010. The Europeanisation of international development policies: The case of Central and Eastern European States. *Europe-Asia studies*, 62 (2), 329–350.

Lum, T., et al., 2009. China's foreign aid activities in Africa, Latin America, and Southeast Asia. Congressional Research Service, Washington DC. Available at http://www.fas.org/sgp/crs/row/R40361.pdf [Accessed 11 May 2011].

Manning, R., 2006. Will 'emerging donors' change the face of international cooperation? OECD DAC Chair. Available from: http://www.oecd.org/dataoecd/35/38/36417541.pdf [Accessed 14 April 2011].

Márquez, H., 2005. Weaving new alliances with cultural threads. IPS News. Available from: http://ipsnews.net/africa/nota.asp?idnews=30807 [Accessed 11 April 2011].

MFA, Republic of Hungary, 2004. Hungary's report on the Millennium Development Goals, taking stock. Budapest, Hungary, October.

Morsbach, G., 2006. Venezuela pushes ties with Africa. BBC, 17 March. Available from: http://news.bbc.co.uk/2/hi/americas/4816478.stm [Accessed 13 April 2011].

MSZ, 2008. Polska pomoc – Afryka. Available from: http://www.polskapomoc.gov.pl/files/dokumenty_publikacje/PUBLIKACJE_2008/494x260-afryka-pol08.pdf [Accessed 14 May 2011].

MSZ, 2010a. Polska współpraca na rzecz rozwoju. Departament Współpracy Rozwojowej, Warsaw, p. 10.

MSZ, 2010b. Program polskiej współpracy rozwojowej udzielanej za pośrednictwem MSZ RP wroku 2011. Available from: http://www.polskapomoc.gov.pl/files/inne%20dokumenty%20PDF/Pomoc%20-zagraniczna%202011/Alokacje%20finansowe_program%20PWR%202011.pdf [Accessed 11 May 2011].

Mürle, H., 2007. Towards a division of labour in European development co-operation: Operational options. Bonn: German Development Institute Discussion Paper, 6/2007. Available at http://www.oecd.org/dataoecd/60/23/46859449.pdf [Accessed 16 May 2011].

Naidu, S., 2008. India's growing African strategy. *Review of African political economy*, 35 (115), 116–128.

Naim, M., 2007. Rogue aid. What's wrong with the foreign aid programs of China, Venezuela, and Saudi Arabia? *Foreign Policy*, 14 February 2007.

Neumayer, E., 2003. What factors determine the allocation of aid by Arab countries and multilateral agencies? *Journal of development studies*, 39 (4), 134–147.

OECD, 2010. *Special review of Poland*. Paris: OECD.

PAP, Współpraca gospodarcza Polski z Afryką – marginalna, 13 April 2011. Available from: http://wiadomosci.onet.pl/kraj/wspolpraca-gospodarcza-polski-z-afryka-marginalna,1,4241724,wiadomosc.html [Accessed 30 June 2011].

Paragi, B., 2010. Hungarian development cooperation. In: Paul Hoebink, ed. *European development cooperation. In between the local and the global*. Amsterdam: Amsterdam University Press.

Polacy o pomocy rozwojowej, 2010. Wyniki badania TNS OBOP dla Ministerstwa Spraw Zagranicznych, Warszawa, grudzień. Available from: http://www.polskapomoc.gov.pl/files/Edukacja%20rozwojowa/Badanie%20opinii%20publicznej/Polacy%20o%20pomocy%20rozwojowej%202010 .pdf [Accessed 11 May 2011].

Richter, J., 2010. Czech foreign ministry closes embassies to cut costs. Radio Praha, 1 April 2010. Available from: http://www.radio.cz/en/section/curraffrs/czech-foreign-ministry-closes-embassies-to-cut-costs [Accessed 3 May 2011].

Slovak Aid, 2009. Strednodobá stratégia oficiálnej rozvojovej pomoci Slovenskej republiky na roky 2009–13. Available from: http://eng.slovakaid.sk/uploads/2009/06/Strategia_ODA_2009_2013.rtf [Accessed 3 May 2011].

Slovak Aid, 2010. Contribution of Slovak Official Development Assistance to the Millennium Development Goals 2004–09. Available from: http://eng.slovakaid.sk/wp- content/uploads/2010/09/studia-MDGs_preklad-proofreading.pdf [Accessed 30 June 2011].

Smith, K., T. Fordelone, T.Y., and Zimmermann, F., 2010. Beyond the DAC: The welcome role of other providers of development co-operation. DCD issues brief, May, OECD.

Szent-Iványi, B., and Tétényi, A., 2008. Transition and foreign aid policies in the Visegrád countries: A path dependant approach. *Transition studies review*, 15 (3), 573–587.

Tarrósy, I., 2011. New South–South dynamics and the effects on Africa. In: I. Tarrósy, L. Szabó and G. Hyden, eds. *The African state in a changing global context. Breakdowns and transformations*. Berlin-Münster: LIT Verlag, 17–32.

The Economist, 2010. Speak softly and carry a blank cheque. 15 July, 42–43.

Villanger, E., 2007. Arab foreign aid: Disbursement patterns, aid policies and motives. CMI report 2/2007. Oslo: Christian Michelsen Institute.

Vittek, M., and Lightfoot, S., 2010. The Europeanization of Slovak development cooperation? *Contemporary European studies*, 1, 21–37.

Woods, N., 2008. Whose aid? Whose influence? China, emerging donors and the silent revolution in development assistance. *International affairs*, 84 (6), 1205–1221.

World Bank, 2010. *Arab development assistance, four decades of cooperation*. Washington DC: World Bank.

Hungarian International Development Cooperation: Context, Stakeholders and Performance[1]

BALÁZS SZENT-IVÁNYI

Department of World Economy, Corvinus University of Budapest, Budapest, Hungary

ABSTRACT *This paper explores the domestic and international context of Hungary's emerging international development policy. Specifically, it looks at three factors that may influence how this policy operates: membership in the European Union (EU) and potential 'Europeanization', Hungary's wider foreign policy strategy, and the influence of domestic stakeholders. In order to uncover how these factors affect the country's international development policy, semi-structured interviews were carried out with the main stakeholders. The main conclusions are: (1) While accession to the EU did play a crucial role in restarting Hungary's international development policy, the integration has had little effect since then; (2) international development policy seems to serve mainly Hungary's regional strategic foreign policy and economic interests, and not its global development goals; and (3) although all the domestic development stakeholders are rather weak, the Ministry of Foreign Affairs (MFA) still seems to play a dominating role. Convergence with European requirements and best practices is, therefore, clearly hindered by foreign policy interests and also by the weakness of non- governmental stakeholders.*

1. Introduction

The Central and Eastern European (CEE) countries, namely the Czech Republic, Hungary, Poland, Slovakia, Slovenia, the three Baltic countries, and later Romania and Bulgaria, all became members of the international aid donor community in the past decade. In fact, 2011 can be seen as the tenth anniversary of the re-emergence of these policies in the CEE, as in 2001, some of these countries accepted their first official documents relating to international development. Therefore, it is increasingly inappropriate to call these countries 'new' donors, although their development policies are still very different from those of the older, more established Western donors or internationally agreed 'best practices'.

This paper takes a closer look at one of these emerging donors, Hungary. Hungary was one of the first CEE countries to re-create its international development policy between 2001 and 2003, but in the past few years, activity in this field seems to have stagnated. There seems to be no clear strategy or direction for the future and no discussion on how and why Hungary should aid poorer countries. Resources spent on development cooperation are low and stagnating, public attention on the topic is negligible and there is no political discourse. This current state of affairs can only be explained partly by Hungary's weak economic performance and the resulting government austerity measures. This paper argues that in order to gain a better understanding of Hungary's international development policy, one must look at other factors. The main goal of the paper, therefore, is to explore the context of Hungarian international development cooperation and its implications for the practice and performance of the country's international development policy. Three contextual sources of influence on Hungary's external assistance policy are discussed: membership in the European Union (EU), wider foreign policy strategy and the influence of domestic stakeholders. Specifically, the following three research questions are formulated: (1) Has membership in the EU had any effect on Hungary's international development policy? (2) Is its international development policy affected by wider strategic foreign policy goals? (3) How do the interests and power relations of domestic development stakeholders affect the policy area?

The main conclusions of the paper are that membership in the EU has had little noticeable effect in shaping Hungary's development policy since 2004; that international development policy seems to serve Hungary's external political and economic interests; and that although all the stakeholders are rather weak, the Ministry of Foreign Affairs (MFA) still seems to play a dominating role. Convergence with European requirements and best practices is clearly hindered by foreign policy interests and also by the weakness of the non-governmental stakeholders. These issues make the creation of a unified vision on why and how Hungary should provide aid to less fortunate countries difficult.

All three of the contextual sources of influence could constitute separate research agendas. Therefore, this paper should be seen as exploratory research, setting the agenda for future, more detailed inquiries into the topic. Also, the paper does not attempt to describe Hungarian international policy in detail; rather, it aims to shed light on the dynamics behind the current state of affairs. Written material and data on Hungary's international development policy are limited and there has not been much scholarly work on the topic either. In order to overcome this problem, seven semi-structured qualitative interviews with representatives of the various stake-holders were carried out. The interviewees included a senior policy official and a desk officer as well as a former mid-level director, all from the Directorate of International Development at the Hungarian MFA. A senior desk officer working on issues related to tied aid credits from the Ministry of National Economy was the fourth respondent. The last three respondents were three experts working at various Hungarian development non-governmental organizations (NGOs), both in policy issues and 'on the field'. For reasons of confidentiality, their identities have not been revealed.

The contribution of the paper to the field is that it expands the rather scarce academic literature on development policies in the CEE countries and provides an

DEVELOPMENT POLICIES OF CENTRAL AND EASTERN EUROPEAN STATES

approach for understanding the evolution of the policy area in the case of Hungary. This sets the agenda for future, more detailed research and can be applied to other CEE countries as well. The paper is structured around the three topics introduced above. Section 2 briefly reviews the history of Hungary's international development policy and its current challenges. Section 3 analyses the effects EU membership has had (or has failed to have) on Hungary's international development policy. Section 4 discusses the domestic policy context and Section 5 looks at the interests and relative power and influence of the development stakeholders. Section 6 concludes the paper.

2. Hungary's International Development Policy: History and Present Challenges

Much of the existing literature on international development policies in the CEE countries focuses on the history of these policies and the current challenges. Studies have discussed the early beginnings (Dauderstädt 2002), the difficulties and deficiencies faced by the CEE donors (Bucar and Mrak 2007) and, more recently, the interactions between these new donors and the EU (Carbone 2004, Lightfoot 2008, 2010, Horky 2010). In the case of Hungary, the works of Kiss (2002, 2007) and Paragi (2010) are the most important sources, in addition to the report published by Hungary's aid implementing agency at the time, HUN-IDA (2004). This section does not repeat the findings of this literature; instead, it provides a brief overview of how development policy emerged in Hungary and what difficulties the country faces today.

All CEE countries, including Hungary, had international development policies during their communist years. While there has been hardly any detailed academic research on these pre-1989 development policies, the most important characteristic is easy to identify – the heavy influence of the Soviet Union's geostrategic objectives. This included providing assistance mainly to Soviet allies or developing countries with heavily leftist governments; no clear distinction between military and development aid; high reliance on technical assistance and tied aid; and the extensive use of scholarships (for more details, see Kiss 2002, HUN-IDA 2004). According to some estimates, the resources Hungary devoted to foreign assistance reached 0.7 per cent of the country's national income in the late 1970s, although this cannot be compared with aid expenditures today due to methodological differences. In most CEE donors, including Hungary, the impact of the communist era development policy can be identified to this date (Szent-Iványi and Tétényi 2008).

After the end of the Cold War, Hungary terminated its international development policy and turned from being a donor country into a recipient of foreign aid.[2] During the 1990s, there was no active bilateral development cooperation, only smaller ad hoc contributions to multilateral development organizations. Hungary restarted its international development policies due to external pressure, stemming from membership in the Organisation for Economic Cooperation and Development (OECD) in 1996 and accession to the EU in 2004. The first strategic document on international development cooperation was accepted in 2001 by the government and the first Hungarian financed bilateral aid projects started in 2003. Due to Hungary's historical, political, financial and economic conditions, the international development policy it created took on a very different nature from those prevailing in the member countries of the OECD's Development Assistance Committee (DAC).

52

Although it is very difficult to talk about a single best practice in bilateral development policies among the OECD DAC members, as all countries have their own national characteristics (Lancaster 2007), nevertheless, in the past decade, an international academic and political consensus has emerged on the desirable traits of effective national bilateral aid policies. This consensus includes increasing the resources spent on aid, the concepts of partnership and ownership, untying aid, better coordination between donors, aligning donor activities with recipient systems, decreasing the administrative burdens of the recipients, larger emphasis on evaluation and results, among other things (see, for example, the outcomes of the Monterrey Conference in 2002, the Rome-Paris-Accra-Busan process on aid effectiveness, or in the case of the EU, the European Consensus on Development accepted in 2006).

Hungary's aid policy, on the other hand, is heavily donor driven and characterized by low spending on bilateral cooperation, a high share of tied aid, the proliferation of small projects, inefficient delivery structures and the almost total lack of evaluation (Paragi 2010). Aid is given mostly to middle income neighbouring countries, which implies that poverty reduction is not a true goal (Szent-Iványi 2011). Table 1 shows the amounts Hungary spent on foreign aid relative to gross national income (GNI) between 2003 and 2010, and compares it to the performance of the other CEE countries and the OECD DAC average. Hungary spent the most on international development in 2006, when official development assistance (ODA) reached 0.13 per cent of GNI. However, this was mainly due to one-off items, such as debt relief to Iraq and Ethiopia. In the past years, a clear stagnation of resources spent on development is visible. The member states of the EU have reiterated the need to increase the resources devoted to international development, but the global economic and financial crisis, which began in 2008, has definitely curbed these ambitions. In 2010, Hungarian ODA was 0.09 per cent of GNI, falling well short of the 0.17 per cent target set within the EU back in 2005 (Bucar and Mrak 2007).

The stagnation of the ODA/GNI level is a symptom of a more general lack of progress within Hungary's international development policy, which cannot be explained solely by deficiency of resources. The law for regulating international development cooperation had not been passed as of late 2011 – it has been 'under

Table 1. ODA/GNI levels among the Central and Eastern European donors

	2003	2004	2005	2006	2007	2008	2009	2010
Czech Republic	0.10	0.11	0.11	0.12	0.11	0.12	0.12	0.12
Estonia	–	0.05	0.08	0.09	0.08	0.10	0.10	–
Hungary	**0.03**	**0.06**	**0.11**	**0.13**	**0.08**	**0.08**	**0.10**	**0.09**
Latvia	0.01	0.06	0.07	0.06	0.06	0.07	0.08	–
Lithuania	0.01	0.04	0.06	0.08	0.11	0.11	0.11	–
Poland	0.01	0.05	0.07	0.09	0.10	0.08	0.09	0.08
Romania	–	–	–	–	–	0.08	0.09	–
Slovakia	0.05	0.07	0.12	0.10	0.09	0.10	0.09	0.09
Slovenia	–	–	0.11	0.12	0.12	0.13	0.15	0.13
OECD DAC Average	0.25	0.26	0.33	0.31	0.28	0.31	0.31	0.32

Source: OECD 2011.

preparation' for five years. No reforms have been started to change the inefficient institutional setting for aid delivery, in which many line ministries are involved with very weak central coordination. The evaluation of projects and learning from their experience is given hardly any emphasis and no attempts have been made to strengthen this. No attempts have been made to start a public discourse on the issue either. The following three sections of the paper map three sources of potential influence on Hungarian development cooperation in order to explain this stagnation: the effects of EU membership, the foreign policy context and stakeholder interests and relations.

3. The Effects of EU Membership

In the last decade, 'Europeanization' has become a very popular concept for understanding changes and dynamics in various policy areas due to membership in the EU or the prospect of it. During the accession process of the CEE countries to the EU, requirements were voiced that these countries should contribute to international development efforts. Thus, the EU was a crucial factor in the re-emergence of the development policies of the CEE countries and this has made the concept of Europeanization an increasingly popular framework to study these new policies (Vittek and Lightfoot 2009, Lightfoot 2010, Horky 2010). The concept can thus be useful in structuring the discussion on how EU membership has affected Hungarian development policy.

Europeanization is most generally understood as the process through which countries adopt formal and informal European rules and policies (Graziano and Vink 2007, p. 7, Schimmelfennig and Sedelmeier 2005, p. 7). The basic model of Europeanization, advocated by Risse, Cowles and Caporaso (2001, pp. 6–12), states that laws (institutions, methods, processes, norms, behavioural rules, etc.) originating from the EU level may be incongruous with the relevant legislation of the nation states. Depending on how large this gap is, pressures arise for the nation state to adapt to the 'European way' of doing things. However, these pressures are mediated through domestic institutions and a multitude of factors will influence whether and how the country actually changes its policies. In the end, some national institutional and policy outcome will emerge, which may eliminate or reduce the original misfit, or even leave it unchanged. The pressures for change may, therefore, still remain and the entire process may start again in a cyclical manner.

The two main channels for Europeanization to happen are through conditionality and socialization (Checkel 2001, Schimmelfennig and Sedelmeier 2005, Juncos 2011). In the case of the former, the member states are obliged to comply with any hard legislation accepted by the EU institutions. The EU can formulate explicit conditions towards the accession countries as well and, often, it can have an even larger leverage on these countries than it has on its own members (i.e., their accession process can be stalled if they do not comply). On the other hand, a more constructivist approach to Europeanization emphasizes the importance of longer term socialization and social learning. This involves the internalization of European values and formal rules as well as the gradual development of the conviction that that is the only proper way to act. While Europeanization through conditionality can be rather explicit and quick, social learning is a slow process and also much more difficult to identify in practice.

However, the two approaches, while relying on different theoretical backgrounds, are not mutually exclusive. In policy areas where conditionality and coercion are not possible, social learning can be the only channel for Europeanization to occur.

The question, therefore, is: Can one find evidence of Europeanization in Hungary's development policy? In the past two decades, the EU has attempted to considerably increase its influence on bilateral member state development policies, but the EU also had a chance to prescribe explicit criteria to Hungary during the accession negotiations.

The EU's influence on member states comes from several sources. The Treaty of Maastricht introduced qualitative requirements for both EU level and member state development policies with the concepts of complementarily, coherence and coordination (the so-called 3Cs, see Hoebink 2004). With regard to quantitative requirements, in 2002, the European Council reaffirmed that member states must increase their aid spending to 0.7 per cent of their gross national incomes by 2015 and set an intermediate goal of 0.39 per cent by 2006. In 2005, a new intermediate goal was established for 2010 of 0.56 per cent and a separate goal was set for the new member states of 0.17 per cent (Bucar and Mrak 2007, p. 7). In 2005, a joint statement by the Commission, the Council and the Parliament, entitled the European Consensus on Development, created a new framework for the EU's common development policy and also laid down many requirements for the individual member states. Other requirements include untying aid (European Commission 2002), focusing aid on Africa, increasing aid effectiveness (European Commission 2006, 2007) and implementing internationally agreed best practices such as the Paris Declaration or the Accra Agenda (Council of the European Union 2011).

Europeanization in the short term can be most effective through explicit conditionality. However, almost all the requirements the EU voices towards member states in the field of international development fall into the category of soft law – they are mainly recommendations. The EU could have formulated conditions during Hungary's accession negotiations, but it did not. It is well documented that international development (included in the negotiating chapter on trade) was neglected during the accession negotiations and no specific requirements were voiced, except for the fact that Hungary, as all the other CEE countries, must create such a policy (Fodor 2003). According to one of the foreign ministry officials who were interviewed, the EU missed its only possibility to exert any true influence on the course taken by Hungary's emerging international development policy. Without any explicit conditions, however, there was no reason for Hungary to adopt the practices advocated by the EU.

The actual 'hard' requirements (the binding rules to which the member states are legally required to conform) the EU has in place in the field are all either highly technical, such as the classification of aid projects and reporting on specific issues such as policy coherence, or related to financial issues, such as contribution to the European Development Fund (EDF). In this sense, according to a ministry official interviewed, there is evidence of Europeanization, but it is rather limited and has no significant influence on actual policies.

If there is no explicit conditionality and no 'hard' pressure, that would leave socialization as the main channel for the Europeanization of Hungary's development policy. Of course, officials at the Hungarian MFA and the other line ministries involved in international development have continuous interactions with the EU as they take part in the comitology system of the integration. They interact frequently with officials from other member states and from the European Commission. It is very difficult to draw any conclusion on the extent of social learning, but there are many factors hindering it, such as the high turnover of MFA staff and the perceptions dominating in the MFA on what interests and comparative advantages Hungary enjoys. According to the respondents, the perception that Hungarian interests dictate a different type of international development policy than the one advocated by the EU seems dominant within the MFA. All the three ministry officials who were interviewed seem to believe that Hungarian development policy should not follow blindly the requirements of the EU, but should take Hungary's situation into account as well. For example, they maintain that Hungary should receive economic and political benefits from giving aid and thus tying aid to exports is justified. They do acknowledge that many issues that the EU raises, such as placing greater emphasis on evaluation and feedback, are generally important, but Hungary has other priorities, such as building a constituency for aid. As these issues are related to the other two sources of influence on Hungarian external development policy, they will be discussed in more detail below.

European values and norms on development are, therefore, far from being internalized by the Hungarian MFA officials. They have learned to 'talk the talk', but the impression from the interviews was that they see the various committee meetings mostly as terrains for pursuing national interest and not opportunities for themselves to learn and adapt.

In sum, the current practice of Hungarian development policy is rather far from the soft requirements of the EU. Conditionality is only present on the technical level and has had no real effect on policies. There seems to be little evidence for social learning either, but this can be due to the fact that Hungary has not been a member of the EU long enough for the mechanics of social learning to kick in. It is concluded that there is little evidence of Europeanization in Hungary's international development policy.

4. Foreign Policy Strategy and Development

The second source of influence on Hungarian international development policy is the wider foreign policy context. It is widely agreed that foreign aid is a tool of foreign policy and can be used to serve specific foreign policy goals, such as influencing other countries, building alliances, creating stability and increasing national security (Degnbol-Martinussen and Engberg-Pedersen 2005). This section identifies the main strategic goals of Hungary's foreign policy and then looks at how these relate to the current allocation of foreign aid.

After the end of communism, a consensual Hungarian foreign policy strategy emerged. This strategy rested on three pillars: (1) integration in the Euro-Atlantic community; (2) the protection of ethnic Hungarians living abroad; and (3) good relations with neighbouring countries. While this strategy served Hungary well throughout the 1990s, it became obsolete when it joined the North Atlantic Treaty Organization (NATO) in 1999 and the EU in 2004. It was also realized that protecting ethnic Hungarians (most of them living in the neighbouring countries) inevitably led to conflicts with the neighbours, and so the two second priorities needed to be reconciled in some manner. After long preparatory work involving more than 100 experts and academics, a new foreign policy strategy was accepted by the government in 2008, meant to be valid until 2020.[3]

The new strategy also rests on three pillars, which to some extent refine the three pillars of the previous strategy and also expand them (Hungarian Government 2008). Pillar One is entitled 'Competitive Hungary in the European Union' and it details Hungary's interests in relation to the EU. These include maintaining and deepening the integration, maintaining community solidarity, keeping the integration open (including future enlargements) and increasing Europe's competitive position and global influence. Pillar Two is 'Successful Hungarians in the Region', which basically attempts to reconcile the contradictions between protecting the interests of the Hungarian minorities and maintaining good relations with the neighbours. This pillar stresses regional cooperation for mutual benefits, emphasizes stability and development in the Balkans and the Eastern countries (and the importance of their EU and NATO accession) and also the need for Hungary to serve as a major investor and trading partner in the region. The support of Hungarian minorities is a further key issue here, but it is placed into an EU framework, and the strategy also emphasizes the protection of non-Hungarian minorities living in Hungary. Pillar Three is entitled 'Responsible Hungary in the World'. This objective includes contributing to global peace, the spread of democratic values and human rights, promoting global governance, combating climate change, reducing global poverty and increasing global security.

The question is how international development policy relates to these three pillars. Due to the nature of development policy and the requirements of the EU, it should be serving mainly the strategic objectives outlined in Pillar Three – issues such as global poverty reduction. Hungary's foreign policy strategy includes three paragraphs on international development cooperation, which seem to reinforce this idea. In these paragraphs, a reference is made to the Millennium Development Goals (MDGs) and how Hungary supports the efforts of the international donor community to achieve them; a commitment to increase ODA and reach the 0.17 per cent and 0.33 per cent ODA/GNI targets set by the Council of the EU for 2010 and 2015, respectively. The third paragraph is meant to discuss the geographic focus of Hungarian aid, which, besides mentioning the importance of Africa, emphasizes maintaining a close relationship with Southern and Eastern Europe and the Far East.

However, based on data on Hungarian aid allocation and interviews with ministry staff and NGOs, it can be argued that the Hungarian international development policy serves mainly Pillar Two of the strategy – helping Hungary and Hungarians become 'successful' in the CEE region. A glance at the aid allocation data from the MFA's report on the implementation of official development and humanitarian assistance in 2010 (Hungarian Ministry of Foreign Affairs 2011) illustrates this point well, but the conclusions are valid for earlier years as well (Szent-Ivanyi 2012). In 2010, Hungary spent US$113 million on

DEVELOPMENT POLICIES OF CENTRAL AND EASTERN EUROPEAN STATES

Table 2. The regional allocation of Hungary's bilateral aid in 2010

Region	Amount (thousand dollars)	Share in total (%)
Southeastern Europe and CIS	8 892	33
of which: support to Hungarian minorities	3 927	15
Afghanistan	5 555	21
Africa	762	3
Other regions	2 932	11
Costs of refugees in Hungary	6 096	23
Unallocated*	2 353	9
Total bilateral	26 590	100

Note: The budget spent by the MFA itself is not broken down in the report. Most of it was probably allocated to Afghanistan, and it also includes the amounts spent on humanitarian aid.
Source: Calculations of the author, based on information from the Hungarian Ministry of Foreign Affairs (2011, pp. 36–47).

ODA, of which approximately $26.6 million were channelled bilaterally. Table 2 shows a breakdown of these bilateral funds.

As can be seen from Table 2, countries in the Balkans and in the former Soviet region received the highest chunk of Hungary's bilateral aid. A significant portion of these resources (15 per cent of total bilateral aid) was actually channelled to support ethnic Hungarians in Serbia and the Ukraine. Only 3 per cent of Hungary's bilateral aid went to African countries, and even that was mainly in the form of scholarships to Hungary, so some may argue that it benefitted Hungary even more in the form of a brain drain than it did the African countries. The single largest aid receiving country was Afghanistan, where Hungary, as a part of the NATO coalition, is in charge of a provincial reconstruction team and, therefore, has an international obligation to contribute to development there. Looking at the aid allocation data, it is clear that it is more in line with Pillar Two of the foreign policy objectives than it is with Pillar Three, global poverty reduction. Developing countries (with the exception of Afghanistan), where poverty is a huge issue, where democratic values and respect for human rights are lacking to a great extent and where the quality of governance is low, receive much smaller amounts of aid than middle income neighbouring countries, relations with which are crucial for Pillar Two of the strategy.

The interviews basically reinforced this conclusion, which was based on the aid allocation data. Respondents from the MFA said that Hungary's main comparative advantages and foreign policy interests dictate giving aid to neighbouring countries and to those countries that Hungarian actors 'know well', the latter clearly implying countries with which Hungary has had more extensive development relations during communism, such as Vietnam, the Palestinian authority and Yemen. Hungarian NGOs and private companies clearly have some advantages in the neighbouring countries, but giving aid to such partners is also underpinned by foreign and security policy considerations, such as the need for regional stability. One respondent cited the case of the Kosovo war in 1999, which had an adverse affect on foreign investments in Hungary. The official interviewed from the Ministry of National Economy mainly emphasized economic interests, saying that foreign aid should be used as a tool to pave the way for Hungarian exports and investments in the neighbouring countries.

Hungary is not perceived to have any comparative advantage in giving aid to Africa. As explicated by an MFA respondent, Africa is for 'the big players'. Building a presence in Africa in order to deliver efficient development aid has high fixed costs, which Hungary cannot afford. As Hungary currently has only two embassies in the Sub-Saharan African countries (in South Africa and Kenya), one can hardly argue that the continent figures high on its list of foreign policy and international development considerations.

NGO respondents complained that poverty reduction was not a true goal of Hungary's international development policy; if it had been, Hungary would have devoted more attention to regions where the return on aid in terms of people lifted out of poverty was higher. They also said that the MFA's lack of attention towards Africa was highly frustrating and made the work of NGOs dedicated to the region very difficult.

One may argue that the relatively large amounts spent in Afghanistan can be attributed to Pillar Three of Hungary's foreign policy strategy, as can multilateral aid (which makes up some 75 per cent of Hungary's total ODA). However, the Hungarian mission in Afghanistan seems to be perceived as an international obligation, and much of Hungary's multilateral aid is based on compulsory membership fees, and so the country has little freedom in deciding how much it pays and how it is spent. References in the foreign policy strategy to global poverty, the MDGs or respect for human rights may thus be a further example of Hungarian politicians and officials having learned to 'talk the talk' of international development, but their talk is not supported strongly by aid allocation.

Summing up this section and answering the second research question, it is clear that Hungary's international development policy is affected by wider foreign policy, as foreign aid is used to a large extent to promote Hungarian political and economic interests in the region, such as maintaining stability, helping ethnic Hungarians and building economic opportunities for Hungarian companies. Aid is used to a much lesser extent in decreasing global poverty and promoting respect for human rights – the goals elaborated in Pillar Three of the country's foreign policy strategy.

5. Development Stakeholders

The third potential source of influence on international development policy is the power relations between domestic stakeholders and their interests. The literature on how domestic dynamics affect international development policy in the OECD DAC member donor countries is still rather sparse, so these dynamics are not well understood. Lancaster (2007) offers one of the few comprehensive works that analyse these interior dynamics in the case of the US, Japan, France, Germany and Denmark.

Major foreign aid stakeholders include political parties, the government organizations and officials actually working on foreign aid, NGOs, business interests and the wider public. Political parties may have their own preferences, as, for example, socialist parties may put more emphasis on solidarity (Hopkins 2000). Governing parties also react to the wider public opinion, although international development – like foreign policy in general – is not highly sensitive to it (Otter 2003).

Within the government, the bureaucracies that take part in the day-to-day practice of international development are also major stakeholders. In fact, ministry officials can often play an important role in shaping policy if political attention on the topic is low or other interest groups are divided. In many OECD DAC countries, it was the foreign ministry officials that pushed for reforms. Lancaster (2007, p. 101) cites the State Department and the United States Agency for International Development (USAID) as important constituents for giving aid in the US. The Commission officials played a leading role in the reform of the EU's common development policy (Carbone 2007). Staff working on international development issues may be more concerned about aid effectiveness because their prestige and future budgets depend on the impact of their work. Thus, such staff may push for aid policies that are likely to increase the impact of aid. As shown below, this is not the case in Hungary.

Other stakeholders include those who are profiting from the 'development business', either financially or otherwise – private companies and development NGOs. It is clear that one cannot lump NGOs and private companies in one single group, as NGOs – while also making a living from international development – do not seek profit, but are motivated by moral and ethical considerations. While private companies most likely prefer aid practices that provide them with clear benefits (such as tied aid), NGOs generally advocate practices that involve increasing levels of aid, that are more beneficial for the partners and that are more in line with international best practices. Lancaster (2007, p. 103) notes that NGOs and business coalitions in the US lobbied together successfully to block cuts of foreign aid in the 1980s.

The remainder of this section briefly analyses the interests and relative power of two major development stakeholders in Hungary, the MFA and the development NGOs. As mentioned earlier, international development issues are not part of the everyday political dialogue in Hungary; in fact, they hardly ever are an issue. Political parties rarely raise the topic, which clearly indicates that they do not figure high on the political agenda. Due to this, the interests of these political actors will not be discussed. While private companies that benefit from the aid business do exist in Hungary, their numbers are definitely low and they are difficult to identify, so their role is discussed only marginally. Due to the lack of political attention, the bureaucracy of the MFA may have larger possibilities to define how international development policy is shaped. The institutional set-up for international development in Hungary is highly fragmented – there is no single budget line for foreign aid, almost all the line ministries are involved to some degree. The MFA has a central, coordinating role and is also in charge of policy formulation. This coordination is carried out by two committees, one on the ministerial level and the other on the level of officials and experts from various ministries working on international development. However, it became clear from the interviews that the MFA usually has no real power to influence the other ministries on how they determine their priorities and how they spend their aid budgets. All the line ministries seem to have their own understanding of what foreign aid is or what it should be used for and the MFA has no authority over their decisions. In 2010, the MFA actually controlled only about 25 per cent of the bilateral ODA (Hungarian Ministry of Foreign Affairs 2011, p. 36).

MFA officials complained that much of their weakness and inability to influence other official actors is related to lack of resources. They said their work has become very difficult in the past few years, as there has been a strong need to cut budget expenditure in Hungary since 2006, a situation that has been further exacerbated by the global economic crisis. The NGO respondents added that the MFA lacked expertise. They said, by way of an example, that the turnaround of staff in the MFA is high and many of them do not seem to have a clear understanding of what international development is actually about.

Still, the MFA officials, while acknowledging their constraints, argued that they do everything they can to promote 'Hungarian interests', including at the EU level. The MFA officials were well aware of the fact that development policy tools often serve foreign policy interests other than global development (as discussed in Section 3). In fact, the most surprising theme in the interviews was that the development staff in the MFA actually seemed to support this approach. They saw no contradiction here and they argued that Hungary should contribute to 'regional' development as it has 'comparative advantages' in the region that other donors do not. According to this argument, poverty stricken regions such as Sub-Saharan Africa are for donors who have more resources and larger and stronger NGOs and private companies to implement projects. Countries such as Hungary, which lack such large actors, need a different approach and must make the fostering of 'local aid champions' a part of their policies. This theme emerged in many different forms during the interviews and it was mostly the government officials, both from the MFA and the Ministry of National Economy, who mentioned it, not the NGOs. One issue closely related to this was the EDF; one of the respondents emphasized the fact that Hungarian companies and individual experts are rarely competitive enough to win international development tenders and grants financed by the EDF. According to this logic, the money Hungary contributes to the EDF (almost €125 million between 2008 and 2013) is effectively lost for Hungary. Apparently, the MFA even lobbied to change the rules of the EDF in order to provide some form of positive discrimination not only for companies and NGOs from the African, Caribbean and Pacific (ACP) countries, but also for the CEE countries. A second related issue is tied aid, which has already been mentioned, but should be reiterated here. The Ministry of National Economy, which is in charge of the budget for tied aid credits, perceives the various forms of tied aid solely as a tool for helping Hungarian enterprises gain international presence.

The need to use development policy to strengthen Hungarian development actors and serve foreign policy interests can explain why Hungary may resist pressures from the EU to untie aid, make greater use of programme based aid, or use practices that may lead to greater ownership for the recipient. It can explain why the MFA failed to act as a catalyst in promoting this adaptation. It is not clear, however, whether this is actually a true conviction of the MFA officials or just rhetoric directed at the Hungarian government, which they think can help them secure funds.

The weaknesses of the development NGOs stem in part from the communist era and Hungary's relatively lower incomes, but it is still a problem they must overcome. Financing their activities can often seem daunting. Raising resources from donations has proved to be difficult, so they must rely on grants from the state or international organizations. The actions and powers of development NGOs, however, clearly depend on the amount of resources they can draw upon, the public support for their cause and also the way governments and ministry officials perceive their activities (and usefulness). So what influence do NGOs have on Hungarian development policy making? Hungarian NGOs, and their platform organization, HAND, are highly active in lobbying. HAND had a high profile during the Hungarian EU presidency in the first half of 2011, organizing a multitude of events and producing policy papers. Recently, a group of NGOs drafted a strategy recommendation for the MFA on Hungarian engagement in Africa. NGOs are also active in monitoring the government, as shown by the Aid Watch Reports published in 2007 (Kiss 2007) and 2011. They are also represented on an advisory committee that meets formally once a year to discuss the implementation of international development policy in the previous year and formulate recommendations for the future. According to the MFA's report on the implementation of international development assistance in 2010, ministry officials also met formally every 'one or two months' with the representatives of HAND and participated in events organized by the platform if invited (Hungarian Ministry of Foreign Affairs 2011, p. 32). Therefore, it is clear that despite their lack of resources, NGOs do try to shape Hungary's international development policy, using both formal institutions and other means. They are committed to increasing the effectiveness of aid, emphasizing global poverty reduction and also increasing the transparency of the MFA and other ministries.

The NGO respondents, however, complained that the MFA did not treat them as partners. The flow of information from the ministry is slow at the best of times and their opinions are rarely sought. Their requests for information often take a long time to be processed, and grant applications often include conditions unfavourable to them, although in the past years, due to austerity measures, the MFA's budget for such grants has decreased greatly. The formal meetings seem to the NGOs as little more than talk shops, as the problems raised in them are rarely followed up or acted upon. In fact, one respondent said that the MFA seemed to treat them with outright hostility, which seems to be in stark contrast with what the ministry officials said about the need to strengthen domestic NGOs. This contradiction may be difficult to explain. While it may point to differences in perceptions, it may also hint at the possibility that helping domestic actors is just rhetoric on the part of the MFA. Or – as one NGO respondent put it – the MFA simply does not like being told what to do.

All these issues may imply that NGOs are not able to exert substantial influence on Hungary's international development policy. Still, most NGOs agree that they did have an important impact in the past years in making the MFA more transparent and forcing it to disclose more information publicly on its activities. Summing up this section, both the MFA and the development NGOs have weaknesses, but it seems that the former is more powerful and thus able to wield more influence on international development. However, the MFA seems to favour a policy that is aligned with Hungarian political and economic interests and not so much with global poverty reduction. The reasons for the MFA's motivations are unclear. Higher level political interest in the issue as well as clear political and strategic guidance are greatly needed.

6. Conclusions

This paper has discussed three potential sources of influence that may have had a role in shaping Hungary's emerging international development policy in the past

DEVELOPMENT POLICIES OF CENTRAL AND EASTERN EUROPEAN STATES

decade: membership in the EU, Hungarian foreign policy priorities, and the relationships and relative power of the domestic stakeholders. These three factors are of course heavily interrelated and all three must be taken into consideration when explaining the evolution of Hungary's international development policy.

The main conclusion that emerges is that in the past decade, Hungary's international development policy seems to have been guided mainly by its political and economic interests, as the close links between the country's foreign policy strategy and aid allocation demonstrate. Foreign aid is used to a much lesser extent to promote global development and poverty reduction. The requirements of the EU in this policy area (mainly in the domain of soft law), which mandate the increase of aid effectiveness in decreasing global poverty, have had little impact on Hungary's practice. One potential reason for this can be found in the dynamics between the domestic stakeholders: The development staff at the MFA seem to support the current approach, because of which the MFA has failed to act as a catalyst in orienting development policy towards a more global, poverty focused approach. Higher level political guidance is lacking and the development NGOs are too weak to achieve any substantial influence.

These dynamics may allow one to draw conclusions on the potential future evolution of Hungarian development cooperation. Most importantly, convergence with EU practices will likely be slow and it will only take place as incomes and development experience in Hungary increase, allowing the country to play more of a global role and also strengthening the development actors. International pressures, which try to push for a quick adaptation of Hungary's international development policy to European or other standards, are likely to be unsuccessful.

As emphasized in the introduction, this research should be seen as exploratory and all three sources of influence need further investigation, especially concerning the causal mechanics. Future research may also attempt to uncover similar dynamics in other CEE countries and thus provide a possibility for comparison.

Notes

[1] The research was funded by the following grant: TÁMOP-4.2.1.B-09/1/KMR-2010-0005.
[2] Hungary was eligible for official aid between 1990 and 2004. During these 15 years, the country received a total of $5.1 billion (at 2009 prices and exchanges rates). On an annual average, this amounted to 0.4–0.5 per cent of Hungary's GDP (World Bank 2011).
[3] The current Hungarian government, in power since 2010 and led by the conservative Fidesz, has signalled the need for a new strategy. However, work on such a strategy has not started and no information on future directions can be found on the website of the government as of late 2011.

References

Bucar, M., and Mrak, M., 2007. Challenges of development cooperation for EU new member states. Paper presented at the *ABCDE World Bank conference*, 17–18 May 2007 Bled, Slovenia.
Carbone, M., 2004. Development policy. In: N. Nugent, ed. *European Union enlargement*. Basingstoke, UK: Palgrave, 242–252.
Carbone, M., 2007. *The European Union and international development*. London: Routledge.
Checkel, J.T., 2001. Why comply? Social learning and European identity change. *International organization*, 55 (3), 553–588.

DEVELOPMENT POLICIES OF CENTRAL AND EASTERN EUROPEAN STATES

Council of the European Union, 2011. *Operational framework on aid effectiveness. Consolidated text.* Available from: http://register.consilium.europa.eu/pdf/en/10/st18/st18239.en10.pdf [accessed 21 July 2011].

Dauderstädt, M., ed., 2002. *EU Eastern enlargement and development cooperation.* Bonn: Friedrich-Ebert-Stiftung.

Degnbol-Martinussen, J., and Engberg-Pedersen, P., 2005. *Aid: Understanding international development cooperation.* London: Zed Books.

European Commission, 2002. Untying: Enhancing the effectiveness of aid, COM (2002) 639 final. Brussels: European Commission.

European Commission, 2006. EU aid: Delivering more, better and faster, COM (2006) 87 final. Brussels: European Commission.

European Commission, 2007. EU code of conduct on division of labour in development policy, COM (2007) 72 final. Brussels: European Commission.

Fodor, E., 2003. Partnerek a fejlődésben – az Európai Unió fejlesztési politikája (Partners in development – the development policy of the European Union). *Külügyi szemle,* 2 (2), 142–170.

Graziano, P., and Vink, M.P., 2007. Challenges of a new research agenda. In: P. Graziano and M.P. Vink, eds. *Europeanization New research agendas.* Houndmills, UK, and New York: Palgrave MacMillan, 3–21.

Hoebink, P., ed., 2004. *The Treaty of Maastricht and Europe's development cooperation. Studies in European development co-operation evaluation no. 1.* Brussels: European Union).

Hoebink, P., ed., 2010. *European development cooperation. In between the local and the global.* Amsterdam: Amsterdam University Press.

Hopkins, R.F., 2000. Political economy of foreign aid. In: F. Tarp, ed. *Foreign aid and development: Lessons learnt and directions for the future.* London: Routledge.

Horky, O., 2010. The Europeanisation of development policy. Acceptance, accommodation and resistance of the Czech Republic. Deutsches Institut für Entwicklungspolitik Discussion Paper 18/2010.

Hungarian Government, 2008. Hungary's external relations strategy. Unofficial English translation, available from: http://www.mfa.gov.hu/kum/en/bal/foreign_policy/external_relations_strategy/ [accessed 20 July 2011].

Hungarian Ministry of Foreign Affairs, 2011. Beszámoló Magyarország 2010. évi hivatalos nemzetközi fejlesztési és humanitárius segítségnyújtási tevékenységéről (Report on Hungary's official development and humanitarian assistance activities in 2010). Budapest: Ministry of Foreign Affairs.

HUN-IDA, 2004. A magyar műszaki-tudományos együttműködés és segítségnyújtás négy évtizedének rövid áttekintése napjainkig (An overview of the four decades of Hungarian technical-scientific cooperation and assistance). Prepared by the Hungarian International Development Agency for the Hungarian Ministry of Foreign Affairs, Budapest.

Juncos, A.E., 2011. Europeanization by decree? The case of police reform in Bosnia. *Journal of common market studies,* 49 (2), 367–387.

Kiss, J., 2002. Hungary. In: M. Dauderstädt, ed. *EU Eastern enlargement and development cooperation.* Bonn: Friedrich-Ebert-Stiftung.

Kiss, J., 2007. A magyar nemzetközi fejlesztéspolitika a számok tükrében (Hungary's international development policy in numbers). Budapest: HAND Aid Watch Working Group.

Lancaster, C., 2007. *Foreign aid. Diplomacy, development, domestic politics.* Chicago, IL: Chicago University Press.

Lightfoot, S., 2008. Enlargement and the challenge of EU development policy. *Perspectives on European politics and society,* 9 (2), 128–142.

Lightfoot, S., 2010. The Europeanisation of international development policy. *Europe-Asia studies,* 62 (2), 329–350.

OECD, 2011. OECD StatExtracts online database. Available from: http://stats.oecd.org/Index.aspx?lang=en [accessed 30 April 2011].

Otter, M., 2003. Domestic public support for foreign aid: Does it matter? *Third World quarterly,* 24 (1), 115–125.

Paragi, B., 2010. Hungarian development policy. In: P. Hoebink, ed. *European development cooperation. In between the local and the global.* Amsterdam: Amsterdam University Press.

Risse, T., Cowles, M.G., and Caporaso, J., 2001. Europeanization and domestic change: Introduction. In: M.G. Cowles, J. Caporaso and T. Risse, eds. *Transforming Europe: Europeanization and domestic change.* Ithaca, NY: Cornell University Press, 1–20.

Schimmelfennig, F., and Sedelmeier, U., 2005. Introduction. Conceptualizing the Europeanization of Central and Eastern Europe. In: F. Schimmelfennig and U. Sedelmeier, eds. *The Europeanization of Central and Eastern Europe*. Ithaca, NY: Cornell University Press, 1–28.

Szent-Iványi, B., and Tétényi, A., 2008. Transition and foreign aid policies in the Visegrád countries. A path dependant approach. *Transition studies review*, 15 (3), 573–587.

Szent-Iványi, B., 2012. Aid allocation of the emerging Central and Eastern European donors. *Journal of international relations and development* 15 (1), 65–89. 23 September 2011, DOI:10.1057/jird.2011.19.

Vittek, M., and Lightfoot, S., 2009. The Europeanization of Slovak development cooperation. *Contemporary European studies*, 1 (1), 20–36.

World Bank, 2011. World development indicators. Available from: http://data.worldbank.org/data-catalog/world-development-indicators [accessed 25 October 2011].

Development Discourse in Romania: From Socialism to EU Membership

MIRELA OPREA[1]

ABSTRACT *In recent years, 12 European countries (re)entered the donors' community. They are said to be 'new', inexpert donors that need to learn from the 'old' ones. Taking Romania's case, this paper argues that the equation, 'new EU member state = new donor', is debatable. Before 1989, Romania had an extensive web of relations with the developing countries and was an active presence in the field of international development. The paper discusses Romania's pre-1989 programme for international development, some important elements of its development discourse and its current strategy for development cooperation. It shows that while encouraged to 'build its capacity' as a 'new' donor, Romania has also been encouraged to – and was willing to – 'unlearn' its previous practices. Romania and its fellow 'new' member states go through a process that sees their cooption to the dominant theory and practice of development cooperation. The above-mentioned equation seems to be only one of the many tools employed by the promoters of this cooption process. The paper is informed by discourse analysis methods and post-development thinking.*

1. Introduction: New Players in a Crowded Market

The aid market is said to literally be 'crush[ed]' under some 90,000 aid projects a year (Frot and Santiso 2009), financed by no less than 200 aid agencies (Riddell 2007, pp. 51–53). One may wonder if additional official donors are needed, but here is what happened a few years ago: Twelve European countries, 'new' member states of the European Union (EU), joined the aid industry as official donors. The 12 see themselves and are seen by the other players as 'new' donors.

In what follows, we will look into this 'newness'. We will do so primarily by means of historical data and discourse analysis, with the underlying assumption that language is not merely a reflection or expression of social processes, but a *part* of these processes; it is a social process in itself, while also being socially conditioned. Analysing language is no less important than analysing politics: Politics consists partly of the disputes and struggles that occur in and over language (Fairclough

2001). The 'new donors' label attached to the 12 new member states (NMS) did not occur by chance – it is the pointer to and the trigger of a specific discourse that has the power of excluding other possible interpretations. As this paper will show, the term, 'new donors', can be seen to be historically inaccurate (at least some of the EU-12 were thought to be donors before 1989) and inadequate today because the present-day 'newness' is 'contaminated' by massive imports of 'old donor' ideology.

2. How Old are the 'New' EU Donors?

Some authors quote EU officials to say, 'The NMS might not be so familiar with concepts such as donor practices harmonization, selectivity and performance-based allocations, the PRSP (Poverty Reduction Strategy Papers) approach and the shift away from projects to sector/budget support' (Lightfoot 2010). And indeed it is arguable that many of these notions are conceptual acquisitions of the last two decades, when the current EU new member states were more concerned with their own development from a recipient stance, rather than international development from a donor perspective. But what is more, scholars and practitioners alike point to the lack of historicity that the new EU member states have as donors. In 2007, at a public hearing organized by the European Parliament, Marián Čaučík, founding member and chairman of the Slovak NGDO platform, referred to 'the lack of history of NMS being donors' (Čaučík 2007), while Ambassador Marija Adanja, head of International Development Cooperation in the Slovene Ministry of Foreign Affairs (MFA), showed that like the other new EU member states, her country was a '*novice* in the field of international development cooperation' (Adanja 2007).

However, older bibliographic resources narrate a more nuanced reality. Writing in 1981, the American political scientist of Romanian origin, Michael Radu, classified the socialist countries according to their Third World policies (Radu 1981). He identified various groups. One of them was formed of the two Eastern superpowers, the Soviet Union and China, the only states with the ability to formulate and implement overall and independent policies. Then came Albania and Yugoslavia, which Radu called the 'separatist' group, given that both Tirana and Belgrade tried to act as separated centres of influence; then the 'free-riders', represented by North Korea and Romania, which, even if not truly independent, seemed to enjoy a certain degree of autonomy in their policy-making, positioning themselves in an intermediary position between the two superpowers; Cuba and Vietnam, or the 'Trojan Horse' of socialist interests in the Third World, as they both enjoy a position of prestige and legitimacy among the developing countries, while promoting communist policies; and last but not least, the 'loyal five', Bulgaria, Czechoslovakia, East Germany, Hungary and Poland, the socialist countries directly subordinated to Moscow as far as their Third World policies were concerned. All these countries were said to use a series of policy instruments, aid included, to advance their interests in the Third World.

Thus, before 1989, some of the current EU new member states were part of at least four different categories of Third World policy-makers. There was the group of the 'loyal five' (at the present time, Bulgaria, the Czech Republic, Slovakia, Hungary and Poland); a so-called 'free-rider' (Romania); an heir of the 'separatists'

(Slovenia); and a group of countries (Estonia, Latvia, Lithuania) that are now independent, but were then part of the Soviet Union, the superpower acknowledged as an important donor for the developing countries. Cyprus and Malta (with its long tradition of international philanthropy) add complexity to this categorization of EU-12 interactions with the developing countries. And still, one notices that in spite of such different historical experiences, the EU-12 all tend to be put together in one single category – that of 'new' donors.

According to Frank Morey Coffin (1964), former deputy administrator of the United States Agency for International Development (USAID), the Eastern European countries played an important role in building the socialist system of development assistance. In the first decade after the Soviet programme for economic aid was established, the Eastern European socialist countries allegedly contributed almost one-third of the total socialist development aid. At times, Poland and Czechoslovakia claimed the leading position among the Eastern European donors, with Czechoslovakia reporting having given as much as 0.74 per cent of its gross domestic product (GDP) (Després 1987, p. 156) to as many as 136 countries.[2] Romania was less keen to advertise its donor budget, but by the beginning of the 1980s, this country was considered by some foreign observers as having 'by far the largest foreign aid budget in Eastern Europe' (Linden 1983, p. 55).

Based on the definition of aid proffered by the Organisation for Economic Cooperation and Development's (OECD's) Development Assistance Committee (DAC), Western donors claimed that the East's development aid was a mere, if complex, system of commercial exchanges, with distinctions between aid and trade systematically blurred so as to make trade agreements look like aid (Little and Clifford 2005, p. 27). The Western observers claimed that the aid figures presented by the Eastern European donors were 'difficult to understand' and pointed to inconsistencies in reporting (Després 1987, pp. 156–157). Countering this, the East warned against the system of conditionality ushering Western aid, which they alleged was aimed at undermining the sovereignty of the South. In Romania, some authors denied the existence of a genuine Western effort for the South's development and Romanian scholar Gavril Horja argued that Western aid was only a veiled form of neo-colonialism (Horja 1981, p. 93).

If the West was the 'inventor' of development (Rist 2003, Escobar 1995), the East soon followed suit and embarked on development vocabulary and programmes. The instruments, the strategies and the rationales for the South's development were a bone of contention between the two 'blocks', with the East constantly criticizing the West for its influence in the South and vice versa, but in spite of apparently conflicting world-views, the capitalist and non-capitalist theories for development had much in common (Raff 1996). The question was not if one should be a 'donor', but how to do this and from which political perspective.

Hence, before 1989, some of the current EU new member states (such as Romania, Bulgaria, the Czech Republic, Slovakia, Poland and Hungary) claimed to be fully ingrained in the complex processes of 'international development' and to be in line with or above the 0.7 per cent UN target. These claims were contested by the 'traditional' donors, but for the purposes of this paper, it is not so important to

DEVELOPMENT POLICIES OF CENTRAL AND EASTERN EUROPEAN STATES

investigate the 'truth' of the matter – who was more of a 'real' donor. Instead, the focus proposed is to acknowledge the very fact that in a previous historical time, these countries did identify themselves as aid donors and correlate this with more recent developments that led these countries to disown or 'disclaim' their previous experience and accept the image that the EU was striving to build for them – that of 'new' donors.

The European Parliament (2008) 'stresses the (recipient) experience of the new Member States, in particular during the transition process', but fails to mention their experience *as donors* before that transition period started. Talking about the 'strengths' that the new member states can bring to the field of development cooperation, the head of the TRIALOG project refers to a coherent list of factors,[3] but their past experience as donors is overlooked (Bedoya 2008). Last but not least, according to the European Parliament (2008), the objective of the EU with regard to the new member states is to 'capitalize' on their experience, 'help them strengthen their role as new donors' and 'bring them into line with the EU's development aid objectives'.

Development workers themselves are keen to emphasize their countries' lack of experience in this field. As a Hungarian practitioner (witnessed by this author) once said emphatically in defence of capacity building for development non-government organizations (NGOs) in the new member states, 'I feel that there is a huge gap between the old Member States (NGOs), which go like a train forward to the (development) policy and manage a lot of projects in parallel; meanwhile, in the new Member States we don't have this development (cooperation) work in our countries; we are absolutely new (to development cooperation); we are, I am so sorry to say, worse than a Southern NGO, because a Southern NGO was until now a recipient, working with you.'

This is a statement that is heard rather frequently in the new member states. The argument as it goes is that Western countries have a longer tradition of donor experience, whilst the transition years (intended here as the years between 1989 and the time of EU accession) were naturally dominated by the new member states' internal development concerns, which is why the new member states are not up to date with current DAC donor practices.

As for the public authorities in the new member states, most of them keep official silence on their past experience as donors and Third World policy-making. Only informally can talk on such experiences be heard, with Romania making references to the 'capital of sympathy' that it still has in the developing countries from the 'old times'.[4] The Czech Republic seems to be the only new member state that makes explicit reference to the past. A report published by the Institute of International Relations says, 'The Czech Republic reintroduced a program of international development cooperation in 1995 as the first transition country in Central and Eastern Europe. The program took up the long and rich tradition of relations between former Czechoslovakia and developing countries...' The acknowledgement is straightforward and rather exceptional if it were not for the rest of the sentence, which is practically a 'disclaimer' of such past experience; the Report goes on to show that such relations were resumed 'with the objectionable ideological encumbrance removed' *(Adamcová et al.* 2006, p. 7).

69

Thus, contrary to historical evidence, the prevalent opinion in the new member states is that development cooperation is a completely new sphere of activity. To 'catch up' with the more established donors, the EU-12 invited 'twinning projects' with the 'old' member states to facilitate institutional learning; strategic partnerships were created with the United Nations Development Programme (UNDP) so that the new member states could benefit from this agency's experience in the field of international development; funding from more established donors was welcome for creating the new member states' 'own' institutions and models of development cooperation.[5] And still, in 2008, four years after the EU enlargement, Ibolya Bárány (2008), director of the Hungarian Agency for Development Cooperation, showed that the new member states were not yet ready to become 'normal' donors as they were not able to keep pace with the volumes of aid assistance and development issues proposed by the 'old' donors. Due to the '50 year gap' in development history, the new member states argue that they need new opportunities to 'learn' from the old member states. But as the experience of the past is apparently rejected, this 'learning' process seems to be paralleling a process of 'unlearning' or in any case of evasion of the knowledge gained before 1989.

3. Socialist Romania and the Global South

At the end of World War II, Romania had diplomatic relations with only one country each in Africa and Asia and only two countries in Latin America. The 1960s saw this state of affairs change radically as Romania steadily broadened its relations with the developing countries; by 1974, Romania had diplomatic relations with no less than 39 countries in Africa, 32 countries in Latin America and 16 countries in Asia (Popişteanu 1976).

President Nicolae Ceauşescu was a keen promoter of his country in the developing world and he was among the few Eastern European leaders to 'tour' the developing countries. These 'Third World Tours' – highly visible foreign policy instruments that became so characteristic of his time – were intensely publicized, official, multi-nation visits. The first of these tours took place in 1972 and included countries in Sub-Saharan Africa (Congo, Zambia, Zaire, Tanzania and the Central African Republic). After Africa, Latin America came into focus, with two dedicated tours in 1973 and 1975; some countries in the Middle East were toured in 1975 and Africa was high on the agenda again in 1977 (Mauritania, Senegal, Ghana, the Ivory Coast and Nigeria), 1979 (Gabon, Angola, Zambia, Mozambique, Sudan and Burundi) and 1983 (Ethiopia, Mozambique, Zimbabwe, Zambia and Somalia) (Barnett 1992). Besides the multi-country tours, which usually lasted 10–20 days, Ceauşescu also made frequent shorter state visits, when not receiving Third World leaders and delegations at Bucharest.

In 'whirlwind diplomacy' style (Barnett 1992, p. 52), the tours were supported by intense summitry – 59 high-level summit participations from 1972 to 1974 (of which 33 were hosted by Romania itself) – as Romania was applying for G-77 membership and keen to convince the Third World countries about the genuineness of its claim of belonging to their group. To show its solidarity with the developing countries, and with those 'struggling' for their independence and against colonialism and neo-colonialism in particular (Vasilescu 1973, p. 30), 'the Romanian people extended political, diplomatic, moral and material support to the African and Asian peoples in their struggle to free themselves from the imperialist and colonialist domination, and to win their right to a free and independent life' (Barac 1977, p. 6).

The displays of Romanian 'solidarity' were so significant as to make some foreign commentators (Barnett 1992, Linden 1983) talk about a substantial 'increase' of Romania's 'aid' budget. In 1973, Nicolae Mǎnescu (1973, pp. 18–19) conducted an overview of the main forms of economic and technical cooperation between Romania and the developing countries. He mentioned four main categories. First, Romania built 'economic objectives and new production capacities' in the developing countries, with Romanian machines, equipment and technical assistance. Second, Romania and the developing countries formed mixed companies to ensure raw material access and to increase Romanian exports. Third, Romania created, in the developing countries, trade companies with '100% Romanian capital' to realize a 'direct contact with that market'. And, finally, Romania made technological and technical assistance available for modernizing the 'existing production capacities' of its developing partners. Technical assistance was mentioned, but this or any other kind of material support did not represent a separate 'form' of economic and technical cooperation. Law no. 1/1971 on Romania's foreign trade distinguished technical assistance from other instruments and clarified that technical assistance was instrumental in Romania's external trade: 'The activity of external trade is given a broad content, by its comprising the commercial operations and of economic cooperation regarding the vending, the procurement and the exchange of goods (. . .), tourism, the design and execution of works, technical assistance or collaboration (. . .)' (Puiu 1974, p. 6).

The ambiguity between 'technical assistance' and commercial forms of cooperation was promoted from the highest levels. Ceauşescu stated: 'Taking into account the fact that socialist Romania is itself a developing country and has limited resources, the main form of help that we can promote towards the developing countries is the cooperation in production (. . .) on mutually advantageous bases.' But immediately after such a clear statement, Ceauşescu (1978, p. 518) added a confusing element when he said, 'Even if this imposes on us some efforts, we grant and will grant in the future too, technical assistance to the developing countries and, at the same time, we will train specialists from these countries in our country.'

However, beyond information regarding the *creation* of a special fund for the national liberation movements,[6] one can find hardly any other official data regarding the size and operations of this particular fund or about the creation and operations of similar funds. On extremely rare occasions, the difficulties in keeping the flow of aid open are alluded to, but never is there a clear indication of the amounts involved. When Ceauşescu refers to the kinds of difficulties that Romania faced when extending its assistance to foreign students, he talks about Romania's determination to overcome such difficulties without producing any concrete data. In one of his speeches, he says: 'Even if we have to face some problems related to the accommodation spaces, our country will go not towards restraining, but towards developing the activity of training, in our education system, of the specialists from these countries' (Ceauşescu 1978, p. 519).

Information about Romanian credit to the developing countries is less difficult to put together and shows hundreds of millions of dollars granted every year.[7]

DEVELOPMENT POLICIES OF CENTRAL AND EASTERN EUROPEAN STATES

However, official sources such as the party journal, *Scînteia*, generally fail to mention whether these credits were export or development oriented, as also other important details regarding the size and scope of the credit contracts.

As regards Romania's technical assistance, this is systematically associated with the number of Romanian specialists working in the developing countries, plus the number of young people from developing countries studying in Romanian universities. Technical assistance, also called 'scientific assistance', included offering state-funded scholarships to developing country nationals; having Romanian professionals train developing country professionals; transferring scientific, techno-logical and teaching equipment to research institutes in developing countries, and so on (Ghibernea 1969, p. 395). If Romanian sources offer limited official and public information about the actual size of Romania's 'material support' to the developing countries, information about the level of technical assistance is frequently provided by the Romanian media. Romanian authors say proudly, 'Thousands of Romanian specialists are presently working in developing countries, while an important number of young people from those countries study in Romania' (Ecobescu and Celac 1975, p. 65).

Data reliability, however, might well be a question of interpretation. In 1979, Călina shows that there were 15,000 Romanian specialists working in 60 developing countries, a sharp increase from 4,000 in the 1970s. At the same time, 15,000 foreign students were studying in Romania. But in 1971, Ceauşescu was pointing to a different picture: 'In the field of technical assistance 642 Romanian specialists work in the developing countries, of which more than 500 are in the African countries. From the developing countries, 665 students study in various training institutions from Romania, of which 166 come from the African continent' (Ceauşescu 1985, p. 232).

Since such a sharp decrease – from 4,000 in 1970, according to Călina, to 642 in 1971, according to Ceauşescu – is unlikely to have taken place at a time when the size of Romanian technical assistance was supposed to be on the increase, it follows that while the programme of 'technical assistance' as such *was* real, its exact size was kept concealed. In any case, it was a matter of national pride that many young people in the developing countries 'dream to accomplish their studies in Romania',[8] and this is given as one of the reasons for Romania's eagerness to enrol them in such large numbers in Romanian universities.

An overview of Romania's 'assistance' to the developing countries needs to acknowledge the fact that Romania took a very broad view of classifying its forms of assistance. Thus, Romania considered that it assisted the developing countries not only when extending credits, scholarships or grants, but also when sharing from its own experience in capitalizing on the country's natural resources; when backing the developing countries' positions in various international forums; and when joining their fight against colonialism, neo-colonialism and imperialism. In addition, Romania was a supporter of East–South multilateral cooperation, a form of cooperation in which two or more socialist countries pooled their efforts to accomplish various economic objectives in the developing countries (Bari and Dumitrescu 1988). Romania took great pride in a special form of industrial cooperation, officially called 'industrial cooperation in two phases' or 'buy-back'. According to Romanian scholars, this form of cooperation came to be known in international forums as 'the Romanian formula for industrial cooperation', given that it was Romania that first proposed it as early as in 1958, at the 13th session of the UN Economic Commission for Europe (Albu 1995).

According to reports, articles and interviews carried in *Scînteia*, this mix of assistance formats was acknowledged by many leaders in the developing countries. An example is the Gabonese Minister of Foreign Affairs, Edouard-Alexis Mbouy-Boutzit, speaking in 1979, on the occasion of Ceauşescu's state visit to Gabon to sign the Romanian-Gabonese Treaty of Friendship and Cooperation: 'In the field of staff training, for instance, it is enough to show that almost 500 Gabonese are now studying in Romania, specializing in various professions. We have high esteem for Romania's participation in joint ventures for the exploitation and valorization of our natural wealth, especially our iron ore, at Benga. For us, also of great importance is the interest of Romania to participate in building the trans-Gabon railway, which, as shown by our President Bongo, is the backbone of the multilateral development of Gabon. Our country shows a special interest towards the Romanian technology and experience, which can help us in the complex capitalization of the national wealth, allowing Gabon to take new steps on the path of underdevelopment liquidation'.[9]

Thus, according to the Romanian approach, development 'assistance' was not so much about hard currency cash transfers as about a transfer of goods and services that needed to be to the advantage of both 'donor' (Romania) and 'recipient' (the developing country). This – the 'mutually-advantageous help', in Romanian, '*întrajutorare*' – can be considered as one last, but very significant, feature of Romania's 'assistance' to the developing countries.

In spite of information scarcity in Romanian public sources,[10] foreign sources report various data regarding the size of Romania's 'aid' programme. Paul Gafton (1979), quoting the 1 April 1977 edition of *The Neue Züricher Zeitung*, estimated that overall Romanian assistance to all developing countries in the period, 1950–75, amounted to $1,767 million. To offer a scale of comparison, the article said that the assistance of the Soviet Union and the East European countries during the same period was $19.87 million. However, the term, 'assistance', is not defined, so it is difficult for the reader to infer how these amounts were spent. Writing in 1983, Ronald Linden quoted a Radio Free Europe Research Report from 29 April 1977, estimating that from 1966 to 1970, Romania contributed an average of $40 million per year in foreign aid, while from 1971 to 1975, its aid commitments 'jumped' to an average of $350 million per year, to a level that was 'by far the largest foreign aid budget in Eastern Europe' (Linden 1983).

Additionally, Thomas Barnett talks about 'Romania's bilateral commitments of capital to non-communist developing countries', showing that with this expression, he actually refers to aid money, but, like other scholars, he also fails to define what 'aid' meant.

4. Transferring Development Knowledge

If language is not a mere channel for transmitting information, but the machine that generates and constitutes realities (Jørgensen and Phillips 2002, p. 9), then the discursive construction of the EU-12 as 'new', 'novice', 'beginner' and 'inexperienced' can be susceptible to having some ideological effects. A possible practical consequence of building the EU-12 as 'new' donors is that they can easily become objects of 'teaching' and ideological work, where ideologies are understood as world representations, which 'contribute to establishing, maintaining and changing social relations of power, domination and exploitation' (Fairclough 2003, p. 9). The transfer of development ideology from the EU-15 (the old member states) to the candidate countries and now the new member states occurred through a whole range of strategies, from so-called 'capacity-building' programmes for NGOs to 'twinning' programmes for public authorities. In what follows, we will look into an apparently 'innocuous' tactic – the use of the various Reports issued by the European Commission to 'monitor' the candidate countries' progress towards accession. Examples are drawn from Romania's case.

The first regular report on Romania's progress towards accession succinctly shows that 'Romania has continued to improve the legal framework for its relations with developing countries, mainly in the fields of economic and trade cooperation', even if '[n]o progress has been achieved concerning development cooperation with ACP countries' (European Commission 1998d, p. 42). Romania, the report said, lagged behind forerunners such as the Czech Republic, Hungary and Poland.

The Czech Republic is acknowledged for having 'continued with its foreign development assistance through its Humanitarian Assistance budget (...) and Foreign Development Assistance budget' (European Commission 1998b, p. 33). Poland 'has continued to play a constructive regional and international role in the field of development' (European Commission 1998e, p. 37), while in Hungary, '[t]here is a foreign aid fund managed by the Ministry of Foreign Affairs through which Hungary provides development and humanitarian aid' (European Commission 1998c, p. 37).

There seemed to be a hierarchy in the candidates' preparedness for taking up responsibilities as donor countries. Leading the group were Poland and the Czech Republic, which already ran a special budget for international development and were not expected to constitute – in the Reports' words – a 'problem' in this sense. Second in range are candidate countries such as Estonia and Latvia, which did not have a special budget or institutions for development cooperation, but still had a certain awareness regarding the challenges of international development and contributed on a 'case-by-case' basis (Latvia) or had started to develop plans for allocating resources for humanitarian and development assistance (Estonia). Third were candidates such as Lithuania, Slovakia, Slovenia and Romania, which either did not take any steps to adopt development policies in line with those of the EU (Lithuania) or achieved no progress in this field. A significant case was that of Bulgaria as the Commission's Report shows that 'Bulgaria traditionally maintains good relations with developing countries and despite its financial difficulties it has invariably responded to appeals and taken part in initiatives of the international community for helping developing countries, including the granting of humanitarian aid' (European Commission 1998a, p. 37). Bulgaria is the only one among the candidate countries that was thus acknowledged for its traditional 'good relations' with the developing countries, even if, historically, other countries in the region used to have equally intense – if not more so – exchanges with the global South.

With little variation, this hierarchy was maintained in the years to follow, with Poland and the Czech Republic continuing to lead, while Romania had a slow and apparently inadequate growth of donor attitude: In 2002, 'Romania is (still) not an international donor and does not have a development policy although contributions are made to certain United Nations development programmes and fund' (European Commission 2002, p. 118). In 2003, the Progress Report reiterates that 'Romania is not an international donor and does not have a development policy', but it acknowledges Romania for building some humanitarian assistance capacities. Some advancement is also acknowledged: The Romanian MFA had established an Office for Development Cooperation 'in order to coordinate Romania's input into EU development policy'. The wording is evocative, suggesting that Romanian 'input' – policies, strategies, ideas – already exists and what is now needed is mere 'coordination'. Further progress was acknowledged by the Regular Report in 2004: An inter-ministerial working group had been established to define the future objectives of Romania's strategy for development cooperation and make an inventory of (already existing) Romanian programmes that might be assimilated and reported as development assistance. Moreover, the Romanian MFA was acknowledged as having closely cooperated with the Commission services in building development capacity, while continuing to provide humanitarian assistance (European Commission 2004, p. 135).

As of 2005, the Regular Reports are replaced by the Monitoring Reports. Issued in October 2005, the Comprehensive Monitoring Report for Romania dedicated eight paragraphs to External Relations, an exceptional length when compared with previous reports. One of these paragraphs is specifically dedicated to humanitarian and development policy. Unlike the Progress Reports, which offered very brief accounts, this Monitoring Report takes a more explanatory, informative, almost instructive stance. Thus, the Romanian readership can learn about new developments in EU policy and is informed that Romania 'must' make adequate budgetary provisions upon accession and develop its institutional framework and administrative capacity for the implementation of the EU acquis in this area (European Commission 2005, p. 75).

Compared to previous reports, this is a rather clear and strong message, formulating an obvious expectation regarding Romania's contribution to development assistance, even if such expectations were not also translated into an unambiguous standard. The adjective, 'adequate', used in conjunction with 'budgetary provisions' softened the 'must' and opened the possibility for any progress to be considered satisfactory. If this is a 'gap', a communication error, then this is a significant one, as the standard could have been easily provided, based on previously approved documents worked at the highest levels: The conclusions of the General Affairs and External Relations Council (GAERC) Council of May 2005 showed that the EU-15 would 'commit' to achieve the 0.7 per cent target by 2015, while the new member states would aim to achieve 0.17 per cent by 2010 and 0.33 per cent by 2015 (Conseil de l'Union Européene 2005, p. 22). But if this is not a communication error, then one may conclude that the aim of this exercise was not so much to force Romania into a quantitative commitment, but to establish the practice, the 'way of thinking', that would make future budget allocations possible in a country that still considered itself a recipient country.

Progress Reports, Monitoring Reports, Strategic Papers, Composite Papers and other documents of this kind were not only creating a communicative discourse, but a type of strategic discourse. The difference between the two is that while the former is oriented towards interpersonal goals, the latter is goal-directed and power-laden (Thornborrow 2002, p. 2). While communicative discourse is about speakers symmetrically engaging in achieving mutual understanding, strategic discourse is about getting results through an intentional use of language and its resources. The Commission's Reports are written not only to *account* for 'progress' towards accession in a neutral and disinterested manner, but they also play a crucial part in *shaping* institutional behaviour by showing what the desired standards are for the candidate country to be acknowledged as achieving such 'progress'. They are not merely witnessing, they are also constituting. By showing, at a time when Romania had the clearly consolidated status of a recipient country, that 'Romania is *not* an international donor', the text of the Report implies that being an international donor is an objective that a candidate country needs to fulfil in the wake of EU accession. Similarly, by showing that Romania 'still' lacks a development policy, the Report implies that this candidate country – as all the others – is expected to take up such a bureaucratic practice. Or, when emphasizing that '[n]o progress has been achieved concerning development cooperation with *ACP* countries', the Report is creating a standard regarding geographical priorities. Objectively, Romania was equally weak in its development cooperation with Latin America or Asia, but these regions are not mentioned.

The Reports are meant to shape the new member states' political choices by setting standards that the candidates need to achieve for them to be acknowledged as making 'progress'. At least three such standards can be identified: putting in place a development policy, as is current practice in the 'traditional' donor countries; establishing and running institutions for implementing the said policy; and ensuring an optimum level of administrative capacity that allows for a sufficient integration and coordination with other donors. The candidate countries are supposed to 'catch-up' with practices developed by the older EU members and this mainly means a certain level of bureaucratization and professionalization of the kind that allows the EU to present itself as the 'biggest provider of development aid in the world'.

The Reports, in theory an instrument for the Commission to merely inform the Council 'on the progress made by candidate and potential candidate countries on their road towards the EU',[11] in practice also generate implicit demands. Candidates are not encouraged to find their own path in development cooperation based on their historical background and present-day experiences. They are required to contribute to international development and do so by the same means and with the same aims as those of the EU. The EU-12 have to abide not only to the over-arching value of international solidarity, but to the whole system of standards and vested interests that the old donors built around international solidarity.

5. Romania's Development Policy: A Complying Discourse

Apparently, Romania's policy for international development is now confidently embraced by the Romanian MFA: It is part of the MFA's government programme; it is the object of a series of legislative initiatives; it is the field of work for a growing unit in the Romanian MFA; it is being mentioned in Romania's Foreign Policy Report.[12] In what follows, we will look at the discursive framework that supports this field of political action and we will look at Romania's national strategy for development cooperation in particular.

The Strategy is a six-page document, organized into nine sections. In the first section, the 'context' of the policy is explained; the second section delineates the eight principles (ownership, differentiation, coordination, coherence, complementarity, effectiveness, transparency and conditionality) for Romanian development assistance; the third sets Romania's objectives for its development aid; the fourth establishes the geographic and 'sectorial' (thematic) priorities; the fifth offers information about the types of assistance that Romania envisages (bilateral, multilateral and trilateral); the sixth explains the institutional framework, putting the MFA in charge as policy coordinator; the seventh discusses financial resources; and the last two sections discuss the role of NGOs and development awareness and education.

Like the other new member states, Romania focuses geographically on the 'near abroad': Eastern Europe, the West Balkans and the South Caucasus. The Strategy shows that Romania will, in principle, also support least developed and low income countries, as 'the list of beneficiary states can be expanded towards Central Asia, Africa and Latin America, once Romanian capacities in the assistance for development field are being consolidated'.

The Strategy enumerates six main areas in which Romania deems itself prepared to offer development assistance: good governance; strengthening of democracy and the rule of law; economic development; education and career development/ employment; health, with a focus on reproductive health, prevention and control of diseases, and the fight against HIV and AIDS; and development of infrastructure and environment protection. In the first phase, Romania will focus on a limited number of areas, with special emphasis on those where it has a so-called strong advantage in comparison to other donor countries. These areas are considered to be human rights promotion, strengthening of democracy, education and career development and economic development.

The Strategy and its Statement of Reasons[13] are heavily impregnated with development jargon. 'Romania will support the objectives established by the international community for guaranteeing prosperity and development at a global level', and in doing so, Romania will give its full support to the Millennium Development Goals (MDGs). 'The main goal of Romania's assistance policy consists in reduction of poverty, as poverty represents the major obstacle for a country's social and economic development' (*Hotărare...* 2006, p. 26).

The two documents have a very similar rhetorical structure. Significantly, both of them, from the very first sentence, talk of the commitments made by Romania in the EU accession negotiation process. The Strategy says, 'Taking into account the obligations Romania will have as an EU member, upon accession, an international development cooperation policy needs to be set-up and implemented.' After this clear overture, the Strategy dedicates almost one full page (out of a total of six) to introducing the EU development policy and to underscore that 'after becoming an EU member, Romania will change its status from receiver to donor of development assistance'. From its very beginning, 'Romania's international development policy is aligned with the European Consensus values, principles and objectives' as '[t]he policy consists in supporting poor people in developing countries, including low income and middle income countries'. Since the fight against global poverty will be the focus of this policy, 'poverty' is then defined in the same general, negative lexical terms that are so frequently used by the 'traditional' donors: 'Poverty is not simply defined as the lack of financial resources but also citizens' deprivation of food, education, health services (...). The poor population is the victim, as well as the cause of the environment deterioration, because it generally lives in ecologically vulnerable areas. (...).'

The Statement of Reasons has an equal strength in what the 'European reason' is concerned with. With only three exceptions, every single paragraph of this document links back to some EU institution, principle or commitment. Unequivocally, this document reads: 'In this sense, Romania has to define, according to the European practice, the institutional and legislative framework that will ensure compliance with the commitments taken (...).' In both the Strategy and the Statement of Reasons, the modality is categorical: Romania *has* to define its development cooperation policy. Even before its debate in the national fora (the Strategy was never discussed in the Romanian Parliament), it was decided that it would be aligned to the European Consensus. The word, 'obligation', comes to the fore more than once, as if to suggest that there is no choice other than compliance, or, perhaps, no other reason stronger than the 'European' one.

The arguments for building the case for this public policy are not articulated to progress from existing problems, through strategic goals, to proposed solutions. The problems are not identified and detailed, the strategic options are not assessed and balanced against each another, the resources needed to achieve the identified goals are never mentioned. The benefits for Romania or for the recipient countries from such a policy are never referred to. The main problem that the Strategy seems to address is the mere non-existence of the policy itself in a context in which Romania is *obliged* to become an international donor according to EU standards. The specific benefits that a development policy could bring come second to the general benefit of showing good-will in the accession process. The legitimacy for this development cooperation policy is built on the need for Romania to comply with European practices and the European 'reason' is sufficient for a new policy area to be initiated, if requested.

From this point of view, what we witness is the shallow Europeanization phenomenon described by other authors when analysing the role of the EU in shaping development policy in the EU-12. Romania – as did the other new member states – joined the EU with administrative structures and policy frameworks in place and a commitment to meet the EU ODA targets and to contribute to the European Development Fund. However, neither Romania nor the other new EU donors are on track to achieve their targets without inflating or tying their aid and the overall ability of these states to meet the development acquis is very much a matter of concern (Lightfoot 2010). If the strategic documents are shallow, then it should also be noted that the MFA staff experience in development aid is limited in Romania, just as in the other EU new member states. And just like the other new EU donors, Romania, too, has failed to build sufficient development expertise and create a professional corps of development public servants (Migliorisi 2003). The general staff in the ODA department/unit of the Romanian MFA has always been diplomatic staff with no background in development work, while the more senior staff (department/ unit directors) only stayed in the unit for short intervals in between diplomatic assignments abroad. With a turnover of approximately one director or interim director per year, the country's development institutional structures could hardly build sustainable results in a context in which development policy appeared to be a second-rate EU integration issue that only needed to be ticked off a list. Through the so-called transition years, Romanian foreign policy lost its pre-1989 interest in the developing world, focusing mostly on the 'euro-atlantic integration' and the EU integration process failed to embolden Romania to regain its capabilities to meaningfully re-engage the developing countries. The so-called 'capital of sympathy', which Romania is supposed to be able to collect from its communist past (when relations with the developing countries were much closer), has remained un-operationalized in spite of some calls from civil society to do so (Oprea and Novac 2009).

Conclusion

Romania and some of the other EU new member states are thought of as new EU donors, but this 'newness' is debatable. On the one hand, these 'new' EU donors were deemed to have had international development programmes in a *previous* historical system (before 1989). On the other hand, their present-day development programmes are heavily influenced by EU/ OECD-DAC development ideology. The EU-12 are not encouraged to become members of the donor community – they are encouraged to join the community of *Western* donors *and* abide by the dominant development discourse represented by the OECD-DAC norms filtered through EU soft development law. The 'new donor' identity is so constructed as to lead to cooption and it allows for limited reflection of anything other than the EU/ OECD-DAC development ideology. While learning 'new donor' behaviour, the EU's new member states are encouraged to marginalize and forget about older experiences, particularly those that could draw them close to non-OECD-DAC development practices. Romania, as some of the other new member states, will join the 'traditional' donors and their efforts to 'fight global poverty' according to a set of standards agreed among the Western players in the last several decades. While a certain alignment with international practices is surely needed, the possible opportunity cost of this massive import of development ideology is a tapering space for alternative development thinking. The new EU donors, due to their previous engagement/ familiarity with non-OECD-DAC practices, could have been a bridge between the OECD-DAC and the non-OECD-DAC donors, but this is obviously not an option considered by either the EU institutions or the new member states themselves. The option considered is the 'mythical' transition experience, as another article in this series shows.

Notes

[1] The author is writing in a personal capacity. The views expressed here do not reflect the views of the World Vision Romania Foundation/ World Vision Institute.

[2] Even 1 per cent, according to Daniel Hanspach, Emerging Donors Policy Specialist at the UNDP Bratislava Regional Centre, as per a presentation witnessed by this author at the Romanian Development Camp in September 2008.

DEVELOPMENT POLICIES OF CENTRAL AND EASTERN EUROPEAN STATES

[3] The transition experience; the dynamism, enthusiasm and the young age of the people involved in development cooperation, given the 'NMS role as new donors'; the knowledge and experience of cooperation with their neighbour countries; and their primary focus on the sector of democratization, human rights and good governance, where they have personal experience. See Bedoya, C., 2008.

[4] Romanian official from the MFA ODA directorate, expressing her views at the Romanian Development Camp in September 2008.

[5] Through the Official Development Assistance in Central Europe (ODACE) programme, the Canadian Agency for Development Cooperation invested $15 million in consolidating the development agencies of Hungary, Poland, the Czech Republic and Slovakia.

[6] *Scînteia*, 16 July 1971. In a first-page article, *Scînteia* presents the conclusions reached and decisions taken at the 'enlarged meeting' of the Executive Committee of the Romanian Communist Party (RCP), chaired by Ceauşescu: 'The Executive Committee, taking account of a series of requests received from different countries and giving expression to the sentiments of international solidarity of the Romanian people with the people's fight for national independence against colonialism, decided on the creation of a Fund for Solidarity and support of the liberation movements, of the young developing states, as well as the support of the population from some countries in case of some natural calamities. This fund will be realized by contributions of the state, of the socialist and community (*obşteşti*) organizations, as well as by the benevolent contributions of the citizens.'

[7] See the list of Romanian credits developed by Gafton, P and the Romanian section, 1979, based on official public sources.

[8] Ioan Grigorescu, reporting for Scinteia on 15 April 1979, on the occasion of President Ceauşescu's visit to Zambia, interviews the 'young Kinje Kumolo', who 'dreams to accomplish his studies in Romania'. He is passionate about chemistry and followed closely the scientific progresses of this discipline in our country'. Kumolo is quoted to say: 'I know that many Zambian students study in your country – he says. This is one of the most concrete forms of cooperation, because tomorrow all these young people will be reliable cadres for our national economy and Zambia's advancement.'

[9] *Scînteia*, 8 April 1979. Author's translation from Romanian.

[10] The author reviewed *Scînteia*, *Lumea* and various Romanian authors such as Sava, Maliţa, Horja, Popişteanu, etc.

[11] See the 2005 Enlargement Package Glossary for Candidate and Potential Candidate Countries. Available from: http://ec.europa.eu/enlargement/archives/key_documents/glossary_2005_en.htm [accessed March 2009].

[12] Ministerul Afacerilor Externe, Raport privind politica externă a României, 2005–08, op. cit., p. 21. Surprisingly, the development cooperation policy is given considerable importance in the text of the Report, as it is being presented immediately after Romania's major 'achievements' – integration into the EU and playing host to the NATO summit in 2008. It is followed by sections on economic diplomacy, the 'trans-atlantic relation', regional cooperation, relations with the Western Balkans, relations with the Republic of Moldova, the Eastern neighbourhood, the Russian Federation, the other regions of the world and so on.

[13] The Statement of Reasons – Expunere de Motive – is a separate, introductory document that accompanies all official documents seeking a government decision.

References

Adamcová, N., 2006. *International development cooperation of the Czech Republic*. Prague: Tiskárna Libertas Inc.

Adanja, M., 2007. Presentation by Ambassador Marija Adanja, Head of International Development Cooperation at the Ministry of Foreign Affairs of the Republic of Slovenia, European Parliament–Committee on Development, Public hearing on new EU donors and development cooperation policy, 30 January Brussels. Available from: http://www.europarl.europa.eu/comparl/deve/hearings/20070130/adanja.pdf [accessed April 2011] April 12.

Albu, A.D., 1995. *Cooperarea economică internaţională: tehnici, virtuţi, oportunităţi*. Bucharest: Editura Expert.

DEVELOPMENT POLICIES OF CENTRAL AND EASTERN EUROPEAN STATES

Barac, I., 1977. Romania and the Developing Countries. *Revue Roumaine d'etudes internationales*, XI Année, 1 (35), 6.

Barany, I., 2008. Presentation at the international conference Development assistance operators from EU new member states: Experiences, trends and challenges, 3–4 June Ljubljiana, Slovenia. Available from: http://www.cef-see.org/oda/ODA_NMS_conference_final_report.pdf [accessed June 14. 2009].

Bari, I., and Dumitrescu, S., 1988. *Sansele unei lumi: Sub-dezvoltarea – un fenomen ireversibil?*. Bucharest: Editura Politică.

Barnett, T.P.M., 1992. *Romanian and East German policies in the Third World*. Westport Praeger Publishers.

Bedoya, C., 2008. Which cooperation between old EU member states and new EU member states? Conclusions from Workshop 2 of the European meeting of development cooperation platforms, Strasbourg, France. Available from: http://www.trialog.or.at/images/doku/EDD-workshop-TRIA-LOG.pdf [accessed 18 March 2009] 15 November, 2008.

Čaučik, M., 2007. Development cooperation in the new member states from NGO perspective. Hearing at the European Parliament, January.

Ceauşescu, N., 1978. Expunere la şedinţa activului central de partid şi de stat. In: N. Ceauşescu, *Romania on the way of building up the multilaterally developed socialist society: Reports, speeches, articles, 1968–88, Vol. 16*. Bucharest: Editura Politică, 518–520.

Ceauşescu, N., 1985. *Interviuri, declaraţii şi conferinţe de presă, iunie 1966-August 1973, Vol. 1*. Bucharest: Editura Politică.

Coffin, M.F., 1964. *Witness for AID*. Boston, MA: Houghton Mifflin.

Council of the European Union, 2005. Communiqué de presse, 2660ème session du Conseil Affaires Générales et Relations Extérieres, 23–24 May Brussels. Available from: http://www.eu2005.lu/en/actualites/conseil/2005/05/23cagre/cagre.pdf (accessed February 2009).

Després, L., 1987. Eastern Europe and the Third World: Economic interactions and policies. In: R.E. Kanet, ed. *The Soviet Union, Eastern Europe, and the Third World*. Cambridge: Cambridge University Press, 156.

Ecobescu, N., and Celac, S., 1975. *Socialist Romania in international relations*. Bucharest: Meridiane.

Escobar, A., 1995. *Encountering development: The making and unmaking of the Third World*. Princeton, NJ: Princeton University Press.

European Commission, 1998a. Regular report from the Commission on Bulgaria's progress towards accession. Available from: http://ec.europa.eu/enlargement/archives/pdf/key_documents/1998/bulgaria_en.pdf [accessed 19 February 2009].

European Commission, 1998b. Regular report from the Commission on Czech Republic's progress towards accession. Available from: http://ec.europa.eu/enlargement/archives/pdf/key_documents/1998/czech_en.pdf [accessed 25 February 2009].

European Commission, 1998c. Regular report from the Commission on Hungary's progress towards accession. Available from: http://ec.europa.eu/enlargement/archives/pdf/key_documents/1998/hungary_en.pdf [accessed 4 February 2009].

European Commission, 1998d. Regular report from the Commission on Romania's progress towards accession. Available from: http://ec.europa.eu/enlargement/archives/pdf/key_documents/1998/roma-nia_en.pdf [accessed 16 February 2009].

European Commission, 1998e. Regular report from the Commission on Poland's progress towards accession. Available from: http://ec.europa.eu/enlargement/archives/pdf/key_documents/1998/poland_en.pdf [accessed 16 February 2009].

European Commission, 2002. Regular report from the Commission on Romania's progress towards accession. Available from: http://ec.europa.eu/enlargement/archives/pdf/key_documents/2002/ro_en.pdf [accessed 16 February 2009].

European Commission, 2004. Regular report on Romania's progress towards accession. Available from: http://ec.europa.eu/enlargement/archives/pdf/key_documents/2004/rr_ro_2004_en.pdf [accessed 6 February 2009].

European Commission, 2005. Romania comprehensive monitoring report, COM (2005)534 final. Available from: http://ec.europa.eu/enlargement/archives/pdf/key_documents/2005/sec1354_cmr_master_ro_college_en.pdf [accessed 6 February 2009].

European Commission Progress Reports, 1998. Available from: http://ec.europa.eu/enlargement/archives/key_documents/reports_1998_en.htm#compo [accessed 6 February 2009].

DEVELOPMENT POLICIES OF CENTRAL AND EASTERN EUROPEAN STATES

European Parliament, 2008. Resolution of 13 March 2008 on the challenge of EU development cooperation policy for the new member states. Available from: http://www.europarl.europa.eu/sides/getDoc.do?pubRef=-//EP//TEXT+TA+P6-TA-2008-0097+0+DOC+XML+V0//EN&language=EN [accessed March 12 2009].

Fairclough, N., 2001. *Language and power*. Essex, UK: Pearson Education Ltd.

Fairclough, N., 2003. *Analysing discourse*. London: Routledge.

Frot, E., and Santiso, J., 2009. Crushed aid: Fragmentation in sectoral aid. *SITE working paper no. 6*, Stockholm. Available from: http://swopec.hhs.se/hasite/papers/hasite0006.pdf [accessed 12 February 2010].

Gafton, P. and the Romanian section, 1979. Romania's presence in Black Africa. Background report/ 118, Radio Free Europe, 23 May.

Ghibernea, M., 1969. Colaborarea tehnică- ştiinţifică şi culturală a R.S.R. România cu alte state. Colaborarea în domeniul ştiinţei şi tehnicii. In: M. Maliţa, C. Murgescu and G. Surpat, eds. *România socialistă şi cooperarea internaţională*. Bucharest: Editura Politică, 395.

Horja, G.N., 1981. *Invingerea subdezvoltării: Cauză a întregii omeniri*. Bucharest: Editura Stiinţifică şi Enciclopedică.

Hotărâre pentru aprobarea Strategiei naţionale privind politica de cooperare internaţională pentru dezvoltare şi a Planului de Acţiune privind politica de cooperare internaţională pentru dezvoltare, Monitorul Oficial al României, Partea I (Legi, Decrete, Hotărâri şi Alte Acte), Anul 174 (XVIII), nr. 506, Luni 12 iunie, 2006, p. 26 This is legislation published in Romania's official journal.

Jørgensen, M.W., and Phillips, J.L., 2002. *Discourse analysis as theory and method*. London: Sage.

Lightfoot, S., 2010. The Europeanisation of international development policies: The case of Central and Eastern European States. *Europe-Asia studies*, 62 (2), 329–350.

Linden, R.H., 1983. Romanian foreign policy in the 1980s: Domestic-foreign policy linkages. In: M.J. Sodaro and S.L. Wolchik Sodaro, eds. *Foreign and domestic policy in Eastern Europe in the 1980s: Trends and prospects*. New York: St Martin's Press, 55.

Little, I.M.D, and Clifford, J.M., 2005. *International aid. The flow of public resources from rich to poor countries*. New Brunswick, NJ: Aldine Transactions.

Mănescu, N., 1973. Forme de cooperare economică şi tehnică între România şi ţări în curs de dezvltare. *Lumea*, 43 (521), 18 October, 18–19.

Ministerul Afacerilor Externe, *Raport privind politica externă a Romaniei 2005–08*. Available from: http://www.mae.ro/poze_editare/2008.11.25_RpMAE_2005-2008.pdf [accessed 12 March 2009].

Moyo, D., 2009. *Dead aid: Why aid is not working and how there is another way for Africa*. New York: Farrar, Straus and Giroux.

Oprea, M., and Novac, R., 2009. *It's our turn to help – development cooperation in Romania*. Bucharest: FOND. Available from: http://www.fondromania.org/eng/pagini/index.php [accessed 14 April 2010].

Popişteanu, C., 1976. *Cronologie politico-diplomatică românească: 1944–74*. Bucharest: Editura Politică.

Puiu, A., 1974. *Comerţul exterior şi rolul lui în realizarea programului de dezvoltare economică a României*. Bucharest: Editura Politică.

Radu, M., 1981. *Eastern Europe and the Third World: East vs. South*. New York: Praeger.

Raff, C., 1996. *Autonomous development: Humanizing the landscape: An excursion into radical thinking and practice*. London: Zed Books.

Riddell, R., 2007. *Does foreign aid really work?* Oxford, UK: Oxford University Press.

Rist, G., 2003. *The history of development: From Western origins to global faith*. London: Zed Books.

Thornborrow, J., 2002. *Powerful talk: Language and interaction in institutional discourse*. London: Longman.

Vasilescu, C., 1973. *Romania in international life*. Bucharest: Meridiane Publishing House.

Involving Civil Society in the International Development Cooperation of 'New' EU Member States: The Case of Slovenia

MAJA BUČAR
Faculty of Social Sciences, University of Ljubljana, Slovenia

ABSTRACT *Accession to the European Union (EU) also meant (re)entry into the donor community for the new member states from Central and Eastern Europe. Human resource constraints seem to be one of the important drawbacks in the government-led cooperation programmes of many of the new member states. This is where, civil society, in particular the national civil society, can play an important role. It can help in the design and implementation of the programmes, in overall awareness raising as well as in keeping 'watch' on government policies. This paper examines the role of non-governmental organizations (NGOs) in development cooperation, focusing on the case of Slovenia: how they have integrated themselves into the development cooperation programmes of Slovenia, what the good practices are and where the difficulties that inhibit cooperation with the government lie. Special attention has been paid to stakeholders' participation in policy design and priority selection as well as to the organizational framework put in place. In Slovenia, the Presidency of the Council of the EU increased the level of the government's cooperation with the non-governmental development organizations (NGDOs) significantly. The 'Europeanization' process has been significant in shaping development cooperation content and delivery in Slovenia, including the participation of NGDOs.*

Introduction

The participation of non-governmental development organizations (NGDOs)[1] in promoting development and reducing poverty and hunger has become a major feature of international development policy. Various donors, from national governments and multilateral organizations to individuals, have turned to non-governmental organizations (NGOs), hoping that their approach to development cooperation would be better suited to achieving their basic goals. It is generally assumed that the advantage NGOs enjoy in the implementation of development cooperation is based on their ability to respond quickly because they are perceived to be unencumbered by the bureaucratic formalities that characterize official agencies (Lorgen 1998, Glenzer 2011).

The multiple possible roles of NGOs in development cooperation are well captured in the following table, as elaborated by Schulpen and Hoebink (2012) in their categorization of Dutch NGDOs.

While this categorization may be difficult to follow in the case of NGDOs in countries with a less developed non-governmental sector, it can still serve us as a reminder of what possible roles NGDOs can play in development cooperation. We will use the table to categorize, not the NGDOs themselves, but their activities and the development of their roles, especially since, in our analysis, we will focus on an NGDO platform as their representative. We have to recognize the fact that, currently, many Slovenian NGDOs have a role in all the mentioned categories and are not yet specialized enough to follow just one activity. For the purposes of this paper, attention is paid primarily to the development of the relationship between the government and the non-governmental sector and less so on development within the non-governmental sector as such.

Accession to the European Union (EU) in 2004 and 2007 meant also a 'graduation' to donor status in the area of international development for the Central and Eastern European states. As new members, they were expected to build up an effective strategy, based on the principles, policies and goals accepted within the EU. However, many of them lack the necessary complex legal and institutional infrastructure to act as efficient donors, they face serious difficulties in increasing resources according to the agreed dynamics, and they face considerable human resource problems in staffing the organizations involved in international development cooperation (Bucar et al. 2007). To overcome this resource gap, the full involvement of the NGDO sector would seem to be a viable alternative for the governments of the new member states, especially if the roles as defined in Table 1 could be performed effectively by the NGDOs.

Table 1. Roles of NGDOs – a typology

	Role	Description/main activities
1	Financer	Funding of Southern partners for their development interventions
2	Advisor	Capacity building, knowledge collection and dissemination, linking Southern organizations to knowledge, expert advice
3	Networker	Bringing organizations (whether governmental, non-governmental and/or commercial) together to increase cooperation and complementarity
4	Implementer	Implementing activities by the own staff of Northern NGDOs. This may be in different fields, but is most clearly seen in humanitarian and reconstruction interventions as well as in more entrepreneurial activities (e.g., fair trade)
5	Lobbyist	Influencing policies of governments, inter-governmental organizations, multilateral agencies and private companies through lobbying and advocacy
6	Changing the North	Stimulating changes in the North with a view to contributing to development in the South. Public support activities take up an important part of this role

Source: Schulpen and Hoebink, 2012.

At the initial stages of official aid programmes in the new member states, NGDOs were de facto not recognized by the state authorities as strategically important partners. A particular feature in all the post-communist societies was a lack of confidence between government and civil society. This attitude has its origins in the pre-transition period, when NGOs often established and articulated themselves as a kind of the opposition to the government and are sometimes still closely associated with the political opposition (Grimm and Harmer 2005). Yet, more recent evidence (Bučar et al. 2008) shows that in several countries, NGDOs are showing increased participation in international development cooperation.

We suggest that in view of the relative novelty of international development cooperation and the lack of qualified human resources, partnerships between government and NGDOs in the new member states are essential for improved policy design, implementation and, in particular, raising public awareness. Yet, both actors are going through a period of 'internal' growth, which also causes friction in the mutual relationship. Systematic building of partnerships requires a responsible and constructive approach on the part of both, taking fully into account the specifics of each partner.

The complexity of the relationship between the government and the NGDO sector is analysed in the case of Slovenian development cooperation. Our assumption is that it is a specific relationship, conditioned by the overall low importance of international development cooperation in Slovenia, which makes the government office for development cooperation and the NGDO platform 'allies' in the promotion of the topic for their mutual benefit.

There are several limitations and simplifications in our paper, which need to be specified at the beginning. We observe primarily the development of cooperation between the Office in Charge of Development Cooperation (Office) at the Ministry of Foreign Affairs (MFA)[2] on the one side and the NGDO platform, SLOGA, on the other. To take the position of the Office as the position of the government is the only operational alternative, yet the Office itself is sometimes faced with opposition within the government when advocating for increased resources for development cooperation as well as for closer cooperation with the NGDOs. On the other hand, while the most active and important NGDOs are all members of SLOGA, the latter is not a synonym for the NGDOs, and even less so for civil society. We see these simplifications as a necessary step in conducting a detailed analysis of the relationship, which, at a later stage and in future research, can be expanded to other forms of cooperation as well as other actors.

Slovenian Development Cooperation: Some Facts

The legal framework of Slovenian development cooperation has been set out by two documents. In June 2006, Slovenia adopted the International Development Cooperation of the Republic of Slovenia Act (UL 2006), which defines the goals and method of long-term planning, financing and implementing international development cooperation. In July 2008, the National Assembly of the Republic of Slovenia adopted the Resolution on International Development Cooperation of the Republic of Slovenia until 2015 (UL 2008). The Resolution sets out the geographical and sector priorities of Slovenia's international development cooperation until 2015 and the mechanisms for its implementation. The guiding principles in selecting geographical and sector priorities have been elaborated taking into account the EU Development Consensus (2006) as well as other specifics of Slovenian foreign policy (Mrak et al. 2007).

Until 2010, Slovenia was able to slowly, but steadily, increase its development assistance. Yet, it seems that achieving 0.33 per cent of GNI is, as for most other new member states, not a realistic target (Bucar and Udovic 2007). Already, the 2010 data reveal a decrease to 0.13 per cent of GNI, with a further drop likely in 2011.

In its documents, the government recognizes NGDOs as important stakeholders in development cooperation. The Resolution dedicates a special chapter to NGDOs with a statement on continuous strengthening of the capabilities of civil society and NGDOs and the promotion of their alliances. Also, following the example of some of the more developed donors, special calls to support NGDOs' development cooperation activities have been introduced in MFA practices on an annual basis since 2009 (see details in the next sections).

Brief History of Civil Society Participation in Development Cooperation

In the 1990s, Slovenia, like the rest of Eastern Europe, was seized by the phenomenon of 'NGO-ization' of civil society, or a gradual transformation of civil society groups into NGOs. NGOs began to emphasize political issues in their activities, parallel to the process of the political transformation of society, which resulted in the political independence of Slovenia in 1991. Particularly important was the development in the 1990s of certain new forms of NGOs that had not existed previously. The legislation on foundations introduced the possibility of founding NGOs for the purpose of obtaining and distributing funds (this is particularly important for NGOs working on development issues).

Another important milestone in NGO development was the establishment of the Centre for Information Service, Cooperation and Development of NGOs (CNVOS) in 2001 by 27 NGOs. With the EU membership, the principle of involving civil society/NGOs in the decision-making process was introduced first only formally, but is now becoming more and more a routine, partly also because the NGOs are more aware of their possibilities as well as their rights.[3] Currently, the Ministry of Public

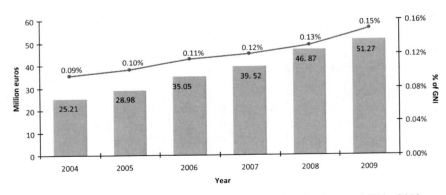

Figure 1. Slovenian ODA, in million € and % of GNI. *Source*: MFA, 2010.

Administration is formally responsible for cooperation and agreements with all NGOs.

SLOGA (SLOvenian Global Action) was established in December 2005 by 19 Slovenian NGDOs, whose aim was to join forces and thus build the capacity of Slovenian non-governmental and non-profit organizations active in the field of development cooperation and humanitarian aid.

Attempts to create a national platform for NGDOs started in 2001, again by the end of 2002. Only the third initiative to establish such a platform, started in 2004, was successful and it was marked by comprehensive NGDO consultations as well as deeper dialogue on a national (with policy makers, especially MFA representatives) and European (with CONCORD, the Directorate General of Development [DG Development], etc.) level.

Those relatively modest beginnings have resulted in today's successful and influential NGDO platform and its widespread activities. By April 2011, SLOGA had 35 (in 2009, 29) member NGDOs[4] and more than 60 supporters.[5] The group of members and supporters is rather heterogeneous in terms of size, fields of work and impact. There are several micro NGDOs with a small number of or no employees (only volunteers) and there are also rather large NGDOs with relatively extensive experience at the national and European levels. From the thematic point of view, the SLOGA members and observers work in the following areas: education, migration, sustainable development, human and child rights, volunteering, global partnership and peace building, among others. If we follow the classification in Table 1, we will have difficulty in assigning them to specific groups since it is quite common for their roles to cross-cut: They could be implementing development projects, lobbying, networking and acting as advisors. Maybe the least pronounced would be the first role – except for the few largest NGDOs, the funding of Southern partners is still beyond the capacities of most of them.

Since SLOGA represents reasonably well the NGDOs in Slovenia, our analysis of the role of NGDOs is based primarily on the relationship that has developed between the government and SLOGA. This does not mean that there is complete agreement between the members of SLOGA as to the handling of this relationship; some members occasionally argue for more confrontation and more radical opposition to the government's strategy in international development cooperation.

Role of Slovenian NGDOs in Policy Development[6]

Chronology

There are several important milestones in the development of the relationship between the government and the Slovenian NGDOs. The entering of Slovenia into the EU in 2004 and the passing of the International Development Cooperation of the Republic of Slovenia Act (UL 2006) are two such milestones. The EU membership committed Slovenia to a more active role in international development cooperation: On the one hand, it was the European Commission, especially DG Development, stressing the need for the regular involvement of civil society in policy making, and on the other, CONCORD as an EU-level confederation of NGDO national platforms was quite active in the new member states, pressing the policy makers and supporting the NGDOs to organize themselves.[7] The Act on International Development Cooperation envisaged the formation of an Advisory Council for the Foreign Minister,[8] in which, as a representative of the NGOs, SLOGA was invited to nominate a member. This gave SLOGA additional visibility and increased its status among its members. The representative of SLOGA in the Council formally cooperated in the process of the drafting the Resolution on International Development Cooperation[9] and, thus, the platform acted on behalf of the NGDOs as a lobbyist and a networker. The Policy Working Group at SLOGA had prepared common NGDO positions and recommendations[10] by getting the SLOGA member and supporter organizations (such as UNICEF Slovenia, Slovenian Caritas, Missionary Centre and Slovenian Red Cross) to join forces.

The Resolution on International Development Cooperation (UL 2008), in Article 15, sets the guidelines and priorities of Slovenian development cooperation. Article 30 of the Resolution is of special importance for further cooperation between the NGDOs and the government and improvement of dialogue between the two, as well as for the empowerment of the Slovenian NGDOs. It addresses the role of civil society in programming and implementing Slovenian development policies. The Resolution also provides for the issuing of special calls for proposals for the NGDOs' development projects and other activities (UL 2008). In this way, the Resolution provides the legal framework for cooperation.

Dialogue between SLOGA and the MFA intensified in the framework of the Slovenian EU Presidency. The MFA agreed to co-finance the main platform conference for the EU Presidency in 2008 and participated at the SLOGA international conferences and seminars.

In 2009, on SLOGA's initiative, a representative of the Office became an observer on SLOGA's Advisory Board, which has the task of forming general guidelines for future activities. This was decided in order to increase the information flow between the Office and SLOGA and vice versa. The government representative has no say in any of the decision-making processes, but is there to brief the Advisory Board on the government's planned activities.[11] There are several other ad hoc meetings between SLOGA and the relevant government representatives on different thematic and operational issues (of special importance here are the organization of common events such as the Slovenian Development Day[12] as well as activities in areas such as development education, aid effectiveness and institutional framework). The most effective 'watchdog role' is played by SLOGA's Working Group on Development Aid, which prepares annually, in cooperation with the CONCORD AidWatch Project, an assessment of Slovenian development cooperation[13] and, on the occasion of publication of the *AidWatch Report*, organizes its public presentation.[14] The Office uses the *AidWatch Report* as a tool to advocate within the government for increased aid spending.

There are some 'NGDOs' and other relevant institutions that are not formal members of SLOGA because of which their cooperation with the MFA was formed on a different basis. These are the organizations that were established in cooperation with the Slovenian government (the government is one of the founders of these organizations).[15] Their role can be best described primarily as implementers of development cooperation, but also partly lobbying, since the Slovenian government is holding regular informal meetings with the representatives of each of these organizations. The government (especially the MFA, the Ministry of Finance and the Ministry of Defence) initially funded their operational activities and projects based on ad hoc requests. Since 2010, the MFA considers them to be government institutions, implementing official government policies. Thus, the MFA now co-funds their annual programmes.

Current Status and Open Issues

It is clear that the cooperation between the government and NGDOs has intensified during the last six years, since the formal establishment of SLOGA. The overall institutional framework for international development cooperation has evolved and become much more firmly embedded within the MFA, with the Office advancing from a unit within a department to an independent department and finally, in Spring 2011, to the level of a directorate. This gives the Office more power in shaping policy and thus also in designing dialogue with civil society. SLOGA has also matured and established clearer policy dialogue within itself (the internal membership scheme, assembly voting on key policies, decision-making procedures, etc.) and can act with more self-confidence as a true representative of the NGDOs in Slovenia. With more stable financing, both from membership fees and special funding provided from the European Social Fund (via structural and cohesion funds), SLOGA has managed to professionalize its services. SLOGA's Policy Working Group is preparing, on a regular basis, various policy proposals and/or amendments on topics such as aid effectiveness and institutional framework of Slovenian development cooperation. Also very active is the Development Education Working Group, which is in regular contact with the MFA and the Ministry of Education.

Potentially, one of the problems identified by SLOGA is formal recognition of the partnership. While certain provisions are included in the Resolution, SLOGA would like to see a more formal agreement with the MFA, specifying its own role and involvement in the policy making and implementation process.[16] This request is based on the fact that due to their specific nature, the personnel at the MFA change relatively frequently, so having a written agreement would hopefully provide for continuity regardless of these frequent changes. The adoption of the formal strategy on cooperation with NGDOs is also a part of the MFA's agenda.

NGDOs as Implementers of International Development Cooperation

Specific Calls for NGDOs: Description of Procedures and Results

Although initially, the government did not provide any direct finance for NGDO activities, the situation changed in 2008. On the basis of the Resolution on International Development Cooperation, the MFA, in cooperation with the Ministry of Public Administration, issued its first call for NGDOs with a total amount of 100,000 euros. The call was aimed at supporting NGDO projects in two areas, the Western Balkans and Eastern Europe region as well as Sub-Saharan Africa. The call was issued again in 2009, 2010 and 2011 in cooperation with other line ministries and has now become a standard practice in the implementation of international development cooperation. SLOGA is active in offering advice on how to improve the public calls for proposals and make the rules and procedures more user friendly. Several suggestions, given before or after the public calls, have been taken into consideration by the government over the years, which has led to improved guidelines and evaluation procedures. SLOGA also advises its members on the preparation of project proposals, especially in the project management area.

In 2009, the MFA included other partners (besides the MFA and the Ministry of Public Administration, the Ministry of Health, Ministry of Environment and Spatial Planning and Government Office for Local-Self Government and Regional Policy were involved) in the call for NGDO projects and increased the financing to 265,000 euros. The call was again aimed at NGDO projects in the Western Balkans and Eastern Europe region and Africa, but a new section was added – humanitarian aid, with the aim of empowering NGOs working in that field.

At the end of 2009, the MFA issued a call for financing development projects in 2010 and 2011 with a substantial increase in funds to 790,000 euros. The following six priority regions/ sectors were nominated: the region of the Western Balkans, Ukraine and Moldova, Sub-Saharan Africa, other regions, humanitarian aid in Sub-Saharan Africa and the Middle East and development education in Slovenia. This was also the first call for biannual projects, with individual projects going up to 40,000 euros.[17]

At the end of 2010 and the beginning of 2011, two additional calls were issued: the call on co-financing the activities of NGDOs, which has already gained the support of the EC with a total amount of 100,000 euros, as well as the regular annual call for co-financing the implementation of development projects by NGDOs with total funding of 960,000 euros. The latter provides for the possibility of three-year financing and is much more specific than the previous calls (priority areas, countries and sectors more defined).[18] This has led to a smaller number of bigger, mostly three-year projects.[19] The reason for this concentration was a feeling that a smaller number of stronger projects would be more effective than a larger number of relatively small ones, in which administrative and monitoring costs would take up a large percentage of the funds.

Assessment of Quality of Projects Proposed by NGDOs and Implementation Experience

Looking at the applications received and the results of the MFA's consecutive calls, one can observe gradual improvements in the guidelines for project proposals on the basis of the experience gained by the MFA and the other cooperating ministries and the comments and proposals received from SLOGA. The selection process has improved – already, in designing the call, the criteria for project evaluation are set. At the same time, the quality of the project proposals has increased: the clarity of the objectives, financial structure of the proposed projects and the expected long-term outcomes are better presented and thus make the selection process more effective.[20] The increase of duration as well as of resources should be beneficial from the viewpoint of the impact of the projects.

Among some of the problems identified in the project proposals is their highly dispersive character with regard to the recipient countries. This can be observed especially in the 2009–10 call in the segment addressing Africa. The selected 12 projects were implemented in ten different African countries, suggesting a wide spread of NGDO activities and practically no cooperation among them, not even where relatively similar projects were being implemented in different countries. Taking into consideration the very small financial values of the projects at the time (between 12,000 and 40,000 euros), this shows a relatively high level of segmentation and opens up the question, not only of the long-term sustainability of the project(s), but also of the immediate impact of such endeavours. What is encouraging is the work of some NGDOs in selected Sub-Saharan African countries, which are applying for funding with project proposals connected to their existing activity in that particular country. This means that they have already gained the relevant experience, have good local partners and can therefore identify the needs of the local communities. One such example is the work of Umanotera in Burkina Faso, which started with the establishment of fair trade arrangements and has expanded into weaving projects, eco-tourism and computer courses, among others.[21] Some of these projects are supported via MFA calls, others by direct collection of donations, still others by raising funds from abroad.

Changing the North: The Key Activity of NGDOs

Cooperation during the EU Council Presidency

The Slovenian EU Council Presidency in the first half of 2008 was an important milestone in the relationship between the government and the NGDO sector. The government turned to the NGDOs for support in organizing a series of events and provided the much-needed financial support for the programmes. The MFA agreed to co-finance the main SLOGA conference for the EU Presidency in 2008 and also participated in the SLOGA international conferences and seminars.

Already in 2007, SLOGA had established the Presidency Steering Group to prepare and implement the Slovenian NGDO Presidency Project. The Project involved seven Consortium members, who aimed to raise awareness about relevant development issues in Slovenia and Europe and to strengthen cooperation between different development education stakeholders at the national level. The project focused on the following development topics: development education, social inclusion (intergenerational dialogue, child advocacy, migration and human trafficking) and climate changes and development. The Project, called 'You Too are Part of This World', was launched in February 2008 with a press conference, presenting the NGDO manifesto for the Slovenian EU Presidency.[22] Alongside, the SLOGA secretariat had been coordinating more than five thematic working groups in order to be able to follow and advocate for the relevant development topics. Among the most active working groups were the groups working in development education, ODA monitoring and evaluation, Africa and migration, sexual and reproductive health and rights and the Global Call against Poverty. The working groups promoted a multi-stakeholder approach to civil dialogue by organizing the series of events in the framework of the Slovenian EU Presidency.[23]

SLOGA's successful implementation of the tasks entrusted to it was recognized by the government and, since then, there have been budget allocations for its functioning. The involvement in the Presidency programme gave SLOGA both national and international recognition and impetus to further professionalize its activities.

Development Days

The Slovenian government decided to promote development issues and international development cooperation by following the EU example of Development Days. Together with SLOGA, the MFA organized Slovenian Development Days in 2009 and 2010.

In 2009, the programme focused on several topics and events. A Global Call for Action on Millennium Development Goal (MDG) 3 was presented by the Danish ambassador to Slovenia, an EU Youth Development Prize was handed to the winners from Slovenia, and Slovenian participation in the 'Stand Up!' initiative was announced. The active participants included the representatives of the European Commission, international organizations, foreign diplomatic representatives, government and NDGOs. The participation of the President of the Republic gave additional media importance to the event.[24]

The 2010 event broadened participation, since it addressed also the business sector's cooperation in development. The participants were addressed by the European Commissioner for Development, Andris Piebalgs, and the Prime Minister of Slovenia.

The cooperation of the MFA and SLOGA in preparing the Development Days has proved to be very successful in terms of attracting public attention. The MFA is in a position to invite high-level representatives from the EC, from other foreign missions in Slovenia as well as high-level officials in Slovenia, which would have been rather difficult for the NGDOs. The NGDOs, in turn, contributed substantially by attending to the practical organization of the main and several parallel events and popularizing these as well.

Development Education

The Resolution on Development Cooperation includes a special chapter on raising awareness about development cooperation and, more generally, on education for development. The introduction of development topics in the education process should help to raise awareness of the importance of development cooperation and increase public support for it. The MFA allotted 145,000 euros in 2011 to awareness raising, of which 125,000 euros went to the NGDOs for various activities in 'Changing the North'.[25]

Mainly, we can distinguish two types of education and training in which the NGDOs are involved. One type provides specialized training and workshops to increase their own skills and capabilities in the implementation process of development cooperation (project management, evaluation, aid effectiveness, communication skills, etc.) Here, SLOGA cooperates closely with CONCORD and Trialog to organize training sessions at the EU/new member state level, which is then often offered to the participating NGDOs free of charge. Internal training sessions are also organized, in which more experienced and larger NGDOs share their knowledge with smaller organizations or newly recruited staff.

DEVELOPMENT POLICIES OF CENTRAL AND EASTERN EUROPEAN STATES

Just as important is the work of the NGDOs, especially SLOGA's Working Group on Global Education, in promoting development content in the education system, from kindergarten upwards. They promote the concept of global education and have prepared several publications: a guidebook for global citizenship; an overview of global education in Slovenia, and a guidebook for global education.[26] The long-term ambition of the group is to introduce global education in the regular curriculum of all elementary and secondary schools in Slovenia.

Assessment of Impact of NGDO Involvement in Development Cooperation and Identification of Good Practices

What the description of the NGDOs' involvement in Slovenian development cooperation shows is a clear correlation: Just as the system of development cooperation has evolved, so has the relationship between the government and the NGDOs. At times, the NGDOs felt that they were not sufficiently involved in policy making, yet, on the other hand, there were occasions when they had difficulty speaking in one voice under SLOGA with the government.[27]

We can examine the relationship between the government and the NGOs by applying the two-dimension approach (Kuhnle and Selle 1992, Kolarič et al. 2002), which distinguishes between:

1. Dependence/ independence between the civil society organizations and the state on the basis of financing and control; and
2. 'Comparative proximity' of the civil society organizations and the state (size and intensity of their communications and contacts).

The first dimension looks at the level of dependency of the NGOs on the government, which can be either very dependent, depending on the conditions of funding, or quite autonomous, if no strings are attached to the funding. The issue of dependency is particularly relevant for those NGOs that are involved in the implementation of certain services/ projects on behalf of the state and are thus subject to state control. Ideally, government funding should not result in increased control of NGO programmes and processes.

The second dimension addresses the issue of proximity of the NGOs and the government. NGOs can be highly integrated in the creation of public policies and decision-making processes or they can be fully distinct from the state. The level of communication and contact depends on the role prescribed by the government to the NGOs: The government may see the NGOs solely as an occasional provider of certain services or it may treat them as a serious partner in policy design and implementation (Kolarič 1994).

Let us look at the findings of broader research projects on the relationship between NGOs and the government in Slovenia, which includes two surveys with extensive data on NGOs (Kolarič et al. 2006), data from the financial reports of NGOs (Črnak-Meglič 2008, 2009) and data from the CIVICUS (World Alliance for Citizen Participation) research study on Slovenia (Rakar and Nagode 2009). This has been supplemented with interviews with representatives of the government, the NGOs and their various platforms. The study found that on an average, Slovenian

NGOs experience medium levels of autonomy. Their income is derived from market sources, public financing and only a small part from donations. While public sector financing has increased in the case of many NGOs, two-thirds of the recipients claim that the funding did not increase as quickly as the amount of services performed (Rakar and Nagode 2009). The study concluded that the level of public financing is still relatively low in the case of the Slovenian NGOs, so we can still talk of low dependency (or relative independence) of the NGOs on the government.

If we compare these general observations for all NGOs to the specific experience of NGDOs, we can observe certain differences. Prior to securing stable government funding at least at the SLOGA level, fewer and less professional activities were carried out. Most of the activities depended on the good-will and skills of the volunteers. Government funding provided for stability in staffing and this provided the ground for applications for funding from other sources as well. At the level of individual NGDOs, the situation is more varied: For some, the annual calls provided the opportunity to grow and expand their existing activity, for others, the funding enabled their very existence. While the government sets certain requirements for project applicants in terms of conditions for receiving funds[28] and reporting of their project related activities, one cannot assess this as an exercise of control over NGDO activity per se. In fact, the subsequent calls for financing NGDO development projects were amended in accordance with the comments and proposals of the NGDOs, as communicated via SLOGA. Therefore, the current relationship, in spite of increased funding, is not one of negative dependency of the NGDOs on the government.

In terms of proximity, the research project mentioned above found that most NGO representatives and experts in the field of civil society participation assess as limited the impact of Slovenian NGOs in the process of policy development and implementation. This differs significantly from the survey carried out by the Government's Office for European Affairs in 2004, where the representatives of the ministries and government agencies and offices were asked their opinion about cooperation with the NGO sector in designing policies. The government felt that the cooperation and the quality of relations were relatively high and had a significant impact on the shaping of policies.

These findings were explained by the authors of the research project as a reflection of the fact that communication at the formal level has indeed increased substantially (at times also as a consequence of the Europeanization of policy processes, because of which the involvement of civil society had to be documented, as, for example, in the programming of structural funds).[29] The relative dissatisfaction of the NGOs can be explained by their expectations that their participation in policy making would bring them a larger role in the implementation process as well.

These general findings relate well to the observation of the proximity relationship of the government and the NGDOs. Here, too, there are several NGDOs who feel that they are under-represented in policy-making bodies and that the government should give them a more prominent role. On the other hand, the Office considers that the NGDOs are well represented through SLOGA and that they play a significant role in policy-making and everyday activities in the field of development cooperation. The activities carried out in cooperation with NGDOs are growing both in number and size, so we can conclude that despite some differences in

DEVELOPMENT POLICIES OF CENTRAL AND EASTERN EUROPEAN STATES

Table 2. Selected NGDO projects for 2010, 2011 (MFA call, 2009)

Region	Number of projects	Amount in euros
Western Balkans	9	206,017
The Ukraine and Moldova	3	84,212
Sub-Saharan Africa	12	396,393
Other regions	2	31,700
Humanitarian aid	1	20,000
Development education in Slovenia	6	51,546
All	33	789,868

Source: Author's own calculations from MFA data.

opinion, the relative proximity is high and increasing, benefiting both partners. The NGDOs perform the roles of networkers, implementers and lobbyists and help raise public support. Their activities could be more intensive and more professional if they were to receive more government support. And the government has a good partner in conducting the several activities it could not otherwise because of staff limitations or simply because the NGDOs do them better.

Not all the NGDOs, not even all the SLOGA members, would evaluate the relationship between the NGDO sector and the government in the same way. It is easy to think of the NGOs as one group. However, as Shah (2005) warns, 'The interests and perspectives are so diverse that summarizing and generalizing anything that can be valid to all NGOs and similar organisations is not possible, neither as criticism [n]or praise.' Yet, by themselves, NGOs and other voluntary associations can rarely secure the level of political consensus that is required to secure and enforce broad-based social reforms – there's too much difference and diversity of opinion (Edwards 2005). Coalitions are essential for civil society organizations seeking to influence events beyond the ordinary scope of small, economically limited, locally based actors. Learning to build bridges across major social, political and economic differences is pivotal to gaining influence (Brown and Fox 2000). This is an important message to the members of SLOGA: Even if some of them feel that the current level of impact NGDOs have on development cooperation policy is inadequate,[30] they need to take on board that as individual NGDOs, their impact would be truly negligible.

We would suggest that coalition building in the area of development cooperation in Slovenia, and quite possibly in other new donor countries, needs to extend beyond sectors: Similar minded people within the government, business, academia and civil society need to put the development agenda on the table, be it in political circles or among citizens. They need to develop a broad support base to assure the increased allocation of public money to issues beyond the Slovenian boarders, which may not always be easy. Here we can quote an observation by Casey and O'Neill (2012, forthcoming) on Irish NGDOs, whose cooperation with the government is well developed – more than 20 per cent of Irish aid is channelled via NGDOs. Still, they warn: 'Broad support cannot be taken for granted and, while starting from a solid base, Irish NGDOs will need to continually strive for effectiveness and impact in the sector, along with clear, coherent communication of their message, in order to be responsive to increasingly demanding stakeholders, public, media, and politicians.'

At the current level of budget allocation for development cooperation in Slovenia, the NGDOs and the Office need to be strong allies in the promotion of ODA

DEVELOPMENT POLICIES OF CENTRAL AND EASTERN EUROPEAN STATES

funding. The Office needs wide external pressure to convince its government colleagues of the need to increase the budget allocation according to the commitments. In turn, the NGDOs benefit from growth of resources since it provides them with stability in their programmes and allows them to grow.

One can speculate that with further growth of international development cooperation and increased public/ political awareness of the importance of Slovenia's engagement in global development issues, the relationship and roles of the NGDOs and the government will change as well. The NGDOs' role of watchdog is likely to increase, in particular. But at the current level of poor understanding of international development cooperation and the low weight this issue bears in political debates, the joint effort of the Office and SLOGA in awareness raising is a pragmatic and, hopefully, productive approach.

Notes

[1] The term, NGO, can be applied to any non-profit organization that is independent of the government. NGOs are typically value-based organizations that depend, in whole or in part, on charitable donations and voluntary service. Although the NGO sector has become increasingly professionalized over the last two decades, the principles of altruism and voluntarism remain the key defining characteristics (World Bank 1995).

[2] Referred to as 'Office' in the text.

[3] One of the environment NGOs even launched a formal appeal to the European Commission since it felt that it had not been properly consulted about the environmental impact of a regional development programme, prepared within Operation Programme to be financed via structural funds.

[4] List of members available from: http://www.sloga.sloga-platform.org/en/clanstvo/members-2 [Accessed 15 October 2011].

[5] Among the observers are all the NGOs with international links as well as several semi-governmental organizations extensively involved in development cooperation. See details available from: http://www.sloga.sloga-platform.org/en/clanstvo/supporting-ngdos/1 [Accessed 15 October 2011].

[6] This section draws on Bucar, Plibersek and Mesic (2008) for the earlier data.

[7] The impact of the EU pre-accession programmes and participation in the 'twinning projects' on civil society has been analysed in the literature. See, for example, Boerzel (2010) and a special issue of *Acta politica* 2010 (45).

[8] Ministry of Foreign Affairs, News, First meeting of the Council of Experts for International Development Cooperation. Available from: http://www.mzz.gov.si/index.php?id=13&tx_ttnews[tt_news]=118 14&tx_ttnews[backPid] [Accessed 25 May 2011].

[9] According to the International Development Cooperation of the Republic of Slovenia Act (ICD), the planning and implementation of development projects is based on the Resolution of International Development Cooperation. The Resolution includes the geographic and sector priorities as well as financing mechanisms and was adopted by the Slovenian parliament.

[10] Internal reports of the SLOGA (Slovenian Global Action Policy Working Group) Policy WG meetings.

[11] Even the Advisory Board has no decision-making power. It only advises the Management Board and Sloga's Assembly on the areas in which SLOGA and its members should develop their activities.

[12] This, among other activities, could qualify as the 'Changing the North' role since the activity is aimed at increasing public support for development cooperation.

[13] Available from: http://aidwatch.concordeurope.org/countries/project/slovenia/ [Accessed 20 October 2011].

[14] Available from: http://www.sloga.sloga-platform.org/en/politicni-informiranje/predaja-aidwatch-poro cila-2011-razvojni-ministrici-bencini [Accessed 25 May 2011].

[15] Foundation Together, the International Trust Fund for Demining and Mine Victims Assistance (ITF), the Center of Excellence in Finance (CEF), the Centre for E-Governance Development (CeGD) and the Centre for European Perspective (CEP) were fully or partly founded by the Slovenian government.

[16] To be more specific, SLOGA wants a written agreement that would commit the government to compulsory consultations with it when it comes to public calls for NGDOs and all other policy matters that relate to NGDOs.

[17] Available from: http://www.mzz.gov.si/fileadmin/pageuploads/Javna_narocila_in_razpisi/RAZPIS NA_DOKUMENTACIJA_NVO_2010_in_2011.doc [Accessed 15 May 2011].

[18] Available from: http://www.mzz.gov.si/fileadmin/pageuploads/Javna_narocila_in_razpisi/Razpisi/Raz pisna_dokumentacija_-_Javni_razpis_NVO_2011-2013.doc [Accessed 15 May 2011].

[19] Thirteen projects were selected altogether, five in the Western Balkan countries (one project each in Bosnia and Herzegovina, Serbia, Montenegro, Macedonia and Kosovo), one in Moldova, five in Sub-Saharan Africa (total value of 249,950 euros), an NGDO consortium won a project in Afghanistan (69,800 euros) and one humanitarian project in Sub-Saharan Africa was awarded 24,600 euros for 2011.

[20] This assessment is based on the personal experience of the author as an external evaluator of the project proposals.

[21] Available from: http://www.umanotera.org/index.php?node=3 [Accessed 26 October 2011].

[22] Details available from: www.tuditi.si [Accessed 26 October 2011].

[23] National Seminar on Development Education for NGO- and GO-Representatives (in collaboration with DEEEP [Development Awareness Raising and Education Forum]); International Seminar on Monitoring and Evaluation of ODA for the Slovenian and European NGO platforms and governmental representatives (in collaboration with the French NGDO platform, CONCORD (European NGO Coordination for Relief and Development), and OECD DAC); side events to the ACP-EU JPA (African Caribbean Pacific - European Union Joint Parliamentary Assembly) in Ljubljana in March 2008 for ACP -EU CSO (Civil Society Organization) and NGOs (for e.g., a seminar on EPAs (European Partnership Agreements) and EDF (European Development Fund)); International Seminar on Sexual and Reproductive Health and Rights (in collaboration with IPPF (International Planned Parenthood Federation) and WPF (World Population Foundation)); photo exhibition on women and children affected by armed conflicts at the launch of the MFA study in Brussels; national high-level round-table on MDGs on World Day against Poverty in 2007 (presence of the Slovenian MFA, MPs, representatives from the EC and the European Parliament).

[24] Available from: http://www.mzz.gov.si/fileadmin/pageuploads/Novinarsko_sredisce/Sporocila_za_jav nost/Slovenski_Razvojni_Dnevi_-_PROGRAM_01.pdf [Accessed 25 May 2011].

[25] The remaining money was planned to be used directly by the MFA Office for its promotional activities, including Development Days.

[26] See details (in Slovenian) available from: http://www.tuditi.si/sl/gradiva/prirocniki.html [Accessed 25 May 2011].

[27] A good example of both was setting the priorities for development cooperation when drafting the Resolution. Some NGDOs complained that they were not sufficiently consulted in the selection process. But when the MFA team invited SLOGA to suggest a small number of priority countries in Africa on which NGDOs would like to focus, SLOGA could not reach a consensus among its members on which countries to nominate. Several SLOGA members already had contacts/projects in various African countries and each felt that the country in which it was working deserved to be given priority treatment.

[28] Such as their annual financial statement, as a proof of their ability to co-finance their share of the project costs, or a statement by the local community/NGO in the developing country, expressing interest in the project, etc.

[29] The process of preparation of the country's National Strategic Reference Framework needs to involve various partners, including NGOs, and the country needs to report on the consultations undertaken. This led to more systematic – or at least formal – involvement of the NGOs in the government's policy making process.

[30] Some NGDOs complain that the resources available for their activities are insufficient and that SLOGA should demand more. The platform has argued for increased resources and, as seen from the values of the calls, some progress has been achieved. Yet, overall, the resources for international development cooperation have not increased as planned due to budget restrictions.

References

Boerzel, A.T., 2010. Why you don't always get what you want: EU enlargement and civil society in Central and Eastern Europe. *Acta politica*, 45(1/2), 1–10.

DEVELOPMENT POLICIES OF CENTRAL AND EASTERN EUROPEAN STATES

Brown, D., and Fox, J., 2000. Transnational civil society coalitions and the WB: Lessons from project and policy influence campaigns. Working paper no. 3, The Hauser Center for Non-Profit Organisations and The Kennedy School of Government, Harvard University.

Bucar, M., Mesic, A., and Plibersek, E., 2007. Development policies of new member states and their participation in EU development cooperation, Annex 1. DIE (Deutsches Institut fuer Entwicklungspolitik) Discussion Paper 6/2007. *In:* H. Muerle, ed. *Towards a division of labour in European development cooperation: Operational options.* Bonn: 47–52.

Bucar, M., Plibersek, E., and Mesic, A., 2008. Development cooperation in new EU member states: The role of non-governmental organisations. EADI General Conference, Geneva, 24–28 June 2008.

Bučar, Maja, and Udovič, Boštjan, 2007. Oblikovanje strategije mednarodnega razvojnega sodelovanja Slovenije ob upoštevanju načel EU (Design of the strategy of international development cooperation of Slovenia in accordance with EU principles). *Teorija in praksa*, 44(6), 842–861.

Casey, E., and O'Neill, H., 2012, forthcoming. *Irish development NGOs and the official aid programme of Ireland: A 'special' relationship?* Basingstoke, UK: Palgrave EADI Development Book Series.

Črnak-Meglič, A., 2008. Obseg in viri financiranja nevladnih organizacij (društev in ustanov) v letu 2007 (Size and sources of financing of NGOS – Report for the Ministry of Public Administration in 2007). Ljubljana: Poročilo za Ministrstvo za javno upravo.

Črnak-Meglič, A., 2009. Obseg in viri financiranja nevladnih organizacij (društev, ustanov in zasebnih zavodov) v letu 2008 (Size and sources of financing of NGOS – Report for the Ministry of Public Administration in 2008). Ljubljana: Poročilo za Ministrstvo za javno upravo.

Edwards, M., 2005. Civil society. In *The encyclopaedia of informal education.* Available from: www.infed.org/association/civil_society.htm [Accessed 20 May 2011].

Glenzer, K., 2011. International development NGOs. *World Bank development outreach*, April, 18–20.

Grimm, S., and Harmer, A., 2005. Diversity in donorship: The changing landscape of official humanitarian aid. HPG Background Paper, ODI, London. Available from: http://www.isn.ethz.ch/isn/Digital-Library/Publications/Detail/?ots591=0c54e3b3-1e9c-be1e-2c24-a6a8c7060233&lng=en&id=91455 [Accessed 28 October 2011].

Kolarič, Z., 1994. Neprofitno volonterske organizacije v Sloveniji (Non-profit voluntary organizations in Slovenia). *Časopis za kritiko znanosti*, 22(168–169), 143–150.

Kolarič, Z., Črnak-Meglič, A., and Svetlik, I., 1995. Slovenia. *In:* Z. Kolarič, M. Ružica, and I. Svetlik, eds. *The profile of the voluntary sector in Eastern Central European countries.* Družboslovne razprave, XI, 77–94.

Kolarič, Z., Črnak-Meglič A., and Vojnovič M., 2002. *Zasebne neprofitno-volonterske organizacije v mednarodni perspektivi.* Ljubljana: Fakulteta za družbene vede.

Kolarič, Z., et al., 2006. *Velikost, obseg in vloga zasebnega neprofitnega sektorja v Sloveniji. Raziskovalni projekt CRP Konkurečnost Slovenije 2001–06 (Celovita analiza pravnega in ekonomskega okvirja za delo nevladnih organizacij).* Ljubljana: Fakulteta za družbene vede.

Kuhnle, S., and Selle, P., 1992. *Government and voluntary organizations: A relational perspective.* Aldershot, UK: Avebury, 1–33.

Lorgen, C.C., 1998. Dancing with the state: The role of NGOS in health care and health policy. *Journal of International Development*, 10, 332–339.

Mesic, A., and Plibersek, E., 2009. *Vloga NVO pri izvajanju mednarodnega razvojnega sodelovanja-primeri drugih držav in priporočila za Slovenijo* (The role of NGOs in the field of international development cooperation – examples of country profiles and recommendations for Slovenia). mimeo.

MFA, 2010. *Mednarodno razvojno sodelovanje Slovenije 2009 (Annual report on international development cooperation of Slovenia in 2009).* Ljubljana: Ministrstvo za zunanje zadeve.

Mrak, M., Bucar, M., and Kamnar, H., 2007. Mednarodno razvojno sodelovanje Republike Slovenije (International development cooperation of Republic of Slovenia). *IB reviya. (Ljubl.)* 41 (3/4), 50–67.

Rakar, T., and Nagode, M., 2009. *Raziskava indeks civilne družbe (2009).* Vmesno poročilo. Ljubljana: Inštitut RS za socialno varstvo.

Schulpen L., and Hoebink, P., 2012, forthcoming. Condemned to each other – NGDO-government relations in the Netherlands.

Shah, A., 2005. Non-governmental organisations on development issues. Available from: http://www.globalissues.org/article/25/non-governmental-organizations-on-development-issues [Accessed 28 October 2011].

DEVELOPMENT POLICIES OF CENTRAL AND EASTERN EUROPEAN STATES

SLOGA, 2010 *Priročnik za NVO: Spremljanje in vrednotenje projektov in programov razvojnega sodelovanja* (Guidebook for NGOs: Monitoring and evaluation of projects and programmes of development cooperation. Ljubljana: SLOGA.

UL, 2006. Zakon o mednarodnem razvojnem sodelovanju Republike Slovenije (Law on international development cooperation). Uradni list RS 70/2006. Available from: http://www.uradni-list.si/1/objava.jsp?urlid=200670&stevilka=2999 [Accessed 20 May 2011].

UL, 2008. Resolucija o mednarodnem razvojnem sodelovanju (Resolution on international development cooperation of the Republic of Slovenia). Uradni list RS 73/2008. Available from: http://zakono daja.gov.si/rpsi/r08/predpis_RESO58.html [Accessed 20 May 2011].

World Bank, 1995. Working with NGOs: A practical guide to operational collaboration between the World Bank and nongovernmental organizations. Operations Policy Department, WB. Available from: http://www-wds.worldbank.org/external/default/WDSContentServer/WDSP/IB/1995/03/01/0000092 65_3961219103437/Rendered/PDF/multi_page.pdf [Accessed 28 October 2011].

Assessing the Aid Effectiveness of the Czech Republic: Commitment to Development Index and Beyond

PETRA KRYLOVÁ, MIROSLAV SYROVÁTKA & ZDENĚK OPRŠAL

Department of Development Studies, Palacky University in Olomouc, Czech Republic

ABSTRACT *This paper aims to analyse the Official Development Assistance (ODA) of the Czech Republic and assess whether the country has progressed towards being one of those well-established donors that are members of the Development Assistance Committee (DAC) of the Organisation for Economic Cooperation and Development (OECD) or whether it has chosen a different direction with reference to its transition experience. The first part of the paper analyses the institutional establishment of Czech ODA and compares it with the OECD DAC management systems of development assistance. The second part of the paper analyses the financial contributions of the Czech development assistance programme and evaluates whether the country complies with internationally agreed commitments. The third part of the paper uses the Commitment to Development Index (CDI) to measure the effectiveness of Czech development assistance. More specifically, the paper focuses on only one component of the CDI – foreign aid. The paper briefly explains the methodology of the component and applies it to the Czech Republic. The results are interpreted and compared with other countries, members of the OECD DAC, for whom the index was computed.*

1. Introduction

The Czech Republic ranks among the 50 wealthiest countries in the world. As a post-communist country, it has gone through many changes and reforms over the past two decades as it has had to adjust rapidly to the fast changing world and integrate into global society. In a relatively short period of time, the country has become part of such international structures as the European Union (EU), the North Atlantic Treaty Organization (NATO) and the Organisation for Economic Cooperation and Development (OECD). Quite quickly, the post-communist countries, and the Czech Republic among them, have shifted from being recipients of foreign aid to becoming so-called 're-emerging donors' and providing Official Development Assistance

(ODA) (Lightfoot and Zubizarreta 2010). Being part of the EU, the new member states have a set target to allot 0.17 per cent of their gross national income (GNI) towards ODA by 2010 and 0.33 per cent by 2015 (EU 2006).

This paper aims to analyse the ODA of the Czech Republic and assess whether the country has progressed towards being one of those well-established donors that are members of the OECD's Development Assistance Committee (DAC),[1] or whether it has chosen a different direction with reference to its transition experience. The first part of the paper analyses the institutional establishment of Czech ODA and compares it with the OECD DAC management systems of development assistance. The second part of the paper analyses the financial contributions of the Czech development assistance programme and evaluates whether the country complies with internationally agreed commitments. The third part of the paper uses the Commitment to Development Index (CDI) to measure the effectiveness of Czech development assistance. More specifically, the paper focuses on only one component of the CDI – foreign aid. The paper briefly explains the methodology of the component and applies it to the Czech Republic. The results are interpreted and compared with other countries, members of the OECD DAC, for whom the index was computed.

2. The Czech Republic, a Non-DAC Donor

2.1 Evolution of Czech Development Assistance

Among the Central European states that belong to the EU-12,[2] the first country to renew its ODA programme was the Czech Republic, approving the Principles for Providing Development Assistance in March 1995[3] (Government Resolution 153 1995), thus providing the newly established programme with basic guidelines. Apart from stating the general principles, the document appointed the Ministry of Foreign Affairs (MFA) as the main coordinating body of development assistance and, at the same time, assigned individual projects to the relevant ministries according to their sectoral focus, thus creating a complex and rather non-transparent system.

After the re-emergence of Czech development assistance, no particular development structures were put in place. International development was kept under the auspices of the MFA. However, the MFA did not possess the necessary legal competencies to execute any coordinating power.[4] In the late 1990s, the development assistance of the Czech Republic was fragmented both territorially and by sector. Assistance was provided to more than 40 recipient countries through nine line ministries, which were in charge of development projects according to their sectoral priority. Consequently, the programme displayed significant systemic fragmentation, which resulted in lack of transparency and lack of inter-ministerial cooperation and coordination. These factors, together with limited financing, resulted in minimal impact of the development interventions. These problems were recognized and, in January 2002, the government acknowledged[5] the Concept of Czech Development Assistance for the time period, 2002–07 (Government Resolution 91 2002). The Concept should have led to a reform of the system in the stated period, but this aim was not fully achieved.

The Concept suggested the establishment of a development agency – an implementing body for Czech ODA. Although such an agency was not established until January 2008, it was an important step in the transformation process of Czech development assistance. During 2008–10, the agency gradually took over the competencies of individual ministries and became the central implementing body for bilateral assistance. Programming and evaluation remained within the competencies of the MFA.

An important milestone in Czech ODA was the admission of the country into the EU in 2004. After the country's acceptance into the EU (Government Resolution 302 2004), and based on the Principles of Development Assistance, the Czech Republic listed eight programme priority countries for the five-year period, 2006–10. This list featured Angola, Bosnia and Herzegovina, Moldova, Mongolia, Serbia, Vietnam, Yemen and Zambia. Later, two more countries appeared on the list as short-term priorities, Afghanistan and Iraq. As part of the transformation process, a new category of 'project' priority countries was also established, supplementing the eight 'program' priority countries. The newly established category included Ethiopia, Cambodia, Kosovo, Georgia and the Palestinian Administered Areas.

In 2007, the Czech Republic was the first post-communist country to receive the DAC Peer Review of development assistance, which provided . . . and provided the following recommendation concerning the number of priority countries (OECD DAC 2007b): '. . . the Czech Government should take the opportunity of the next Concept for international development co-operation to reduce the number of priority countries to enhance Czech ODA's development impact. It should reassess its sectoral and thematic orientation with a view to concentrating on areas for which the Czech Republic has a clear comparative advantage[6] and value added.'

The new Concept for 2010–17 (MFA of the Czech Republic 2010) was approved by the government in May 2010. Although the document decreased the number of programme priority countries to five, overall, the number of partner countries remained the same (Table 1). The category of project priority countries also remained. In fact, a new category of 'phase-out' countries was created. This category includes mainly former programme priority countries that are not included in either category for the upcoming planning period. According to the Concept, the main purpose was to ensure the sustainability of projects that had already been implemented and to eventually move out of those countries.

In March 2010, Parliament approved the Act on Development Assistance (Act 151/2010), which came into force on 1 July 2010. According to the OECD methodology (Chang *et al.* 1999), such a model corresponds with the category of 'Policy ministry with separate implementing agency'. This system can also be seen in Norway, Sweden and other member countries of the DAC. It can be concluded that in this respect, the Czech Republic has made the necessary changes to increase

Table 1. Czech ODA priority countries for 2010–17

Programme countries	Project countries	Phase-out countries
Afghanistan, Bosnia and Herzegovina, Ethiopia, Moldova, Mongolia	Cambodia, Georgia, Kosovo, Palestinian Admin. Areas, Serbia	Angola, Zambia, Vietnam, Yemen

Source: Concept for 2010–17 (MFA of the Czech Republic, 2010).

effectiveness, enhance transparency and improve the overall performance of Czech development assistance.

2.2 Financial Commitments

Over the past 60 years, the international community has established various institutions and funds devoted to supporting the developing world and has agreed to many targets related to the provision of development assistance. In 1969, the Pearson Commission,[7] under the auspices of the World Bank, recommended that, by 1975, developed countries should provide 0.7 per cent of their Gross National Product (GNP) for development assistance, if there was to be sustained growth in the developing world. More than 30 years later, very few countries have managed to reach this target.[8]

In 2005, the EU member states agreed on the Barcelona II commitments for providing development assistance. Under the agreement, the EU-15 (the old member states) were supposed to strive for an individual target of 0.51 per cent of their GNI for ODA by 2010, 0.56 per cent collectively, and to reach 0.7 per cent by 2015. For the EU-12, the targets were set at 0.17 per cent of GNI for ODA by 2010 and 0.33 per cent by 2015. Although financial volumes have been growing steadily in the past decade, in 2010, most new member states, including the Czech Republic, were far from reaching the recommended volumes (OECD 2011). However, the other EU members were also not meeting their targets.

Figure 1 shows the ODA to GNI ratio of the Czech Republic and the DAC members over the past six years. As can be seen, Czech development assistance has been increasing steadily since 2004. In 2009, as the economy experienced the effects of the global economic crisis, budget cuts did not exclude the development budget. Compared to the previous year, development assistance was decreased by almost US$35 million; however, its share of GNI remained at 0.12 per cent.

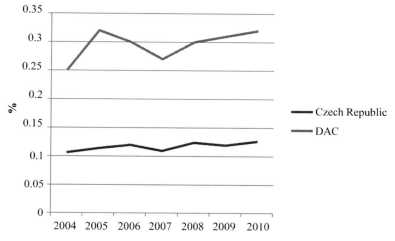

Figure 1. ODA/GNI 2004–10: Comparison of the Czech Republic and the DAC. *Source:* OECD Aid Statistics (2011).

When assessing the financial aspects of ODA, it is important to take into account the proportion of bilateral and multilateral ODA, as this demonstrates countries' engagement outside the mandatory contributions to international development and financial institutions. According to OECD DAC (Rusnak *et al.* 2002), the recommendation for transition countries is to focus their ODA during the initial phase on multilateral cooperation as they do not yet have the essential capacities required for effective contribution to bilateral ODA. ODA analyses of most new member states of the EU support this argument. Most Baltic countries as well as Romania and Bulgaria devote the majority of their ODA to multilateral cooperation (Vencato 2007, AidWatch 2009). However, it should also be taken into account that the countries cannot affect the mandatory contribution to the European Commission (EC), hence to a large extent, it is not a question of decisions, but a result of international commitments.

Considering the bilateral and multilateral ratio of development assistance in the examined period (Figure 2), the levels were mostly consistent, accounting for 45–48 per cent of bilateral assistance; the only exceptions being 2004, when bilateral ODA represented 59 per cent of development assistance,[9] and 2010, when multilateral assistance accounted for 65 per cent. In comparison, the OECD DAC countries provided 70 per cent of total ODA as bilateral assistance in 2009.

3. Assessing Development Impact – Commitment to Development Index

3.1 Methodology of the Aid Component

Donor countries affect the development of poor countries through various policies. These are not only confined to foreign aid, but also include trade and environmental policies, among others. In 2003, the Centre for Global Development constructed the Commitment to Development Index (CDI) (Birdsall and Roodman 2003) to assess a much wider range of policies that affect the development of poor countries. The CDI is a composite indicator that embraces seven policy components: aid, trade, investment, migration, environment, security, and technology. Each of the seven

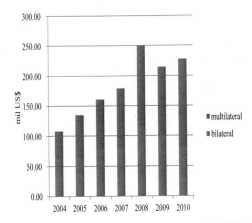

Figure 2. Bilateral and multilateral aid, 2004–10. *Source:* OECD Aid Statistics (2011).

components consists of several sub-indicators. The weight of these indicators differs within each component. However, the seven components are weighted equally in the final index.

The authors have decided to use the aid component of the CDI rather than other indicators because it assesses donors on both quantity and quality of aid. As a quantitative indicator, it allows for the meaningful ranking of donors.

Although, in the broad sense, foreign aid represents only one aspect of development policy, it is the most direct and, therefore, the most visible policy. The aid component consists of (1) quality-adjusted aid and (2) quality-adjusted private charity induced by public policy. In this paper, we will focus closely only on aid policy and we will present a preliminary result for the whole dimension of the Czech Republic. The general assumption underlying the calculation of the aid component is that aid is beneficial for the recipient countries (more aid is better than less) and that the degree of its usefulness differs (some aid is better than others).

The methodology is based on ODA as reported to the OECD DAC and adjusts aid quantity by its quality. More specifically, aid quantity is discounted in the case of (1) tying[10] (a requirement of the donor that goods and services that are to be provided as aid need to come from specific countries, mainly from the donor country), (2) selectivity[11] (providing aid to relatively rich and poorly governed countries is penalized, which reflects the view that aid is more needed and effective in poor and well-governed countries), and (3) project proliferation[12] (aid that is fragmented into small projects is penalized since it is considered less effective due to high transaction costs and other reasons). This is done for both bilateral and multilateral aid; the final number is called total quality-adjusted aid. Since it would make no sense to compare small and large countries in absolute quantity of (quality-adjusted) aid, the total amount is expressed as a percentage of the donors' GNI (in US$, market exchange rates). These percentages are then translated onto a standardized CDI scale (0–10) to be comparable with other components.

3.2 Results for the Czech Republic

As mentioned above, the Czech Republic renewed its development assistance programme after its acceptance into the OECD in 1995. After its admission into the EU, Czech ODA has been improving significantly in many areas. However, it needs to be underlined that the Czech Republic is still not a member of the DAC and, therefore, does not report some of the data necessary for the computation. Thus, in order to calculate the aid component for the Czech Republic, various data sources were used – mainly OECD aid statistics, information provided by Czech non-governmental development organizations (NGDOs) and other sources, including data collected by David Roodman (2011) from the Centre for Global Development. In particular, data for CDI 2010 (aid reported for 2008) was used.

3.2.1 Quality-Adjusted Aid

As explained previously, quality-adjusted aid takes into account tying, selectivity and project proliferation. Quality-adjusted aid is calculated for both multilateral and bilateral ODA as reported to the OECD DAC. In 2008, the Czech Republic reported US$249.21 million as ODA, of which multilateral aid accounted for 53 per cent (US$132.07 million) and bilateral aid for 47 per cent (US$117.14 million). Gross bilateral ODA is cleared of debt cancellation, amortization and interest. The latter two are not reported for the Czech Republic, so only debt relief is taken into account. In 2008, it represented US$1.2 million, which was deducted from gross bilateral ODA, resulting in US$115.94 million of net bilateral aid.

In the next stage, both bilateral and multilateral aid are adjusted to take into account tying costs, selectivity and size–weight. The Czech Republic does not report tying to DAC and, according to the MFA, this data is not recorded. According to the Monterrey questionnaire, the only aid provided to non-governmental organizations (NGOs) is tied. However, analysing individual components of bilateral aid, we can speculate that the majority of Czech bilateral aid is indeed tied. This conclusion is also supported by anecdotal evidence from various representatives of the MFA as well as NGO, academia and other Czech development assistance participants (Horky 2010). Therefore, we calculated tying costs using an average ratio of tying costs to net aid for the three worst performers among the CDI countries in 2008, Austria, Greece and Korea.

Aid is assumed to be more needful and effective in poor and well-governed countries. Therefore, for each donor-recipient pair, aid is multiplied by a selectivity weight that takes into consideration these two aspects. The indicators used for calculating selectivity weight are Gross Domestic Product (GDP) per capita converted to US$ by exchange rates and the Kaufmann-Kraay composite governance indicator (Kaufmann, Kraay and Mastruzzi 2008). Initially, the scaling was done using 2001 data and, for the purpose of valid comparisons, remained fixed over the monitored period. Therefore, some scores can lie slightly outside the 0–1 range (e.g., Ghana's score in 2007 was 1.03).[13] Although Czech bilateral net aid to Ghana in 2008 was almost eight times less than to Iraq, after adjustment by selectivity, the aid given to both countries was almost equal. The reason was a very high selectivity weight for Ghana and a very low one for Iraq. In other words, 98 per cent of Czech net aid to Ghana was included in quality-adjusted aid, whereas only 14 per cent was included in the case of Iraq. Emergency aid is excluded from the selectivity discount as it is provided on an ad hoc basis where needed. In 2008, this represented US$5.09 million. This again re-enters the calculation in the process of size–weight adjustment when it is added to the selectivity-adjusted aid and then multiplied by size–weight to arrive at quality-adjusted aid.

Assessing the approved list of countries for the next planning period (Table 1), only one African country has remained among both categories of priority countries, Ethiopia,[14] and there are only three least developed countries (LDCs) on the list, Afghanistan, Ethiopia and Mongolia. The rest of the aid will be aimed at lower and upper middle income countries. This trend is clearly contradictory to international commitments; on the other hand, it might be in line with the recommendations of the DAC Peer Review, referring to the comparative advantages of the Czech Republic (OECD DAC 2007b). Similarly, the recently published Peer Review of the Polish ODA acknowledged the possible contribution of Polish ODA 'towards the development of its neighbors in Eastern Europe where it has a comparative advantage' (OECD DAC 2010).

When assessing fragmentation and proliferation of aid, it is essential to look at the total number of ODA recipients in the past six years. Since the country's entry into the EU in 2004, the number of recipient countries increased gradually from 86 in 2004 to 105 in 2008 and fell again to 94 in 2009. The main cause of such fragmentation is government scholarships. In 2009, scholarships were provided to 75 developing countries (MFA of the Czech Republic 2009).

Given the abovementioned data, clearly, the Czech Republic increased the number of partner countries. Although the number of programme priority countries declined to just five, other categories of partner countries were formed. This leads to greater fragmentation and proliferation of aid and is inconsistent with the DAC recommendations and the Code of Conduct on Complementarity and the Division of Labour in Development Policy (EC 2007), which emphasizes that donors should 'designate a limited number of priority countries and concentrate the activities on a limited number of national sectors'.

Calculating size–weight tends to be more complicated than calculating selectivity, the main reason being the complexity of factors it considers. The effectiveness of aid depends on the size of the projects. It is assumed that there is an optimal project size that depends on size of the recipient country, volume of aid received by the country, and the quality of its governance. Both small and large projects are discounted. As with selectivity weight, it is calculated for each donor-recipient pair and the average size–weight score is then applied to selectivity-adjusted aid and the previously omitted emergency aid. Among the recipients of Czech development assistance in 2007, the Republic of Congo had the highest size–weight score of 0.9, while China had the lowest of 0.48. Overall, the average size–weight of Czech aid in 2008 was 0.76. Size–weight can only be computed using detailed Creditor Reporting System (CRS) statistics related to the donor's activities. The Czech Republic does not yet provide full reporting on ODA commitments, so the average size–weight that is assigned to each recipient represents the average of other donors.

If we look at the financial volumes received by the partner countries as shown in Figure 3,[15] it is clear that too many partner countries receive too few contributions. Out of the total number of recipient countries, most receive less than US$1 million. Even more worrying is the fact that almost half of the recipients receive a negligible amount of less than US$0.1 million. This leads to a significant fragmentation of Czech ODA and, most importantly, to the diminishing impact of the implemented interventions.

Figure 4 shows the ODA received by the LDCs. During 2004–09, Czech ODA to the LDCs was rather inconsistent. During 2004–06, aid accounted for less than 15 per cent of bilateral aid. However, with the Czech Republic's greater involvement in Afghanistan, the ratio rose to 45 per cent of total bilateral aid provided in 2008; with the exclusion of Afghanistan, it was only 5 per cent. On the other hand, the ODA of the DAC donors has been relatively stable and increasing since 2005. Unlike in the case of the Czech Republic, the pattern is not distorted by ODA provided to Afghanistan.

An interesting comparison can be made among the top 15 recipients of Czech development assistance in the period under study. As can be noted from Figure 5, the

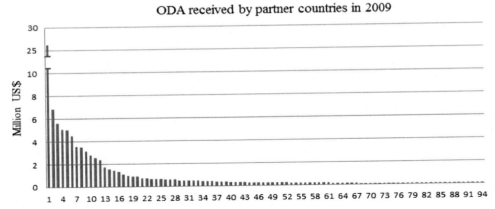

Figure 3. Czech partner countries in 2009 and amounts of ODA received. *Source:* OECD Aid Statistics (2011).

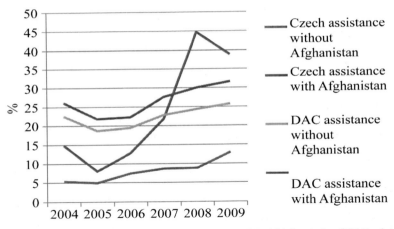

Figure 4. Share of ODA received by LDCs. *Source:* OECD Aid Statistics (2011), data for the Czech Republic based on disbursements, data for the DAC based on commitments.

first four recipient places are taken by priority countries. The fifth place is taken by the Ukraine, which received US$12.81 million in the given timeframe. The other five priority countries also rank among the top 15. However, there are only two LDCs on the list, Afghanistan and Angola. In total, ten priority countries rank among the top 15 recipients of Czech ODA, which can be considered a mixed success. Although the Ukraine is not a priority country for development cooperation, it is a priority for transitional cooperation. At the same time, humanitarian aid also needs to be taken into consideration as it is not a question of selectivity, but provided on an ad hoc basis where needed. The share of bilateral ODA aimed at priority countries has been increasing since 2005, reaching 68 per cent in 2008.[16] The growing trend can be classified as positive, although priority countries should eventually receive around 75 per cent of the total bilateral ODA.[17]

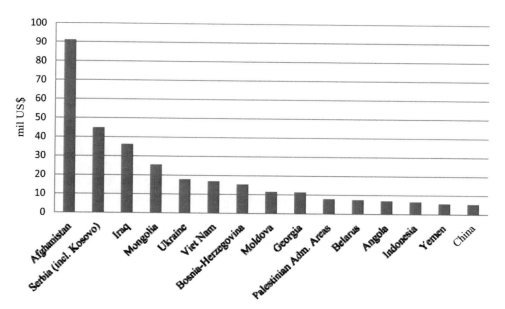

Figure 5. Top 15 recipients of Czech ODA 2004–09. *Source:* OECD Aid Statistics (2011), priority countries displayed in red.

Although most international commitments focus mainly on the LDCs, a recent 'shift of poverty' from low to middle income countries, as noted by Chandy and Gertz (2011), should be taken into consideration when assessing aid allocation. As stated in many official documents of Czech ODA, the promotion of democracy and support for democratic states is an integral part of Czech development assistance. The Czech Republic aims to focus development assistance on countries in transition and thus strives to transfer its own transition experience. Although such a policy is less favourable towards the LDCs, it enables Czech ODA to make use of the comparative advantages it has acquired during the transition period.

The calculation of multilateral quality-adjusted aid is similar, to the extent that it also takes into consideration selectivity and size–weight. However, it excludes tying costs as multilateral agencies are not thought to apply tying measures to aid. The calculation of multilateral adjusted aid is more complex because it considers each individual multilateral donor and evaluates its selectivity and size–weight. For each bilateral donor, the share of its contribution to the multilateral's total net ODA is computed; the share is then multiplied by the quality-adjusted aid of each scored multilateral. Not all multilateral donors are scored. Therefore, the average quality-adjustment measure is calculated as a ratio of quality-adjusted aid to scored multilaterals and net aid to scored multilaterals. The ratio becomes the final component for calculating multilateral quality-adjusted aid. Firstly, aid is assigned to each multilateral based on the contribution of the Czech Republic as reported to the OECD DAC. Secondly, the share of this contribution on the recipients' total ODA is calculated. This share is then multiplied by the quality-adjusted aid of each multilateral donor.

The final average multilateral quality discount is the ratio of quality-adjusted aid to scored multilaterals and net aid to scored multilaterals. The average quality discount is then applied to the total net multilateral aid.

Adding the two separately computed quality-adjusted bilateral (US$32.79 million) and multilateral (US$80.79 million) amounts of aid, the final figure is US$113.57 million. This represents 45.57 per cent of the ODA reported to the OECD DAC. While ODA represents 0.12 per cent of GNI, quality-adjusted aid accounts for only 0.0566 per cent. However, a very interesting aspect becomes apparent when we compare the rates of deduction applied on bilateral and multilateral aid. Whereas bilateral assistance has been deducted by 68 per cent, in the case of multilateral assistance, the deduction was only 38.83 per cent. This supports the conclusion that for the Czech Republic, providing development assistance through multilateral donors is more effective than providing development assistance bilaterally. However, this result should be interpreted with caution. Currently, it is not possible to calculate precisely the size–weight for each recipient of Czech bilateral ODA, therefore an average is used, which might improve or worsen the final result. Furthermore, there are other factors that the index does not take into consideration (e.g., comparative advantage) and, as a result, Czech bilateral aid might be discounted more than would be appropriate.

3.2.2 Quality-Adjusted Private Charity Induced by Public Policy

The second part of the aid component of the CDI focuses on public policies that promote charitable giving. Unlike the DAC members, the Czech Republic does not report data on private charity, nor does the Czech Statistical Office collect such information that could serve as a baseline for the computation. Therefore, we used information provided by the major NGOs. Overall, there are around 50 NGOs working in the field. Most of them receive their funding from official sources such as ministries and European funds and foundations; only a very few organizations receive any significant private funding. The authors have researched the financial reports of most NGOs that are members of the national platform, FoRS (Czech Forum for Development Cooperation), in order to calculate a proximate value of private funding.[18] In order to stay in line with the official OECD DAC reporting, the analysis followed the DAC guidelines and, therefore, the calculations included 'grants by national NGOs and other private sources, including foundations and other private bodies, for development assistance and relief' (OECD DAC 2007a, p. 31). The findings show that the examined organizations received slightly less than US$10 million for development and relief purposes in 2008. A figure of US$9.95 million was included in the computation because the analysis omitted other organizations, which receive only negligible private contributions.

The component aims to assess what proportion of charitable giving is attributable to public policies. Therefore, it takes into consideration various aspects of state policies concerning tax issues as shown in Table 2.

According to the OECD (2010b), the relevant marginal income tax rate for the Czech Republic in 2008 was 20.2 per cent.[19] Because the Czech Republic sets a maximum that can be deducted from taxable income, the tax incentive is taken as half of the marginal income tax rate − 10.1 per cent.[20]

DEVELOPMENT POLICIES OF CENTRAL AND EASTERN EUROPEAN STATES

The tax incentive (10.1 per cent), together with the estimated price elasticity of giving (-0.5) produces an increase in giving of 5.5 per cent. The increase in giving because of a smaller government (35.5 per cent) is a product of three factors – the share of Czech tax revenue on GDP (36.6 per cent), the benchmark share of tax revenue on GDP (51.9 per cent) and the estimated income elasticity of giving (1.1). Both factors produce a combined increase in giving of 43 per cent ($1.055 \times 1.355 = 1.430$). When we divide current private giving by this multiplier, the calculated figure shows the estimated private giving without the effect of tax policies (US$6.96 million). Deducting this amount from the current private giving, we isolate the effect of tax policies on private giving (US$2.99 million) as shown in Table 2.

Table 2. Public policies for charitable giving and charitable giving, 2008

Increase in giving with incentive	Increase in giving because of smaller government	Combined increase	Current giving (million US$)	Giving in absence of favourable tax policies (million US$)	Giving attributed to tax policies (million US$)	Quality-adjusted private giving (million US$)
5.5%	35.5%	43.0%	9.95	6.96	2.99	1.24

Sources: OECD Tax Database, Table O.1, Table 1.4 (OECD 2010b); Authors' calculations

In the final stage, giving attributed to tax policies is subjected to quality adjustment. Given the limited information on the effectiveness of aid from private sources, the average quality discount was set as an average of all donors' bilateral quality aid adjustment (58 per cent in 2008). After this adjustment, private giving accounts for US$1.24 million, which represents 0.0006 per cent of GNI.

Summing up both public and private quality-adjusted foreign aid, we arrive at US$114.81 million for 2008, which amounts to 0.057 per cent of GNI. Translating the percentage onto the standardized CDI scale, the Czech Republic gains a score of 1.7. With this score, the country is placed at the bottom of the list, having the third least favourable aid policy towards developing countries (Figure 7). Although it is a relatively poor performance, it should be viewed in a broader context. Twenty years after the country started upon the cumbersome journey of economic and social transformation, the Czech Republic has made significant progress towards a market economy and a democratic political system. With regard to development policies over the past 15 years, the Czech Republic has attempted to institutionalize its development assistance programme and make it more effective. However, some policies tend to evolve more slowly, and development policies are among them. Should the Czech Republic improve its development policy and move up the CDI ladder, some general recommendations can be derived.

3.2.3 Discussion of Results

Although among the OECD DAC members, the Czech Republic ranks last in absolute as well as relative volumes of aid provided in 2008, the computed aid component indicates that the quality of Czech aid is slightly higher than that of South Korea and Japan.[21]

111

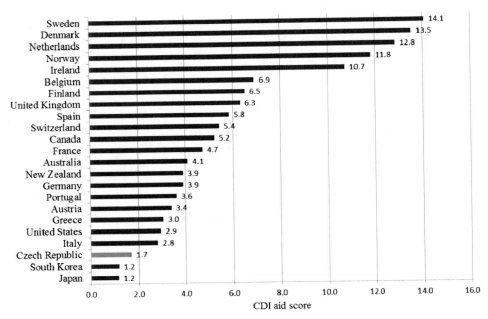

Figure 6. Aid component results for DAC member countries and the Czech Republic. *Source:* Authors' calculations; Roodman (2011).

The territorial focus of Czech aid is slightly controversial. The index penalizes the Czech Republic for supporting mainly the middle income countries, rather than the LDCs. However, taking into consideration the historical context and comparative advantages of Czech development assistance, the question remains whether the LDCs benefit as much from Czech aid as countries now undergoing the transition process. This argument is also supported by a recent OECD DAC Peer Review of Poland's ODA. The report states: 'Poland has an important and welcome contribution to make to international development co-operation, particularly the development of its neighbors in Eastern Europe where it has a comparative advantage' (OECD DAC 2010). However, reflecting on the comparative advantages of individual donors would be, without a doubt, too complex (and also disputable) to incorporate it into the index.

Tied aid is a burning issue of Czech aid. No official statistics assessing tied aid exist. However, by analysing each component of bilateral assistance individually, we can speculate that most bilateral aid provided by the Czech Republic is tied. However, how other DAC members calculate and report their tied aid is questionable. Being aware of this fact, we decided to calculate the average of the three worst performers, which might again improve or worsen the overall result of the Czech Republic.

Considering the multilateral aid provided, unlike in most EU-12 countries, the provision of multilateral assistance is not dominant over bilateral assistance. This fact improves the overall quality-adjusted aid because aid provided through multilateral organizations is discounted less than aid provided bilaterally.

Charitable aid is difficult to analyse as there are no official statistics. However, the brief survey we conducted showed that Czech charitable giving accounts for more than Portuguese and Greek charitable giving and that the Czech policies for giving are more favourable than those in Sweden and Finland.

4. Conclusion

It needs to be underlined that there are vast differences among the DAC members in providing development assistance. In terms of the institutional and legislative establishment of development assistance, it can be concluded that the Czech Republic has progressed towards being a well-established donor and made the proper arrangements essential for the greater effectiveness of Czech development assistance. Currently, it has the same management system of aid as Norway and Sweden. Improvements in financial contributions have not been as positive. However, it could be argued that any increase of funds prior to the institutional re-arrangements would not be justifiable. Regarding its commitments on the European level, the Czech Republic, like most EU member countries, failed to achieve the first Barcelona II recommendations.

The final results of the aid component show that, although the Czech Republic is at the bottom of the list, its development assistance is not incomparable with the members of the DAC. The Czech Republic is in third place from the bottom, above South Korea, which joined the DAC only recently, and Japan, which is the second biggest donor in absolute terms. It is evident that the territorial focus of Czech aid is oriented towards countries undergoing the transition process rather than the LDCs, which are included sporadically (Afghanistan and Ethiopia). Afghanistan is among the priority countries mainly due to international commitments in NATO. It is clear that in this respect, the Czech Republic, like some other re-emerging donors, will take its own path in providing development assistance. Although it might be contradictory with regard to some international commitments, it complies with other recommendations as it enhances the comparative advantage – transition experience – of Czech aid.

Notes

[1] It can be argued whether all the DAC members can be considered 'well-established' donors; however, this is not the purpose of this paper.

[2] The EU-12, sometimes also referred to as the new member states, is a group of 12 countries which entered the EU in 2004 and afterwards: Bulgaria, Cyprus, the Czech Republic, Estonia, Hungary, Latvia, Lithuania, Malta, Poland, Romania, Slovakia and Slovenia.

[3] Only three days after the official entry into the OECD.

[4] In 2002, the Development Centre was established under the auspices of the Institute of International Relations. The Centre was supposed to serve as an advisory body to the Ministry and assist in the coordination of development assistance. However, the Centre did not have any coordinating power either.

[5] The Concept was not approved, only acknowledged.

[6] As examples of comparative advantages, the report mentions transformation to a market economy and pollution control.

[7] The Pearson Commission was established under the auspices of the World Bank in 1968 with the aim of evaluating the state of development assistance and to draw up recommendations for the future. The published report, *Partners in Development*, represents one of the first complex and comprehensive studies of development assistance (World Bank 2003).

[8] Based on the OECD (2010a) Development Co-operation Report, only Denmark, Luxembourg, Norway and Sweden have provided more than 0.7 per cent of GNI for development assistance in the past couple of years.

[9] However, the main reason was an increase in multilateral assistance in the consecutive years (caused by entry into the EU), rather than a decrease in the volume of bilateral aid. The latter continued to increase until 2008.

[10] Jepma (1991) claims that tying of aid decreases the value of aid by 10 per cent to 30 per cent.

[11] Studies on aid selectivity and conditionality show that these approaches have been used increasingly by donors since the 1980s (e.g., Dollar and Levin 2006), while there is a clear shift from the economic to political conditioning of aid (e.g., promoting good governance). Most debates focus on the objectives and impacts of aid conditionality. The conclusions of Burnside and Dollar (2000) show that aid promotes growth in a good policy environment. However, Easterly (2003) disputes these conclusions and states that the relation between aid conditionality and economic growth is not evidential.

[12] Acharya *et al.* (2006) claim that aid fragmentation and proliferation increase the transaction costs of aid on both sides – the donor and the partner – which results in decreased aid efficiency.

[13] The value is a result of two multipliers: 1.68 for GDP per capita (Ghana is relatively poorer than other developing countries) and 0.61 for governance (among developing countries, it is relatively well governed).

[14] Horky (2010) states that '. . . the inclusion of a Least Developed Country in Africa was initially justified only by public and external acceptability'.

[15] Contributions not allocated to a particular country, but to a group of countries, as, for example, North Africa, were excluded.

[16] However, it should be noted that Afghanistan received more than 50 per cent of total bilateral aid provided to priority countries in the given time period.

[17] This percentage has been mentioned by the representatives of the MFA and the Czech Development Agency on several occasions.

[18] The authors would like to thank Eva Komlossyová and Simona Pathová for collecting data on Czech NGOs.

[19] Marginal income tax rates used for calculation do not include social security contributions paid by the employee and those paid by the employer, which are higher for the Czech Republic than for most other OECD members. Also, this share has not been stable in the last decade. From 2000 to 2005, the relevant marginal income tax rate was below 22 per cent; in 2006 and 2007, it was 28 per cent;, and in 2008, it fell to 20.2 per cent.

[20] Individuals can deduct up to 10 per cent of taxable income, companies up to 5 per cent of taxable income. Interestingly, the Czech Republic also applies a minimum limit (i.e., lower giving cannot be deducted) of 2 per cent of taxable income or CZK 1,000 for individuals and CZK 2,000 for companies (see Act No. 586/1992 Coll. on Income Taxes, as amended).

[21] In 2008, South Korea provided only 0.09 per cent of GNI for ODA, less than the Czech Republic. South Korea joined the DAC in 2010.

References

Acharya, A., Lima, A.T.F., and Moore, M., 2006. Proliferation and fragmentation: Transaction cost and the value of aid. *Journal of development studies*, 42 (1), 1–21.

Act No. 586/1992. Coll. on Income Taxes, as amended.

Act No. 151/2010. Coll., Czech Republic: Act on development assistance and humanitarian aid provided abroad (Zákon o zahraniční rozvojové spolupráci a humanitární pomoci poskytované do zahraničí).

AidWatch, 2009. *Lighten the load: In a time of crisis, European aid has never been more important.* Brussels: CONCORD.

Birdsall, N., and Roodman, D., 2003. *The Commitment to Development Index: A scorecard of rich-country policies.* Washington, DC: Center for Global Development.

Burnside, C., and Dollar, D., 2000. Aid, policies and growth. *The American economic review*, 90 (4), 847–868.

Chandy, L., and Gertz, G., 2011. Poverty in numbers: The changing state of global poverty from 2005 to 2015. Available from: <http://www.brookings.edu/~/media/Files/rc/papers/2011/01_global_poverty_chandy/01_globa l_poverty_chandy.pdf> [Accessed 10 July 2011].

DEVELOPMENT POLICIES OF CENTRAL AND EASTERN EUROPEAN STATES

Chang, H., Fell, A., and Laird, M., 1999. A comparison of management systems for development cooperation in OECD/DAC members. OECD working paper. Available from: <http://www.oecd.org/dataoecd/40/28/2094873.pdf> [Accessed 3 March 2010].

Dollar, D., and Levin, V., 2006. The increasing selectivity of foreign aid, 1984–2003. *World development*, 34 (12), 2034–2046.

Easterly, W., 2003. Can foreign aid buy growth? *The journal of economic perspectives*, 17 (3), 23–48.

EU (European Parliament, Council and Commission), 2006. Joint statement by the Council and the representatives of governments of the member states meeting within the Council, the European Parliament and the Commission on the European Union Development Policy: The European Consensus. Available from: <http://ec.europa.eu/development/icenter/repository/european_consensus_2005_en.pdf> [Accessed 15 July 2011].

European Commission, 2007. EU code of conduct on division of labour in development policy. Available from: <http://eur-lex.europa.eu/LexUriServ/LexUriServ.do?uri=COM:2007:0072:FIN:EN:PDF> [Accessed 15 July 2011].

Government Resolution 153, 1995. Principles for providing development assistance (Zásady pro poskytování zahraniční pomoci), approved on 15 March. Available from: <http://kormoran.vlada.cz/usneseni/usneseni_webtest.nsf/0/7897B04C221A1F30C12571B6006BDB3E> [Accessed 23 June 2011].

Government Resolution 91, 2002. Concept of Czech development assistance for the time period of 2002–07 (Koncepce zahraniční rozvojové pomoci České republiky na období let 2002 až 2007), acknowledged on 23 January. Available from: <http://kormoran.vlada.cz/usneseni/usneseni_webtest.nsf/0/CD08EB02CBB63F2AC12571B6006D20EA> [Accessed 23 June 2011].

Government Resolution 302, 2004. The principles of development assistance of the Czech Republic after the country's acceptance into the EU (Zásady zahraniční rozvojové spolupráce po vstupu České republiky do Evropské unie). Available from: <http://racek.vlada.cz/usneseni/usneseni_webtest.nsf/0/66E45F679EF975CAC12571B6006E B537> [Accessed 23 June 2011].

Horký, O., 2010. Development cooperation in the Czech foreign policy. *In*: M. Kořan, *et al.*, eds. *Czech foreign policy in 2007–09: An analysis*. Prague: Institute of International Relations, 347–361.

Jepma, C.J., 1991. *The tying of aid*. Paris: Development Centre of the OECD.

Kaufmann, D., Kraay, A., and Mastruzzi, M., 2008. Governance matters VII: Aggregate and individual governance indicators 1996–2007. Policy research working paper 4654. Washington, DC: World Bank.

Lightfoot, S., and Zubizarreta, I.R., 2010. The emergence of international development policies in Central and Eastern European states. *In*: P. Hoebink, ed. *European development cooperation. In between the local and global*. Amsterdam: Amsterdam University Press, 176–193.

Ministry of Foreign Affairs of the Czech Republic, 2002. Concept of Czech development assistance for the time period of 2002–07 (Koncepce zahraniční rozvojové pomoci České republiky na období let 2002 až 2007). Prague: Ministry of Foreign Affairs of the Czech Republic.

Ministry of Foreign Affairs of the Czech Republic, 2009. Report on official development assistance of the Czech Republic in 2009 (Informace o zahraniční rozvojové spolupráci České republiky v roce 2009). Available from: <http://www.mzv.cz/jnp/cz/zahranicni_vztahy/rozvojova_spoluprace/koncepce_publikace/informace_o_zahranicni_rozvojove.html> [Accessed 9 April 2011].

Ministry of Foreign Affairs of the Czech Republic, 2010. Concept of Czech development assistance for 2010–17 (Koncepce zahraniční rozvojové spolupráce České republiky na léta 2010–17). Available from: <http://www.mzv.cz/jnp/cz/zahranicni_vztahy/rozvojova_spoluprace/aktualne/koncepce_zrs_cr_2010_2017.html> [Accessed 8 August 2011].

OECD, 2010a. Development co-operation report 2010. Paris: OECD Publishing.

OECD, 2010b. OECD tax database. Available from: <http://www.oecd.org/ctp/taxdatabase> [Accessed 10 April 2011].

OECD, 2011. Aid statistics database. Available from: <http://www.oecd.org/document/49/0,3746,en_2649_34447_46582641_1_1_1_1,00.html> [Accessed 10 August 2011].

OECD DAC, 2007a. DAC statistical reporting directives. Paris: OECD.

OECD DAC, 2007b. DAC special review of the Czech Republic. Available from: <http://www.oecd.org/dataoecd/37/34/45367897.pdf> [Accessed 11 April 2011].

OECD DAC, 2010. DAC special review of Poland. Available from: <http://www.oecd.org/dataoecd/58/43/45362587.pdf> [Accessed 12 June 2011].

Roodman, D., 2011. *Commitment to Development Index electronic database* provided by David Roodman.

Rusnak, U., Szep, A., and Brzica, D., 2002. Development aid and co-operation (Rozvojová pomoc a spolupráca). Bratislava: Slovak Institute for International Studies.

Vencato, F., 2007. The development policy of the CEECs: The EU political rationale between the fight against poverty and the near abroad. Thesis (PhD). Katholieke Universiteit Leuven, D/2007/8978/2. Available from: <https://lirias.kuleuven.be/bitstream/1979/1008/2/PhdThesis-MFV07.PDF> [Accessed 10 July 2010].

World Bank, 2003. Pages from World Bank history: The Pearson Commission. Available from: <http://web.worldbank.org/WBSITE/EXTERNAL/EXTABOUTUS/EXTARCHIVES/0,,contentMDK:20121526~pagePK:36726~piPK:36092~theSitePK:29506,00.html> [Accessed 25 April 2011].

Development Cooperation of the Baltic States: A Comparison of the Trajectories of Three New Donor Countries

EVELIN ANDRESPOK*[1] & ANDRES ILMAR KASEKAMP**

*Department of Political and Economic Studies, University of Helsinki, Finland
**Institute of Government and Politics, University of Tartu, Estonia

ABSTRACT: *Estonia, Latvia and Lithuania initiated development cooperation as part of their European Union (EU) accession process. As members of the EU since 2004, the Baltic States have eagerly latched onto the European Neighbourhood Policy (ENP) as a vehicle for their bilateral development cooperation. Analysing the choice of priority partner countries for bilateral aid, this article shows that the development cooperation of the Baltic States is driven primarily by national foreign policy agendas. Of the three countries, Estonia appears to have progressed furthest in fostering development cooperation, whereas Latvian efforts have suffered due to deep cuts in its state budget.*

Introduction

Since the Baltic States are newcomers to development cooperation, as yet, there is hardly any scholarly literature on the subject. The available sources are limited mainly to official government strategy papers and some analyses produced by non-governmental organizations (NGOs). Our paper is a modest attempt to fill this gap by providing an empirical foundation for future theoretical research. We first contextualize the historical background to the establishment and practice of development cooperation by Estonia, Latvia and Lithuania. Then we examine the legislative framework, financing, priorities, public discourse and the role of civil society. It is quite clear that development cooperation has evolved in the Baltic States as the direct result of European Union (EU) conditionality. However, when we look at the priority partner countries selected by the Baltic States, the importance of national interests and geopolitical considerations is quite noticeable.

---

[1] Evelin Andrespok is writing here in a personal capacity.

Historical Background

Unlike some of the other Central and Eastern European countries, the Baltic States had no experience with the developing world during the Cold War era. At that time, Estonia, Latvia and Lithuania were constituent republics of the Soviet Union and not even nominally sovereign countries like Czechoslovakia or Poland, which had diplomatic representations and other external links. After the restoration of their independence in 1991, the Baltic States were themselves recipients of foreign assistance during the 1990s and concentrated on consolidating their own statehood (Kasekamp 2010, ch. 8). Similar to most other Central and Eastern European countries, the Baltic States started their development cooperation programmes as a part of their EU accession process. Estonia was the first to become a donor of development assistance in 1998, when its parliament first dedicated funds from the state budget for such purposes (Estonian MFA 1999). Latvia followed in 1999, with the first ad hoc development projects (TRIALOG 2008) and Lithuania, in 2003, when the government adopted the decision on its development cooperation guidelines for 2003–05 (Bernotas 2006).

Rokas Bernotas, Director of the Multilateral Relations Department in the Lithuanian Ministry of Foreign Affairs (MFA), admitted that the EU membership was one of the most important incentives in the transformation process from recipient of aid to international donor. He believed that the EU commitment to reaching the Millennium Development Goals (MDGs) 'have spurred the expansion of Lithuanian development cooperation policy in many aspects – financial, administrative, legal and public' (Bernotas 2006). According to Kāle (2007, p. 46), in the early days of development cooperation by Latvia, 'the symbolic act of aid giving was more important than the kind or level of aid given and this symbolic act of giving aid had a simple objective – that of integrating Latvia into [the] larger world picture, and preferably at the Western side.'

Here, the impact of EU conditionality can be seen clearly. During the EU accession process, Lithuania, Latvia and especially Estonia strove to be the 'best pupils in the class' (Ehin 2011). Since they had a less favourable starting position than the Central and Eastern European countries (in terms of geopolitics and wealth), they consciously avoided creating difficulties during the accession negotiations, realizing that their success depended entirely on their speedy fulfilment of the Copenhagen Criteria (the EU's membership requirements). There was little demand on the part of the Estonian, Latvian or Lithuanian publics that their governments should become donors. However, the governments were eager to demonstrate that their countries were not only recipients of assistance of various kinds, but that they were becoming 'contributors' themselves. Thus, the initiative to launch development cooperation was largely the consequence of the EU accession process.

The Baltic States had to reconceptualize many of their policies, including their development policy, after joining the EU in 2004. In Estonia, the change in political rhetoric was quite noticeable. In his speech to the parliament in 2005, Foreign Minister Urmas Paet stated 'that the true goal of Estonia's foreign policy is to improve the security and well-being of Estonia and its people, and that joining the EU and NATO is merely a means to an end not an end in itself' (Paet 2005). Both in

Estonia and in neighbouring Latvia and Lithuania, there has been a gradual shift in the self-perception since 1998 from individual countries zealously guarding their sovereignty to states that see themselves as integral parts of the European community and 'as having a moral responsibility to improve global problems regardless of whether it is directly suffering from their effects or not'. (Andrespok 2008, p. 50).

In joining the EU (and also the North Atlantic Treaty Organization [NATO]), the Baltic States seized on the opportunity provided by the European Neighbourhood Policy (ENP) to show themselves in a positive light and to channel their bilateral assistance to countries of the former Soviet Union, thereby furthering their own geopolitical interests. The newly-created ENP was an ideal vehicle for them to demonstrate the 'added-value' of their membership since many in the old member states were asking what the new members could possibly 'contribute'. The ENP and its more refined version, the Eastern Partnership, established in 2009, perfectly coincided with the pragmatic interests of Estonia, Latvia and Lithuania. In fact, development cooperation has often been used by the Baltic States as a tool to implement the ENP (Bruge and Bukovskis 2009, p. 113).

Legislative Framework

All three Baltic States declare in their development cooperation policy documents that they are contributing to development efforts not only to increase global well-being and to reach the internationally agreed MDGs, but also to promote the interests of their own countries. Latvia is the most straightforward in this regard and says that its cooperation aims to integrate Latvia into the European economic and political structures, participate in projects that have a positive direct or indirect impact on Latvian economic development, and present Latvian history and culture, thus expanding the level of information on Latvia globally (Latvian MFA 2003, § 3.3). Such an approach is not usually so explicit nowadays in the Western development community, which is mostly focused on poverty reduction goals. Estonia is the only one of the three countries to outline the unique moral aspect of development cooperation for the newer EU member states; because Estonia has developed rapidly with the support of international donors during the last decade, it perceives it as its moral responsibility to provide similar support for less developed countries (Estonian MFA 2003, § 3.a).

As is clearly stated in the respective legislations in all three countries, the Baltic States designed their development policies based on EU norms. The first governmental decisions in this policy area were taken simultaneously with the first financial allocations to projects. For example, the Estonian parliament established the legal foundations for Estonian development cooperation by adopting the Development Cooperation Principles for 1999–2000, which it later updated in 2003 (Estonian MFA 2003, § 3.a). The latter decision established that the money for development cooperation would be allocated through the MFA budget and required that the quantity of these funds grow in proportion to the country's economic development and international principles.

Three years after the adoption of the principles document, development experts in Estonia criticized the fact that despite having finally joined the EU and NATO and having established the above-mentioned guiding principles for development work, Estonia still did not have an official long-term strategy for development cooperation and that there was a lack of open and constructive debate on the topic (Kuusik 2006, p. 51). However, in May 2006, after long discussions with a number of stakeholders, the government adopted the Development Plan of Estonian Development Cooperation and Humanitarian Aid 2006–10, which named six priority sectors for Estonia's development assistance and identified four priority partner countries for bilateral aid (Estonian MFA 2006). This document has now been updated with a follow-up plan for 2011–15, which makes minor changes to the priority sectors, adds Armenia, Azerbaijan and Belarus (thus including all of the six EU Eastern Partnership countries) to the priority partners' list, and attempts to bring about policy coherence with the Eastern Partnership.

While the other two Baltic States also developed their development policies at a similar pace with Estonia, the Latvian government still did not consider Latvia as a full-fledged aid donor in 2006 because of its 'yet insufficient' level of wealth and envisioned a gradual change towards full-fledged donor status (Kāle 2007, p. 45). It should also be noted that the MFAs are responsible for the implementation of development policy in all three Baltic States. The relevant departments or bureaus have always had to manage with a relatively small number of staff and, therefore, have weak administrative capacities. Furthermore, foreign ministry officials frequently rotate, which means that they have little opportunity to build up in-depth knowledge and competencies in the field.

Financing

The Baltic States, along with the rest of the newer EU member states, have committed to spend 0.33 per cent of their gross national income (GNI) on official development assistance (ODA) by 2015 as the EU Council of Ministers' decision on 25 May 2005 prescribes. The Estonian strategic plan for development cooperation for 2006–10 set out that by 2010, Estonia would spend 0.17 per cent of its GNI on development assistance, but the government reduced this goal during the global economic crises to 0.10 per cent by 2010, still keeping the final goal of 0.33 per cent by 2015. The Estonian plan for 2011–15 is less ambitious and promises to reach the minimum goal of 0.17 per cent by 2015, while aiming for 0.33 per cent as internationally agreed (Estonian MFA 2010). Latvia and Lithuania have not agreed on a year-on-year timetable for reaching the promised 0.33 per cent level, but civil society organizations find it highly unlikely that such an ambitious goal can be met without significant changes in their respective budget policies. In 2010, Estonia and Lithuania dedicated 0.10 per cent of their GNI for development assistance, while Latvia contributed 0.06 per cent of its GNI. Overall, Estonia is the only Baltic State to show a constant rise in ODA over the past few years. The Latvian aid level has decreased because bilateral aid has been practically non-existent since the economic crisis. Lithuania has also cut its aid contributions, but not as severely as Latvia (Lithuania contributed a record 0.11 per cent of its GNI in 2008) (Lithuanian NDGO Platform 2011). Latvia was the European country initially hit hardest by the financial crisis in 2008, with its gross domestic product (GDP) plunging by 18 per cent in 2009. The dramatic impact of the economic crisis can be clearly seen from the

DEVELOPMENT POLICIES OF CENTRAL AND EASTERN EUROPEAN STATES

Table 1. Latvian bilateral aid

Year	Funding in LVL [Latest (6 January 2012): EUR 1 = LVL 0.6977]
2007	450,000
2008	600,000
2009	9,000
2010	807
2011	269

figures for the amount of money dedicated to bilateral aid by the Latvian government over the past five years (Latvian MFA 2011b)[1:]

The Baltic States' economies are small compared to their European counterparts and it is, therefore, crucial that each euro be spent effectively and towards the achievement of set goals. While aid effectiveness has been at the heart of global development policy debates for nearly two decades, it has not gained real momentum in the Baltic States. The discussions on this topic are held on the technocratic level, but few concrete policy measures have been taken in this regard. The pan-European report, AidWatch, on EU member states' aid performance explains that the EU-12 countries generally lack experience in development assistance, aid levels are low and an even smaller part is made up of bilateral assistance, making the aid effectiveness question seem of little importance (CONCORD 2010, p. 14).

Looking at the cost distribution in more detail, we see that out of all the money spent on ODA, nearly a fifth is used for humanitarian aid (€2.3 million in 2009) and the rest for bi- and multilateral development initiatives. In the Baltic case, humanitarian aid is an even smaller fraction than the EU-12 average. Multilateral aid constitutes 75 per cent of Estonia's development spending, amounting to almost €11 million in 2010. By far, the largest channel for Estonian aid money is the European Commission, which received 55 per cent of all ODA and 73 per cent of all multilateral assistance in 2010. Multilateral aid constitutes more than 90 per cent of Latvia's development spending, amounting to almost €10.5 million in 2010, and 80 per cent of Lithuania's, amounting to €23 million in 2009 (Lithuanian NDGO Platform 2011, p. 17). Similar trends appear in all the newer EU member states (OECD 2009, p. 31) that have become aid donors only recently and have limited experience, resources and contacts for increasing their share of bilateral activities. The older EU member states spend a considerably smaller portion of their development assistance multilaterally, and among OECD-Development Assistance Committee (DAC) members, it constitutes approximately a third of all aid spending (OECD 2009, p. 31). Even though the reliance on multilateral partners can be justified by the requirement to coordinate development activities more effectively among the numerous donors, there still remains a need for the Baltic States to evaluate the effectiveness of the current balance of bilateral and multilateral aid spending.

In terms of the transparency of aid financing, Estonia, in particular, has made exemplary progress compared not only to its neighbouring countries, but also to other European donors. The online database of all aid allocations makes it considerably more pro-active in information sharing than many other European countries (CONCORD 2010, p. 16). The government has also improved the national legislation on how bilateral aid grants are given. Furthermore, a new governmental regulation on the conditions and procedures for the provision of development assistance and humanitarian aid (Estonian Government 2010) was adopted in January 2010 under the leadership of the MFA and after consulting with various stakeholders, including civil society actors. The regulation clarifies the concrete ways in which grants can be awarded and evaluated, simplifies the development cooperation process and makes it more unequivocal to the applicants. Until the adoption of the regulation, the involvement of non-state actors in the implementation of development cooperation was relatively limited because the grant application procedures were perceived to be ambiguous and based on ad hoc decisions in the MFA. The first impressions of the new system indicate that more diverse actors are now interested in working in the development cooperation sector. The other two Baltic States have not yet adopted such legislations.

On the negative side, the transparency of the Baltic States' development cooperation is still limited by the lack of bilateral partnership agreements and national strategies on multilateral assistance. None of the Baltic States have signed bilateral agreements with priority partners; these are critical in sending a clear message to their partners about the substantive and financial support they can expect from the donor and would outline the roles and responsibilities of all the related actors. However, Estonia and Lithuania, with the support of the European Commission, are creating a positive precedent by currently working on signing such agreements with Georgia. Latvia will not make such plans until it restores its bilateral aid programmes. Additionally, none of the Baltic States have adopted multilateral aid strategies to explain how the multilateral partners are selected and financed. Evidence from donors with such strategies shows that it would enhance the (inter)national aid coordination efforts, simplify the planning of development cooperation policy and, most importantly, improve aid effectiveness in the long run (OECD 2009, p. 14).

Former World Bank official Hilmar Þór Hilmarsson (2011) argues that the Baltic States should follow the Nordic states and switch from their small projects based approach in bilateral assistance to budget support and policy dialogue with the recipient countries, through which, he believes, they can maximize their impact. While that approach might indeed bring the Baltic States in line with the general trend among international donors, it undervalues the significance of new donor countries being able to show their flags and thereby build up public support for development cooperation expenditure. Furthermore, bilateral assistance enables the state and NGOs to build up their experience and competence. This is vital for helping the young, small Baltic NGOs to qualify for participation in larger EU funded projects.[2]

In order to reach the promised levels of aid quantity and improve the quality of aid, all ministries in the Baltic States have to increase their development activities, which is likely to be the greatest challenge in the process. The low involvement of many state institutions in development activities has been a problem throughout the years and this can only be changed by making the strong political decision that development cooperation should be a relevant horizontal topic in Estonian, Latvian and Lithuanian foreign policy, and not limited to foreign policy.

An issue actively discussed by civil society organizations in the Baltic States has been the unwillingness of the Baltic States to allocate a significantly larger part of their ODA to the least developed regions, primarily Sub-Saharan Africa. For example, Estonia spent merely 1 per cent of its bilateral aid on African countries in

DEVELOPMENT POLICIES OF CENTRAL AND EASTERN EUROPEAN STATES

2009. The MFAs have responded to this criticism by pointing out that the Baltic States favour supporting the poorest countries in Africa through multilateral means as hardly any expertise or experience exists in cooperation with African countries to offer meaningful added value to their development through bilateral means. None of the Baltic countries has an embassy in Sub-Saharan Africa. However, the situation is different for the non-state actors, who have increasingly more connections with the region. A number of civil society organizations have reliable partnerships with organizations from the global South and there is a considerable number of entrepreneurial people with personal experience of living and working in the region, who feel that their governments should support their efforts to build links between the Baltic States and the least developed countries. The debates are ongoing and with no concrete outcome yet, but they centre around the question of how to reach the best development results and include more diverse development actors while staying focused on both the strategic and policy implementation levels.

Priority Sectors and Partner Countries

The governments of the Baltic States declare that the priority sectors for development cooperation have been selected based on where they have a comparative advantage. All three countries see promotion of democracy, human rights and various aspects of good governance as one of their best transition experiences to share through development cooperation. Furthermore, they focus on economic reforms, environment protection, social reforms (health and social care) and education. In addition, Estonia's development work deals with improving aid effectiveness and transparency, while Lithuania cooperates on the topics of euro-integration processes and cultural heritage preservation (AidWatch 2011). Latvia does not identify the specific areas in which it has a comparative advantage and simply states that it will work in the areas where the EU as a whole has identified its greatest potential added value for developing countries (Latvian MFA 2011a, pp. 13–14). All three Baltic States also see gender equality as a horizontal value and support women and they also inform their own public about global development issues through global education.

The Baltic States' distinctive priorities become more evident when one looks at their priority partner countries. Bilateral aid is a much smaller, yet much more politicized and visible part of the Baltic States' development cooperation. All three countries have identified Afghanistan, Belarus (Estonia since 2011), Georgia, Moldova and Ukraine as the primary partners for their bilateral development cooperation. In addition, Lithuania has been working with Azerbaijan and, since 2011, Estonia is establishing development-related contacts both with Azerbaijan and its neighbour, Armenia. Estonia explains that its priority partners have been selected on the basis of which countries can get the most added value from Estonia's experiences and which are ready to move towards a democratic society built on human rights (Estonian MFA 2010, p. 4). Latvia's priority partners had long been the Commonwealth of Independent States (CIS) and the Balkan countries, but the new development policy guidelines for 2011–15 bring to the fore the EU's Eastern Partnership countries, Central Asia, and the countries where the Latvian government sends military contingents or civilian experts (Latvian MFA 2011a, p. 13). Both Estonia and Latvia argue that focusing on ENP

DEVELOPMENT POLICIES OF CENTRAL AND EASTERN EUROPEAN STATES

countries increases the coherence between the different policies. Analyses of the distribution of Estonian aid among recipients over the past three years demonstrate that the aid is often more influenced by politics than the policy documents. For example, after the 2008 war between Russia and Georgia, the Baltic States significantly increased their development assistance to Georgia and gave a notable amount of humanitarian aid (Andrespok 2010, p. 106).

The Lithuanian diplomat, Bernotas, who participated in the writing of the Lithuanian development cooperation policy guidelines, explained that partner countries are selected based on historical experiences and a history of long and close relations with those countries, as 'it is Lithuania that knows best the mentality, language and main problems of former Soviet republics' (Bernotas 2006). This partly explains why Lithuania has paid more attention than Estonia or Latvia to Belarus and Ukraine: it is not just because of their closer proximity, but, perhaps, also due to their historical roots in the Polish-Lithuanian Commonwealth.

The Estonian parliament has decided that the country will direct its development cooperation to regions that are starting or undergoing reforms similar to what it had itself implemented (Estonian MFA 2003). This political discourse is common to all three Baltic States since establishing development work. The underlying assumption is that the other former Soviet republics were at the same starting point as the Baltic States in 1991, but whereas the Baltic States were successful in their transition to a free market and democracy in the 1990s, the other have been less fortunate in various ways. Thus, it is felt to be the moral duty of the Baltic States to help those countries with which they previously shared a common fate or system. Furthermore, the Baltic States were successful in their integration into Euro-Atlantic organizations and they now want to help these countries along the same path. Similarly to its neighbours, Estonia always stressed the importance of sharing its transition experience with other countries, but also outlined the moral obligation and 'an opportunity to pay back the assistance that [Estonia] once received' (Ilves 1999).

The Baltic States found a niche for themselves where they could claim to have a unique expertise. This is probably the only case in which having been part of the former Soviet Union has been turned into an advantage! And indeed Baltic experts appear to be particularly welcomed in countries such as Georgia and Moldova. Georgia is the country that has most clearly sought to emulate the Baltic States in their rapid transition and Euro-Atlantic integration and Moldova shared the fate of the Baltic States as a victim of the 1939 Nazi-Soviet pact.

In addition to EU development cooperation, bilateral assistance was also often related to NATO and its Partnership for Peace (PfP) programme. In the same manner as the Baltic States sought to demonstrate their value to the EU, they tried to show to the NATO allies that they were no longer 'consumers' of security, but 'producers' of security with their contributions to various democratization and integration projects in the former Soviet Union, especially Georgia, the most eager reformer and keenest to follow the Baltic model (Kasekamp and Pääbo 2006).

Finally, however, there is the Russia factor since almost all the priority countries are neighbours of Russia. These are claimed by Russia, in the words of President Medvedev, as its 'privileged sphere of interest'. An underlining, but not officially articulated, assumption of development cooperation with these neighbourhood countries is that it is a means of reducing Russian influence over them and helping

DEVELOPMENT POLICIES OF CENTRAL AND EASTERN EUROPEAN STATES

them to consolidate their sovereignty (Galbreath *et al.* 2008, p. 130). Thus, we see once again how national security considerations are intertwined with development cooperation goals.

Political Discourse and Public Attitudes

All three Baltic States see development cooperation as a tool of foreign policy and 'all decisions are taken under consideration of political goals and results' (Bernotas 2006). The Estonian government's action plan for 2011–15 even states that development cooperation is a tool for security policy (Estonian Government 2011). The security context is particularly relevant in terms of Afghanistan for all three countries. While Estonia and Lithuania are still trying to explain their partnership with Afghanistan specifically as an attempt to conduct development cooperation with the least developed countries, Latvia is the only one to clearly state in its development policy that Afghanistan is a priority partner because of its military's presence there. Nevertheless, it is obvious that all three countries are cooperating with Afghanistan primarily out of their own security interests. The Baltic governments are strongly committed to maintaining their troops in Afghanistan since the mission has been defined as the greatest priority for the NATO Alliance. As NATO is the main security guarantor of the Baltic States, they have a vital national interest in the NATO mission succeeding and in ensuring that NATO's credibility is not damaged by failure in Afghanistan.

In Estonia, spending on development action in Afghanistan increased in 2009 when both the Estonians and the international community at large started expressing stronger discontent with the military actions there (Andrespok 2010, p. 106). While a majority of the Estonians have always supported participation in international military missions, public support for the Afghanistan mission has always been weak. Estonian public support for the mission in Afghanistan in the latest opinion poll in September 2010 was 39 per cent, while the percentage of people opposing the mission was 54 per cent (Estonian MoD 2010). The criticism forced the government to increasingly stress the importance of civilian cooperation with Afghanistan and to put more effort into development actions aimed at poverty reduction and other humanitarian causes such as access to health care and education, which is in line with the trend in other European countries. Lithuania has been the most ambitious Baltic nation in Afghanistan, leading a Provincial Reconstruction Team in Ghor province. This has required Lithuanian military and civilian experts to work together and necessitated raising their cultural awareness, which has proven to be quite challenging for a small country with little experience (Racius 2007).

Public support for and awareness of development cooperation in the new member states of the EU in general, and the Baltic states in particular, has been significantly lower than in the old member states, but has been converging. According to the latest Eurobarometer conducted in 2010, 89 per cent of Lithuanians, 86 per cent of Latvians and 84 per cent of Estonians considered it important to help developing countries; this is close to the EU-27 average of 89 per cent (European Commission 2010). The main difference with the old EU member states (the EU-15) is in the intensity of support: Only 38 per cent of Lithuanians, 33 per cent of Latvians and 32 per cent of Estonians considered it 'very important' to help developing countries, compared to 47 per cent of those in the old member states. Nevertheless, despite the ongoing financial crisis, the support figures in all three Baltic countries had increased considerably compared with the 2009 opinion survey.

There does appear to be a notable difference between the three countries on levels of support for EU member states working together on helping developing countries. Lithuania has the most go-it-alone attitude within the EU, with only 54 per cent in favour, which is also in marked contrast with Latvia (78 per cent in favour) and Estonia (84 per cent) (European Commission 2010). Estonians, Latvians and Lithuanians are among the least individually involved in the entire EU in giving assistance to developing countries. Unsurprisingly, Latvians, in the midst of the deepest economic crisis, are clearly the least active Europeans on an individual level. Also expectedly, a greater percentage of people in Latvia than in any other EU member state favour reducing aid to developing countries because they can no longer afford it. The fact that the current (since 2009) European Commissioner for Development, Andris Piebalgs, is Latvian has apparently not made much of an impact in helping to raise the profile of the subject in Latvia.

The primacy of foreign policy in shaping bilateral assistance is also evident when examining the results of public opinion surveys. The general public overwhelmingly views Africa as the most deserving recipient of development aid. However, opinion leaders tend to have quite a different perspective – they clearly prioritize countries of the former Soviet Union, rather than African nations, as being the countries which the Baltic States should help most (TNS Emor 2008, p. 7). Here the influence of the national foreign policy agenda is once again revealed.

The Role of Civil Society

It has been a common practice in European democracies to include civil society in the policy making and implementing process. This has been the case in the development cooperation sector, too. All three Baltic States mention the importance of the involvement of civil society in development cooperation in one way or another. It is noteworthy that there were practically no non-governmental development organizations (NGDOs) in the Baltic States when the governments initiated their development cooperation policies, while in countries with longer traditions in this field, NGDOs have played a significant role both in policy making and implementation (Kāle 2007, p. 44). However, soon after the establishment of the national development cooperation policies, civil society groups emerged that were interested in and eager to participate in the implementation of development work. Based on the European example, national platforms of development NGOs were created (Berzina 2006, p. 219). Latvia was the first of the Baltic States where such an official network, called the Latvian NGDO Platform, was formed in 2004. The new organization immediately started participating in the European NGO Confederation for Relief and Development (CONCORD) and its working groups as well as planning various projects. The first projects were implemented in 2006. From the beginning, there was cooperation with the MFA and several donors (including the United Nations Development Programme [UNDP] and the Soros Foundation) (Berzina 2006, Skujda 2005). The platform, now called the Latvian Platform for Development Cooperation (LAPAS), has 29 member organizations.

The Estonian development NGO roundtable first met in 2002 to present the consolidated opinion of civil society organizations about the development cooperation principles document being prepared by the MFA. This was an informal network of interested individuals and organizations, which continued implementing activities under the Open Estonia Foundation and, later, the European Movement Estonia until 2007, when an independent legal entity was established as a result of a successful EU-funded Estonian-Finnish-Swedish capacity building project, FEST (Finland, Estonia, Sweden Together for Development). After overcoming the self-defining difficulties of any new organization, the Estonian Roundtable for Development Cooperation (AKÜ), which currently has 21 member organizations, has been involved in the making of development policy in Estonia, provided capacity building services for Estonian NGOs and worked actively on raising the awareness of the general public about global development challenges. AKÜ has a strong working relationship with the MFA.

Lithuanian NGOs, similarly to their Latvian counterparts, decided to create an independent platform in 2004, but the idea was not realized until 2008. The first push for creating such an organization came from the Canadian programme, Official Development Assistance in Central Europe, and the TRIALOG project in association with CONCORD, the European NGO Confederation for Relief and Development, which aims to strengthen civil society and raise awareness of development issues in the enlarged EU (Norvila 2005). The organization's priorities were to create a system for proper information exchange between its members, to offer capacity building training and to represent the interests of the Lithuanian development NGOs at the national and EU level (Norvila 2005). However, the registration of the organization took nearly four years because, due to various internal reasons, a competing platform was created in 2005. The parallel organizations in Kaunas and Vilnius have created a fair amount of confusion and frustration among the stakeholders as well as hindered the organizational development of both platforms financially and in terms of credibility. Recently, there have been talks about joining the two organizations in some form, but concrete steps have not yet been taken in that direction.

For the NGO platforms of all three Baltic States, the common challenges most often identified by member organizations are the need for further capacity building of fundraising and advocacy skills. Currently, most of the platforms' members are more active in global education activities [3] than in actual development cooperation projects because of limited experience, partnerships and difficulties in finding funding. However, an increasing number of NGOs, many of whom are as yet non-members of the platforms, are starting work in developing countries both in the EU's Eastern neighbourhood as well as in Africa and Latin America. The new projects mainly emerge from personal contacts of NGO members who have travelled overseas and contacts from international networks.

The platforms' relationships with the government sector vary quite a bit in the three Baltic States, but are improving in all of them. In the broader sense, the platforms share a common belief that global education and raising the awareness of the general public are prerequisites for society-wide debates on global development issues and that is why a majority of the member organizations are focused on this goal. The three platforms have recently started their first joint awareness raising project, which will last until December 2012 and has led to several pan-Baltic events, but no other cooperation projects. The above-mentioned different financial situations in the Baltic States might affect the NGO cooperation, too. Funding from the private sector is marginal in all three countries.

Conclusion

In the roughly dozen years that Estonia, Latvia and Lithuania have been donor countries, they have made significant strides towards convergence with the mainstream of the EU. Having been part of the Soviet Union and not sovereign countries, their starting point was even further behind that of the other new donors of Central and Eastern Europe who are now in the EU. The levels of development assistance, however, suffered a setback in recent years, particularly in Latvia, because of the impact of the financial crisis. There are some differences in nuances between Estonian, Latvian, and Lithuanian development cooperation policies, but, on the whole, these are very minor compared to the overwhelming similarities. If one compares and evaluates the progress of the three countries, it appears that Estonia has a slight lead because of its advances in legislative framework, transparency and financing. One explanatory factor is the fact that Estonia's GDP per capita is greater than that of Latvia or Lithuania and that Estonia has generally moved quicker and been more successful in its post-communist transition (Norkus 2011, p. 22–30). There are a few differences between the priority sectors emphasized and the time that it has taken one or the other of the three to draft relevant documents, but since they have all begun their development cooperation at the same time and from the same starting point, with EU conditionality being the primary factor motivating or influencing their decisions, unsurprisingly, they are nearly identical in their profiles. All three contribute 75–90 per cent of their ODA through multilateral organizations, first and foremost, the EU. Thus, it is their bilateral assistance that reveals their preferences most clearly. They have all chosen the same priority countries in the former Soviet Union plus Afghanistan. Though their official discourse on development cooperation adheres to the EU mainstream, here it is evident that it is not the fulfilment of the MDGs that is the primary concern of the Baltic States, but rather, that it is their geopolitical interests and foreign policy that determine their development cooperation priorities.

Notes

[1] The authors thank Karlis Bukovskis for his assistance.
[2] The authors thank Toms Rostoks for this observation.
[3] For pioneering work on global education in the Baltic States, see Helin, J., 2009. Development education in school curricula in Europe: Global challenge for schools in Estonia. *Citizenship, social and economics education*, 8 (2 & 3), 128–143.

References

AidWatch, 2011. Lithuania [online]. Available from: http://aidwatch.concordeurope.org/static/files/assets/72dac546/Lithuania.pdf [Accessed 13 April 2011].

Andrespok, E., 2008. Estonians as Europeans: A constructivist analysis of Estonia's development cooperation. Unpublished thesis (Bachelor's). Towson University, USA. Available from: http://www.terveilm.net/uploads/files/thesis_Andrespok.pdf [Accessed 1 November 2011].

DEVELOPMENT POLICIES OF CENTRAL AND EASTERN EUROPEAN STATES

Andrespok, E., 2010. Estonia's development cooperation from a civil society perspective. *In:* A. Kasekamp, ed. *Estonian foreign policy yearbook 2010.* Tallinn: Estonian Foreign Policy Institute, 101–122.

Bernotas, R., 2006. Priorities for Lithuania's development cooperation policy. Paper presented at the EuroNGOs conference, Vilnius, Lithuania, 8–9 June 2006. Available from: www.eurongos.org/Files/Filer/EuroNGOs/bernotas-kalba06eurongo.pdf [Accessed 5 September 2011].

Berzina, G., 2006. Learning to give as well as receive. *In: Social watch report 2006: Impossible architecture.* Montevideo: Instituto del Terver Mundo. Available from: http://www.socialwatch.org/sites/default/files/SW-ENG-2006.pdf [Accessed 5 September 2011].

Bruge, I., and Bukovskis, K., 2009. The EU and the Eastern neighbours. Relations with Russia and implications for the ENP: The case of the Baltic States. *In:* G. Fóti and Z. Ludvig, eds. *EU-Russian relations and the Eastern Partnership. Central-East European member-state interests and positions.* Budapest: Institute for World Economics of the Hungarian Academy of Sciences, 86–131.

CONCORD, 2010. AidWatch. Penalty against poverty: More and better EU aid can score Millennium Development Goals. Available from: http://www.concordeurope.org/Files/media/0_internetdocuments ENG/4_Publications/3_CONCORDs_positions_and_studies/Positions2010/CONCORD_report_light.zip [Accessed 13 April 2011].

Ehin, P., 2011. Estonia's integration with the EU: Excelling at self-exertion. *In:* Simon Bulmer and Christian Lequesne, eds. *The member states of the European Union .* Oxford: Oxford University Press, forthcoming.

Estonian Government, 2010. Conditions and procedures for the provision of development assistance and humanitarian aid. Available from: http://www.vm.ee/sites/default/files/Abi_andmise_kord.pdf [Accessed 1 November 2011].

Estonian Government, 2011. Vabariigi valitsuse tegevusprogramm 2011–15. Available from: www.valitsus.ee/et/valitsus/tegevusprogramm [Accessed 1 November 2011].

Estonian Ministry of Defence, 2010. Public opinion and national defence: September 2010. Available from: http://www.kmin.ee/files/kmin/nodes/10645_Avalik_arvamus_ja_riigikaitse_2010_september.pdf [Accessed 26 July 2011].

Estonian Ministry of Foreign Affairs, 1999. Estonia's humanitarian aid and development cooperation projects in 1998. Available from: http://www.vm.ee/est/kat_425/3220.html [Accessed 2 May 2011].

Estonian Ministry of Foreign Affairs, 2003. Principles of Estonian development co-operation. Available from: http://www.vm.ee/?q=en/node/8323 [Accessed 2 May 2011].

Estonian Ministry of Foreign Affairs, 2006. Development plan of Estonian development cooperation and humanitarian aid 2006–10. Available from: http://web-static.vm.ee/static/failid/344/Development_plan_2006-2010.pdf [Accessed 1 November 2011].

Estonian Ministry of Foreign Affairs, 2010. Strategy for Estonian development cooperation and humanitarian aid 2011–15. Available from: http://www.vm.ee/sites/default/files/Arengukava2011-2015_ENG.pdf [Accessed 1 November 2011].

European Commission, 2010, Sept. Europeans, development aid and the Millennium Development Goals. *Special Eurobarometer*, 352. Available from: http://ec.europa.eu/public_opinion/archives/ebs/ebs_352_en.pdf [Accessed 1 November 2011].

Galbreath, D.J., Lasas, A., and Lamoreaux, J.W. 2008. *Continuity and change in the Baltic Sea region: Comparing foreign policies.* Amsterdam: Rodopi.

Hilmarsson, H., 2011, June. The Baltic States and their transition from being recipient countries to becoming donor countries. Paper presented at the 9th Baltic studies conference in Europe, Södertörn University, Stockholm, 12–15 June 2011.

Ilves, T.H., 1999. Estonia's main foreign policy priorities. Address by Toomas Hendrik Ilves, Minister of Foreign Affairs, on behalf of the Government of the Republic of Estonia to the Riigikogu, 25 November 1999. Available from: http://www.vm.ee/?q =en/node/3491 [Accessed 25 October 2011].

Kāle, M., 2007. *The European Union and development aid: A case study of the Republic of Latvia.* Unpublished thesis (Master's). Albert-Ludwigs-Universität Freiburg, Germany. Available from: http://www.politika.lv/temas/fwd_eiropa/14384/ [Accessed 25 October 2011].

Kasekamp, A., 2010. *A history of the Baltic States.* Basingstoke: Palgrave Macmillan.

Kasekamp, A., and Pääbo, H., eds., 2006. *Promoting democratic values in the enlarging Europe: The changing role of the Baltic States from importers to exporters.* Tartu, Estonia: Tartu University Press.

Kuusik, R., 2006. Estonia's development cooperation: Power, prestige and practice of a new donor. *In:* A. Kasekamp, ed. *Estonian foreign policy yearbook 2006.* Tallinn, Estonia: Estonian Foreign Policy Institute, 51–68.

DEVELOPMENT POLICIES OF CENTRAL AND EASTERN EUROPEAN STATES

Latvian Ministry of Foreign Affairs, 2003. The basic principles for the development cooperation policy of the Republic of Latvia. Available from: http://www.mfa.gov.lv/en/DevelopmentCo-operation/Basic-Documents/BasicPrinciples/ [Accessed 5 April 2011].

Latvian Ministry of Foreign Affairs, 2011a. Attīstības sadarbības politikas pamatnostādnes 2011–2015. gadam. Available from: http://www.mfa.gov.lv/data/file/AttistibasSadarbiba/asppamtnostadnes.pdf [Accessed 1 November 2011].

Latvian Ministry of Foreign Affairs, 2011b. Latvijas sniegtās palīdzības apjoms. Available at http://www.am.gov.lv/lv/Attistibas-sadarbiba/palidziba [Accessed 1 November 2011].

Lithuanian NGDO Platform, 2011. Development cooperation. The commitment of Lithuania and the world. Available from: http://www.pagalba.org/userfiles/file/Brosiura%20vyst%20bendradarb-EN.pdf [Accessed 1 November 2011].

Norkus, Z., 2011. Estonian, Latvian and Lithuanian post-communist development in the comparative perspective. *In: Estonian human development report 2010/2011: Baltic way(s) of human development: Twenty years on.* Tallinn, Estonia: Eesti Koostöö Kogu, 22–30.

Norvila, J., 2005. Lithuanian NDGO platform working towards increased development awareness and international partnership. *In: Trialog 4.* Available from: http://www.trialog.or.at/images/doku/trialog_news_2005.pdf [Accessed 26 July 2011].

OECD, 2009. 2008 DAC report on multilateral aid. Available from: http://www.oecd.org/dataoecd/59/11/42901553.pdf [Accessed 25 October 2011].

Paet, U., 2005. Main guidelines of Estonia's foreign policy. Address by Urmas Paet, Minister of Foreign Affairs of the Republic of Estonia to the Riigikogu on behalf of the Government of Estonia. Available from: http://www.vm.ee/?q=en/node/3655 [Accessed 6 April 2011].

Racius, E., 2007. The 'cultural awareness' factor in the activities of the Lithuanian PRT in Afghanistan. *Baltic security and defence review,* 9/2007, 57–78.

Skujda, I., 2005. The Latvian NDGO platform got started and develops its profile in Europe. *In: Trialog 4.* Available from: http://www.trialog.or.at/images/doku/trialog_news_2005.pdf [Accessed 23 October 2011].

TNS Emor, 2008. Avalik arvamus arengukoostööst. Available from: http://web-static.vm.ee/static/failid/444/Arengukoostoo_avalik_arvamus_2008.ppt [Accessed 26 July 2011].

TRIALOG, 2008. Development cooperation in Latvia. Country study. Available from: http://www.trialog.or.at/images/doku/lv_countrystudy_final_jan2008.pdf [Accessed 26 July 2011].

Index

Page numbers in **Bold** represent illustrations.

accession 77, 84
Accra Agenda for Action 20, 55
acquis communautaire 2, 22
Adanja, Marija 67
Afghanistan 12, 38, 42, 102, 113, 123; Czech
  Republic 106–7; Hungary 59; NATO 125
Africa: aid donors 33; pull factors 35; V4 aid
  policies-reality 38–41; V4 aid policies-
  rhetoric 35–8
Africa Day (2007) Budapest 37
African, Caribbean and Pacific (ACP)
  countries 61
aid: analysis of domestic and international
  factors on targets 7–9; conditionality 33;
  definition 68; evolution of quantity in CEE
  countries (2001–10) 5; fatigue 6;
  fragmentation 107; gap (2010) 6; political
  parties 7
aid component results: OECD DAC **112**
aid financing: transparency 121
aid market: new players 66–7
aid quantity: selectivity 105; tying 105
AidWatch 5, 6, 62, 121
AidWatch Report 88
Albania 67
Andrespok, Evelin 12
Angola 38, 40, 41, 102
apartheid: South Africa 39
Arab Spring 18
Armenia 12
Austria 106
Azerbaijan 120, 123

Baltic States: bilateral aid 123
Baltic States and development cooperation:
  conclusion 128; financing 120–3; historical
  background 118–19; introduction 117;
  legislative framework 119–20; political
  discourse and public attitudes 125–6;
  priority sectors and partner countries 123–
  5; role of civil society 126–8
Barcelona II: commitments 103;
  recommendations 113

Barnett, Thomas 73
Barthes, Roland 27
Belarus 24, 41, 120, 123
Bernotas, Rokas 118, 124
bilateral aid **104**; Baltic States 123
Bosnia and Herzegovina 102
Brazil 34; aid 46
Bretton Woods institutions 22
Bučar, Maja 11
Bulgaria 3, 5, 74, 104
Burkina Faso 91

Cambodia 102
Canada 127
Canadian International Development Agency
  (CIDA) 3
capacity building: programmes 74; training
  127
Ceaușescu, Nicolae 70, 71
Central and Eastern European states (CEE):
  development policies post-accession 4–7;
  donors 2–4; ODA/GNI levels 53
Centre for Experience Transfer in Integration
  and Reform (CETIR) 27
Centre for Global Development 105;
  Commitment to Development Index (CDI)
  104
Centre for Information Service, Cooperation
  and Development of NGOs (CNVOS) 8
Changing the North 92
charitable giving: public policies *111*
China 23, 33, 107; Africa 43, 44; aid 46
CIVICUS (World Alliance for Citizen
  Participation) 93
Civil Society: participation in development
  cooperation 86–7
civil society organizations 95
climate change 57
coalition building 95
colonialism 43
Commitment to Development Index (CDI):
  Centre for Global Development 104; Czech
  Republic ODA 105; discussion of results

INDEX

111–13; methodology of aid component 104–5; quality-adjusted aid 105–10; quality-adjusted private charity induced by public policy 110–11
Commonwealth of Independent States 123
communism 58
comparative advantage 44–5
CONCORD 92, 126, 127
CONCORD AidWatch Project 88
conditionality 117; Europeanization 54
Congo 107
Copenhagen Criteria 118
Council for Mutual Economic Assistance (CMEA) 3
Croatia 4
Cuba 24, 67
Cyprus 68
Czech Development Agency 8, 25, 26, 36
Czech NGOs: Department of Human Rights and Transition Policy (2004) 24
Czech Republic 3, 5, 69; Africa 39; DAC Peer Review 102, 106; Department for Development Cooperation and Humanitarians Aid 24; foreign development 74; priority countries 38; Serbian project 25–6; tax 110; transition experience 23–6, *see also* Visegrad
Czech Republic ODA: commitment to development index 105; comparison of ODA/GDI and DAC **103**; conclusion 113; evolution of development assistance 101–3; financial commitments 103–4; introduction 100–1; partner countries (2009) **108**; priority countries 102; priority countries (2010–17) *102*; share received by LDCs **108**; top 15 recipients **109**
Czech Trust Fund 19, 25
Czechoslovakia 68

debt cancellation 106
debt relief 33
democracy 2; promotion 123
democratization 27
Development Assistance Committee (DAC): Organisation for Economic Cooperation and Development (OECD) *see* OECD DAC
Development Cooperation: Poland 9; Principles 119; Resolution 92
Development Days: Slovenia 92
development education 92–3
development ideology: OECD-DAC 79
development knowledge: transferring 73–6
development policies: Central and Eastern European states (CEE) 4–7
domestic dynamics: international development policy 59

donors: Central and Eastern European states (CEE) 2–4; old and new 67–70

Eastern Partnership 13, 119, 120
economic crisis 120
Egypt 27
emergency aid 106
environmental assessment 25
Estonia 3, 4, 74, 127; Development Cooperation Principles 119; Development Plan of Estonian Development Cooperation and Humanitarian Aid 120; financing plan (2011–15) 120; multilateral development 121; Paet 118, *see also* Baltic States
Estonia Roundtable for Development Cooperation 127
Ethiopia 38, 39, 40, 53, 102, 106
EU Presidency: Slovenia 88
EU-Africa Strategy 35
Euro crisis 4, 13
Euro-Atlantic integration 124
Eurobarometer 7; Baltic States 125
European Consensus on Development 35, 55; (Article 33) 20, 22
European Consensus values, principles and objectives 77, 78
European Development Fund (EDF) 42, 55, 61, 78
European Movement Estonia 127
European Neighbourhood Policy 12, 13; conditionality 22
European Neighbourhood Policy (ENP) 119
European NGO Confederation for Relief and Development: CONCORD 126
European Social Fund 89
European Transition Compendium 18, 20, 22, 24, 28
Europeanization 11, 54, 78; conditionality 54; socialization 54

FEST (Finland, Estonia, Sweden Together for Development) 127
Finland 127

Gabon 73
Gafton, Paul 73
Gemesi, Ferenc 37
Georgia 41, 102, 122, 123
Ghana 106; Poland 37
Global Call against Poverty 91
global development 63
Göncz, Kinga 37
governance 25, 123
Greece 4, 6, 7, 106
Grimm, S. 4

INDEX

Hallet, M. 8
HAND 62
Harmer, A. 4
Hilmarsson, H.P. 122
HIV/AIDS 25, 37, 77
Horja, Gavril 68
Horký, O. 9–10
human rights 27, 57, 123; Estonia 123
humanitarian aid 90
humanitarian assistance 75
Hungarian Agency for Development Cooperation 70
Hungarian EU Presidency project 27
Hungarian Heart Foundation 37
Hungary 3, 5; Afghanistan 59; NGOs 62; priority countries 40; regional allocation of bilateral aid (2010) 58; Soviet Union 52; three pillars 57, 58, 59, see also Visegrad
Hungary's international development policy: conclusions 62–3; development stakeholders 59–62; EU membership 54–6; foreign policy strategy and development 56–9; history and present challenges 52–4; introduction 50–2

India 33; aid 46
industrial cooperation 72
Institute of International Relations 69
institutional learning 70
Instytut Globalnej Odpowiedzialnosci (IGO) 40
International Development Cooperation: NGDOS 89–91; Slovenia 85, 87
International Monetary Fund 7
Iraq 5, 53, 102, 106
Irish NGDOs 95
Italy 7

Japan 111, 113

Kasekamp, A. 12
Kenya 39
Kiss, J. 40, 52
Klaus, Vaclav 36
Kopinski, D. 10
Korea 106
Kosovo 102
Kosovo war 58
Kragelund, P. 2, 4
Krylová, Petra 12
Kukan, Eduard 9

Lancaster, C. 59, 60
Latvia 3, 74; bilateral aid 120; budget policy 120; insufficient wealth 120; multilateral development 121, see also Baltic States
Latvian NGDO Platform 126

Latvian Platform for Development Cooperation (LAPAS) 126
least developed countries (LDCs) 35, 36, 106, 109; share of ODA **108**
Libya 27
Linden, Ronald 73
Lisbon Summit (2007) 39
Lithuania 3; Afghanistan 125; budget policy 120, see also Baltic States
local aid champions 61

Maastricht: Treaty of 55
Malta 5, 68
Mănescu, Nicolae 71
Manning, R. 4
market economy 2
Mbouy-Boutzit, Edouard-Alexis 73
Medvedev, D. 124
Meislová, A. 7
military aid 52
Millennium Declaration (2000) 36
Millennium Development Goal 3 (MDG3) 92
Millennium Development Goals (MDGs) 22, 35, 36, 41, 57; Baltic States 118; Romania 77
modernization 22
Moldova 6, 40, 102, 123
Mongolia 102, 106
Montenegro 37
Mozambique 39
Mugabe, Robert 39
multilateral aid **104**
multilateral cooperation 104
multilateral development 121
Myanmar 24

NATO: Afghanistan 125
Nazi-Soviet pact 124
New Member States (NMS): donors 67–70
Non-governmental development organizations (NGDOs) 7–8, 83–5; assessment of impact of involvement in development cooperation and good practice 93–6; Baltic States 126; implementers of International Development Cooperation 89–91; projects proposed 89–90; roles of 84; selected projects 95; specific calls for 89–90
North Atlantic Treaty Organization (NATO) 56, 100
Norway 102; Africa 43

Obama, Barack 17
OECD DAC 2, 22, 101, 104, 110; aid component results **112**; aid definition 68; development ideology 79; peer review 4

INDEX

Official Development Assistance (ODA) 2; 2010 budgets 6; aid levels and GNI 5, *53*, 120
Open Estonia Foundation 127
Oprea, Mirela 11
Opršal, Z. 12
Orbie, J. 13
Organisation for Economic Cooperation and Development (OECD): Development Assistance Committee (DAC) *see* OECD DAC

Paet, Urmas: Estonia 118
Palestinian authority 58, 102
Paragi, B. 40, 52
Paris Declaration 44, 55
Paris Declaration (2005) 4
Partnership for Peace 124
Pearson Commission 103
People in Need 25
Piebalgs, Andris 92, 126
Poland 3, 4, 5, 8, 112; Africa 35; African embassies 44; Development Cooperation 9; Ghana 37; ODA 106, *see also* Visegrad
Polish Bureau for Development Cooperation 9
political parties: aid 7
Portugal 4, 7
positive discrimination 61
poverty 63, 78, 109; knowledge of 14; reduction 53, 57
Poverty Reduction Strategy Papers 67
privatization 45

quality-adjusted aid 105–10
quality-adjusted private charity induced by public policy 110–11

Radu, Michael 67
recession: priorities 7
reform 123
Riddell, R. 3
Romania 3, 6, 104; development policy 76–9; donor status 75, 76; foreign trade 71; Millennium Development Goals (MDGs) 77; progress towards accession 74; size of aid programme 73; socialist 70–3
Romanian-Gabonese Treaty of Friendship and Cooperation 73
Roodman, David 105
Russia 34; influence 124

scholarships 72
Schwarzenberg, Karel 39
scientific assistance 72
Scînteia 73
security 125

selectivity: aid quantity 105
Serbia 25, 37, 102
Sikorski, Radek 37, 44
SLOGA 85, 87–91, 95; Working Group on Global Education 93
Slovak Aid 9, 39
Slovak ODA 9
Slovak Republic 5
Slovakia 3; Africa 39; Russian language 43; Serbia and Montenegro 41; transition experience 27, *see also* Visegrad
Slovenia 3, 4; development cooperation 85–6; Development Days 92; EU Presidency 88, 91–2; International Development Cooperation 85; NGO-ization 86; ODA/ GNI **86**
Slovenian Development Day 88
Slovenian NGDOs in Policy Development 84; chronology 87–9; current status and open issues 89; Presidency Project 91
social inclusion 91
socialism 67
socialist development aid 68
socialization: Europeanization 54
solidarity 71
South Africa: apartheid 39
South Korea 111, 113
Soviet Union 118
structural adjustment programmes 33
Sudan 39
Sweden 102, 127; Africa 43
Syrovátka, M. 12
Szent-Iványi, B. 10, 11, 23, 42

Tanzania 40
tax reform 45
technical assistance 72
Tétényi, A. 10, 42
Third World policy-makers 67, 69
Third World Tours 70
transferring development knowledge 73–6
transition experience: channels of transferring *21*; conclusion 26–8; contradictions 19–23; Czech Republic 23–6; introduction 17–19
TRIALOG 127; project 69
Tunisia 27
twinning projects 70
tying: aid quantity 105

Ukraine 41, 123
UN World Summit (2005) 36
United Nations 2
United Nations Development Programme (UNDP) 3, 70; Regional Centre Bratislava 19, 25; Trust Fund 39
USAID 60, 68

INDEX

Venezuela 34
Versluys, H. 13
Vietnam 25, 58, 67, 102
Visegrad aid policies: Africa-reality 38–41;
  Africa-rhetoric 35–8; conclusion 45–6;
  introduction 33–5; matching rhetoric with
  reality 41–5
Visegrad Group (V4) 7

Walesa, Lech 18
Warsaw Pact 34

World Bank 103, 122

Yemen 58, 102
You Too are Part of this World 91
Yugoslavia 67

Zambia 38, 102
Zukrowska, K. 19

www.routledge.com/9780415676076

Related titles from Routledge

Eastern Partnership: A New Opportunity for the Neighbours?

Edited by Elena Korosteleva

This volume offers a collective assessment of the development and impact of the European Neighbourhood Policy and the Eastern Partnership Initiative on its eastern neighbours - Belarus, Ukraine and Moldova in particular, with Russia's added perspective. Founded on extensive empirical and conceptual research, the volume uniquely bridges the perspectives of all parties across the EU's eastern border, in an attempt to understand advantages and problems related to the effective implementation of the EU policies in the eastern region.

This book was published as a special issue of the *Journal of Communist Studies and Transition Politics*.

Elena Korosteleva is Senior Lecturer in European Politics and Director of the Centre for European Studies at Aberystwyth University.

September 2011: 216 x 138: 200pp
Hb: 978-0-415-67607-6
£85 / $133

For more information and to order a copy visit
www.routledge.com/9780415676076

Available from all good bookshops